POLICING FOR PEACE: INSTITUTIONS, EXPECTATIONS, AND SECURITY IN DIVIDED SOCIETIES

In communities plagued by conflict along ethnic, racial, and religious lines, how does the representation of previously-marginalized groups in the police affect crime and security? Drawing on new evidence from policing in Iraq and Israel, *Policing for Peace* shows that an inclusive police force provides better services and reduces conflict, but not in the ways we might assume. Including members of marginalized groups in the police improves civilians' expectations of how the police and government will treat them, both now and in the future. These expectations are enhanced when officers are organized into mixed rather than homogeneous patrols. Iraqis indicate feeling most secure when policed by mixed officers, even more secure than they feel when policed by members of their own group. In Israel, increases in police officer diversity are associated with lower crime victimization for both Arab and Jewish citizens. In many cases, inclusive policing benefits all citizens, not just those from marginalized groups.

MATTHEW NANES is Assistant Professor of Political Science at Saint Louis University. He researches policing, security, and counterterrorism. His work is published in journals including Comparative Political Studies and Journal of Peace Research, and he has worked with various NGOs, international organizations, and police departments to design evidence-based policies for peace.

CAMBRIDGE STUDIES IN LAW AND SOCIETY

Founded in 1997, Cambridge Studies in Law and Society is a hub for leading scholarship in socio-legal studies. Located at the intersection of law, the humanities, and the social sciences, it publishes empirically innovative and theoretically sophisticated work on law's manifestations in everyday life: from discourses to practices, and from institutions to cultures. The series editors have longstanding expertise in the interdisciplinary study of law, and welcome contributions that place legal phenomena in national, comparative, or international perspective. Series authors come from a range of disciplines, including anthropology, history, law, literature, political science, and sociology.

A list of books in the series can be found at the back of this book.

POLICING FOR PEACE

Institutions, Expectations, and Security in Divided Societies

Matthew Nanes
Saint Louis University, Missouri

CAMBRIDGE
UNIVERSITY PRESS

CAMBRIDGE
UNIVERSITY PRESS

University Printing House, Cambridge CB2 8BS, United Kingdom

One Liberty Plaza, 20th Floor, New York, NY 10006, USA

477 Williamstown Road, Port Melbourne, VIC 3207, Australia

314–321, 3rd Floor, Plot 3, Splendor Forum, Jasola District Centre, New Delhi – 110025, India

79 Anson Road, #06–04/06, Singapore 079906

Cambridge University Press is part of the University of Cambridge.

It furthers the University's mission by disseminating knowledge in the pursuit of education, learning, and research at the highest international levels of excellence.

www.cambridge.org
Information on this title: www.cambridge.org/9781108839051
DOI: 10.1017/9781108979580

First published 2021

A catalogue record for this publication is available from the British Library.

Library of Congress Cataloging-in-Publication Data
Names: Nanes, Matthew J., author.
Title: Policing for peace : institutions, expectations, and security in divided societies / Matthew Nanes.
Description: Cambridge, United Kingdom ; New York, NY : Cambridge University Press, [2021] | Series: Cambridge studies in law and society | Includes bibliographical references and index.
Identifiers: LCCN 2020052346 (print) | LCCN 2020052347 (ebook) | ISBN 9781108839051 (hardback) | ISBN 9781108969680 (paperback) | ISBN 9781108979580 (ebook)
Subjects: LCSH: Police – Middle East. | Police-community relations – Middle East. | Multiculturalism – Middle East. | Conflict management – Middle East. | Reconciliation – Middle East.
Classification: LCC HV8241.9.A2 N36 2021 (print) | LCC HV8241.9.A2 (ebook) | DDC 363.2/30956–dc23
LC record available at https://lccn.loc.gov/2020052346
LC ebook record available at https://lccn.loc.gov/2020052347

ISBN 978-1-108-83905-1 Hardback

CONTENTS

FIGURES

TABLES

PREFACE

As I finalize this manuscript in summer 2020, the role of identity in policing is at the forefront of the news. From my apartment in St. Louis, I can hear protesters marching and demanding justice for victims of police violence. The incidents in Minneapolis, Louisville, and elsewhere that sparked these protests reignited a collective consciousness that arguably began six years earlier, just eight miles from where I now sit, when a White police officer in Ferguson, Missouri, shot and killed an African American civilian. It was certainly not the first African American death under questionable circumstances at the hands of the police, but it sparked riots, protests, and a national conversation about the relationship between racial minorities and the police.

This is not a book about law enforcement in the United States. Yet, it is impossible to ignore the similarities between the experiences of citizens in Oakland, Baltimore, and New York and those of citizens in Jerusalem, Baghdad, and Mosul. The levels of violence vary, but the underlying mistrust between minority citizens and the police is familiar. It is therefore not unreasonable to ask whether the demographic makeup of the police in the United States impacts our society in the same ways, as I show in this book, that it affects the citizens of Israel and Iraq. Are there common mechanisms that might allow us to draw conclusions about the United States from evidence in the Middle East, or are these different worlds where identity affects policing in different ways?

Throughout this book, I show that perceptions link demographics with security. Integration is more than just a tally of officers by religion or skin color; it is the perceived empowerment of a group within an institution. In societies where group identity and political fortunes are deeply intertwined, integration of the police creates the perception that the government is committed to certain treatment of vulnerable groups and the expectation that this treatment will continue into the future.

Negative perceptions certainly characterize police–citizen relations in the United States. Large swaths of society perceive the police as an occupying force designed to subjugate them. The US Department of Justice's report on the shooting in Ferguson pointed to institutionalized structures "shaped by the City's focus on revenue rather than by public safety needs," leading to "clear racial disparities that adversely impact African Americans."[1] This summer, militarized police responses to protests in dozens of cities prompted perceptions among citizens that the police themselves had antagonized the situation. "The tone that we felt from the police is: This is their rally ... They are going to control it from the beginning. They are going to dictate what happens. It's a very offensive type of approach."[2] While there is no evidence that militarized policing protects officers or citizens, it appears to diminish the public's perceptions of the police (Mummolo 2018). These negative perceptions become magnified when a community is simultaneously under- and over-policed, causing dual problems of insecurity at the hands of both criminals and officers.

Negative perceptions and mistrust between citizens and law enforcement run in both directions. Speaking at the University of Chicago Law School in 2015, FBI director James Comey said, "I imagine two lines: one line is law enforcement and the other line is the folks we serve and protect, especially in communities of color. I think those two lines are arcing away from each other, at an increasing rate." Later in the speech, Comey attributes this divergence between police and society to officers' perceptions that the public has turned against them.

> In today's YouTube world, are officers reluctant to get out of their cars and do the work that controls violent crime? Are officers answering 911 calls but avoiding the informal contact that keeps bad guys from standing around, especially with guns? I spoke to officers privately in one big city precinct who described being surrounded by young people with mobile phone cameras held high, taunting them the moment they get out of their cars. They told me, "We feel like we're under siege and we don't feel much like getting out of our cars."[3]

[1] United States Department of Justice Civil Rights Division. *Investigation of the Ferguson Police Department*, March 4, 2015. p. 2.

[2] Dewan, Shaila and Baker, Mike. "Facing protests over use of force, police respond with more force." *The New York Times*, June 2, 2020, https://www.nytimes.com/2020/05/31/us/police-tactics-floyd-protests.html.

[3] Comey, James B. "Law enforcement and the communities we serve: Bending the lines toward safety and justice." *Remarks delivered at the University of Chicago Law*

Former NYPD Commissioner Howard Safir called it a "war on police," and the president of the Federal Law Enforcement Officers Association described a "contagion of anti-cop rhetoric."[4]

This perception of society as the enemy is hardly a new phenomenon. William Westley writes that when it comes to people in lower-class neighborhoods, "the policeman sees them as lacking in morality, ready to commit a crime, ignorant of the law . . . if rough treatment is not used these people will get out of hand and take advantage of the police" (99). Of the 85 officers Westley surveyed, 62 (73 percent) perceived that the public is "against the police, hates the police" (93). One officer told him, "The use of force is necessary to protect yourself. You should always show that you are boss. Make them respect the uniform and not the man" (126). Westley began the research that sparked these words in 1949. While societal norms no longer permit the police to admit such attitudes publicly, their behavior suggests that a nontrivial subset of officers still view the public as a threat, and violence as the primary response to that threat. Indeed, an op-ed written in 2014 by a former St. Louis police officer claims that his colleagues "routinely called anyone of color a 'thug,' whether they were the victim or just a bystander."[5]

If police officers view the entire civilian population as the enemy, it should not come as a surprise when they seize on any hint of disobedience as an excuse to exert their dominance. In perhaps the most blatant instance of turning "to serve and protect" on its head, dozens of St. Louis police officers took to the streets in September 2017 chanting, "Whose streets? Our streets!" at citizens protesting the acquittal of an officer accused of murdering a civilian. Shortly afterward, Interim Police Chief Lawrence O'Toole told reporters, "We're in control. This is our city and we're going to protect it."[6] The police view the city as

School. Chicago, Illinois. October 23, 2015, www.fbi.gov/news/speeches/law-enforcement-and-the-communities-we-serve-bending-the-lines-toward-safety-and-justice

4 Chiaramonte, Perry. "'War on police': Line-of-duty deaths rise amid racially-charged rhetoric, anti-cop climate." FoxNews.com, January 12, 2017, www.foxnews.com/us/war-on-police-line-of-duty-deaths-rise-amid-racially-charged-rhetoric-anti-cop-climate

5 Hudson, Redditt. "Being a cop showed me just how racist and violent the police are. There's only one fix." *Washington Post*, December 6, 2014, www.washingtonpost.com/posteverything/wp/2014/12/06/i-was-a-st-louis-cop-my-peers-were-racist-and-violent-and-theres-only-one-fix/

6 Hogan, Susan. "St. Louis officers chant 'whose streets, our streets' while arresting protesters." *Washington Post*, September 18, 2017, www.washingtonpost.com/news/morning-mix/

"theirs," to be protected *from* society, rather than a city society entrusts to them for protection.

So, can altering the demographic makeup of the police reduce this "us versus them" mentality by both citizens and police officers? The overwhelming majority of police officers are well-intentioned men and women who genuinely want to serve their communities. There is no reason to think that most officers, regardless of their race, are incapable of or unwilling to police African Americans fairly. Yet, good people operating in a flawed institutional context sometimes behave differently than they might otherwise behave. I explain in the pages that follow that integrating the police changes citizens' perceptions of government. Though my evidence on officer behavior is limited, I suggest that integration changes the context in ways that should reshape officers' perceptions of citizens as well. Under normal circumstances, a disproportionate share of officers' interactions are with the individuals from whom society needs protecting. Add this skewed experience to centuries of institutionalized racism, and one begins to understand how the police acquire the impression that society is out to get them, that African Americans are "thugs," and that the police are the last bastion of order in an otherwise chaotic society. Changing these perceptions and helping officers see that the vast majority of people are law-abiding citizens worthy of their respect and protection must be the goal of any reforms.

The police often talk about fellow officers as though they are family. These uniformed men and women work together toward a common cause in the face of danger, day in and day out, creating a sense of attachment. When the men and women in uniform overwhelmingly look and talk a certain way, a way that differs systematically from the rest of society, it is easy to view citizens as "others" worthy of mistrust. Creating a diverse police force in which officers from different groups work side by side might change officers' perceptions of citizens who look different than they do, helping them see citizens worthy of protection rather than out-groups to be feared. As James Comey said in the very same speech quoted earlier, "It's hard to hate up close. It's hard to hate someone once you sit and stare into their eyes and start to understand where they're coming from, and why they feel the way they do." Generating positive interactions between police officers and citizens is

wp/2017/09/18/st-louis-officers-chant-whose-streets-our-streets-while-arresting-protesters-against-police-killing/

obviously an important part of making hate hard. Given the potential for structured, positive interactions between members of different groups to improve attitudes toward out-groups (Allport 1954), perhaps officers with police "family" of other races will find it easier to view civilians of other races as allies, not adversaries.

This book presents evidence on citizens' behaviors and perceptions, but one can imagine a similarly powerful narrative about police officers' perceptions of citizens like the one I described earlier. More than anything, I hope the research in this book helps to recognize and address some of the institutionalized causes of insecurity in divided societies and contributes to the peaceful coexistance of all people, regardless of race, religion, or uniform.

ACKNOWLEDGMENTS

This is, at its heart, a book about people. The thousands of individuals who make up my "data points" are real people who have something important to say. I am grateful to them for lending their experiences and voices to my research. My ultimate hope for this work is that it contributes to the welfare of these individuals and others like them.

Many people contributed to this book and the research behind it. First and foremost, the members of my doctoral committee at the University of California San Diego (UCSD), Karen Ferree, Claire Adida, Eli Berman, David Lake, and Phil Roeder, provided inspiration and guidance as the project developed from a seminar paper to a dissertation, and from a dissertation to published research. I sincerely thank each of them for entrusting me with the tools and resources to pursue the research I envisioned. During my time at UCSD, I also benefited from the guidance of Clark Gibson, Zoli Hajnal, Simeon Nichter, Nico Ravanilla, and other faculty. My cohort-mates in the "Best Cohort Ever" and members of the neighboring cohorts also provided frequent input and, more importantly, lasting friendship. I thank Konstantin Ash, Matt Bergman, Shannon Carcelli, Dotan Haim, Andy Janusz, John Kuk, Nazita Lajevardi, David Lindsey, Brandon Merrell, Kelly Matush, Inbok Rhee, Debbi Seligsohn, Zachary Steinert-Threlkeld, Abigail Vaughn, and Jack Zhang for contributing formally and informally to this work.

I spent the summer of 2014 in Jerusalem where I appeared unannounced and uninvited on the doorstep of Hebrew University's Institute of Criminology. Badi Hasisi, Simon Perry, and David Weisburd generously shared their time and contacts, providing me with an indispensable introduction to policing in Israel and to the academic study of policing more generally. I am deeply indebted to them and hope they do not mind a political scientist reinventing a wheel that their field developed decades ago.

From September 2017 to June 2018, Stanford University's Center on Democracy, Development, and the Rule of Law (CDDRL) provided me with the greatest gift an academic can receive: time. During my postdoc at CDDRL, my work benefited from helpful feedback from Lisa Blaydes, Seung Cho, Natt Hongdilokkul, David Laitin, Jane Yeonjae Lee, Rebecca Perlman, Kerry Persen, Ryan Tans, and Samantha Vortherms.

In fall 2018, I found a new home in the Political Science Department at Saint Louis University (SLU). My colleagues here have overwhelmed me with kindness and support. I especially thank J.D. Bowen, Ellen Carnaghan, Ali Fisunoglu, Morgan Hazelton, and Steven Rogers for their comments on various stages of my work. In spring 2019, I had the privilege of hosting a workshop for my manuscript at SLU. Rob Blair, Jim Gilsinan, Guy Grossman, Caroline Hartzell, and Jake Shapiro generously spent the better part of a day picking apart my work and then helping me put it back together again in ways that undoubtedly made it stronger.

I was fortunate to receive funding from several sources. From 2015 to 2017 I received a predoctoral fellowship from the Israel Institute, which allowed me to study the Israel Police. The University of California Institute on Global Conflict and Cooperation, and UCSD Policy Design and Evaluation Lab also provided critical funding. SLU funded additional interviews and fieldwork as I developed the manuscript. I collected data with the help of two research firms: IPSOS in Israel and IIACSS in Iraq. Both played an instrumental role in accessing respondents and interviewees in hard-to-reach places, adding richness to this project. Special thanks go to Munqith Daghir for his guidance and commitment to this project. At Cambridge University Press, Jackie Grant devoted many hours to ensuring this project reached fruition. I also appreciate the editors of the Law and Society series taking a chance on my work. Two anonymous reviewers provided extremely helpful feedback.

Finally, neither this book nor my career could have come to fruition without my family's love and encouragement. No doubt my parents never expected their son to go wandering around the Middle East asking questions about sectarian violence and policing. The knowledge that I have their unwavering support every step of the way gives me the courage to take the professional risks necessary to achieve my goals. My brother Ben sets a positive example, both in scientific research and in life, that I strive to follow every day. I could not ask for a better role model.

1

INTRODUCTION: THE CHALLENGE OF INSTITUTION-BUILDING IN DIVIDED SOCIETIES

Aisha suspected trouble as soon as the police officer approached her. "Where are you from?" he asked, code in Baghdad at the time for "to what sect do you belong?" Aisha, a twenty-five-year-old housewife, is Shia, but at that moment she was walking down the street in Saidiya, one of the city's predominantly Sunni neighborhoods. To Aisha's relief, however, the officer was a fellow Shia. "When he saw how I talked [with an accent], and I told him I'm from Karbala [a Shia city], he said 'welcome, you are one of us, and since you are one of us you will leave here without trouble.' He protected me like I was one his family members; his treatment was different."[1]

Ahmed, a thirty-two-year-old Sunni, describes a very different encounter with the police. Officers initially stopped Ahmed at a checkpoint because his name was similar to a wanted man's name. When it became clear that Ahmed was not the man they were looking for, the officer who stopped him, who was Shia, told him he could fix the mix-up. At the officer's request, Ahmed gave him 100,000 Iraqi dinar, about $85 US, and the officer told Ahmed he would receive an official letter in a week. "A week passed [without any resolution] and people told me to be thankful that the officer did not do anything to me or arrest me at the checkpoint. It's about sectarianism. There are some people who read the surname [which signals sect] and get you into trouble at the checkpoint . . . he took 100,000 Iraqi dinar just because I'm from

[1] IIACSS interview 06SF, Baghdad, February 2019. As with all references to civilians in this book, the name is a pseudonym.

[Anbar, a mainly Sunni province]." Ahmed says that if the officer had been Sunni, he would not have taken his money.[2]

Interactions like these between civilians and rank-and-file police officers occur millions of times every day around the world. In divided societies like Iraq, where political competition and violence occur along group divisions like religion, ethnicity, or race, it stands to reason that officers' identities shape citizens' perceptions of encounters. This book argues that the demographic makeup of the police shapes attitudes and expectations far beyond these specific interactions. The police are the primary point of contact between citizens and the state and play a central role in enforcing the government's laws, making rank-and-file officers the face of both government service provision and state coercion. Citizens' experiences with the police, therefore, have far-reaching effects on their broader relationships with the law.

Rank-and-file officers' demographic makeup signals to citizens the way the government intends to treat their group. In doing so, it serves as an important intervening variable in the bridge between law and society. Inclusion in the police rank and file gives citizens reason to expect better treatment on two main dimensions, protection under the law and service delivery. In the anecdotes mentioned earlier, there is no conclusive evidence that either citizen would necessarily have been treated differently had the officer been from a different sect. Yet, each citizen perceived that sect played a role in their treatment by the police, and these perceptions will undoubtedly shape their future behavior toward the police and the government. Officers rely on citizens' cooperation for everything, from crime prevention (Skolnick and Bayley 1988; Tyler 2004; Weitzer and Tuch 2006) to counterinsurgency (Department of the Army 2006; Kalyvas 2006; Berman et al. 2011b; Lyall et al. 2015). A breakdown in this cooperation threatens the very fabric of society.

THE ARGUMENT: POLICE INCLUSION SHAPES EXPECTATIONS OF FUTURE TREATMENT

Rank-and-file officers possess a unique combination of three key characteristics, namely, visibility, discretion, and capacity for violence, which shape citizens' expectations of how they will be treated. Police

[2] IIACSS interview 09NM, February 2019

officers are in the public eye as they conduct patrols and provide services, and ordinary civilians interact far more frequently with police officers than with elected officials. Government uniforms and vehicles branded with the name of the jurisdiction ensure that citizens associate officers' actions with the government. Media reports and conversations with family and friends reinforce personal experiences and observations (Mazerolle et al. 2013; Saunders et al. 2013). Thus, in settings in which group identity is highly salient, citizens observe the police's demographic makeup and associate what they see with police and government intentions.

Unusually high levels of discretion amplify the importance of these interactions. While it is technically illegal to drive even slightly faster than the posted speed limit, officers stop and punish only a small subset of offenders. When applied correctly, this discretion makes service delivery more efficient by allowing rank-and-file officers to use their knowledge of the community to allocate their time and energy appropriately (Lipsky 1980). In conflict-prone societies, however, officers' discretion allows them to differentiate service delivery and harm civilians.

Finally, the police distribute the most important service of the modern state, public safety (Olson 1993), and are typically the only institution legally authorized to use violence against civilians. The importance of public safety raises the stakes of policing above other service-providing bureaucracies. When the state represses civilians, it often does so through the police.

These characteristics of the police mean that when citizens perceive that their well-being is linked with their identity, their group's inclusion in the police rank and file shapes expectations of how the police will treat them. Citizens may interpret exclusion from the police as a signal that the police do not care to serve their community. Officers may fill ticket quotas by over-policing certain neighborhoods where out-groups live or develop a department culture of "roughing up" suspects from certain groups. Even if exclusion does not affect officers' *actual* behavior, it creates the *perception* that mistreatment by the police, including insufficient devotion of resources, lack of effort by officers, or harassment, is due to identity. If left unchecked, these perceptions can spiral into poor citizen–state relations and anti-state violence. It is not for nothing that US officials informally referred to anti-government insurgents in Iraq as "POIs," or "pissed-off Iraqis" (Patel 2015). On the other hand, just as citizens may attribute mistreatment by the police to sectarianism if the officer comes from an out-group, they may be more willing to discount mistreatment by a coethnic officer in an integrated institution, viewing it as the behavior of a single bad apple that does not reflect on the police or government overall.

Group-based police inclusion shapes citizens' expectations of whether the state intends to harm them. Included groups have access to weapons, vehicles, equipment, and information that rebels could use to identify and exploit government vulnerabilities. In the event of attempted repression, officers might refuse to help the government harm members of their own group. When fighting broke out in Syria in 2011, the rank and file of Syria's security forces included a diverse range of religious and ethnic groups. Police officers and soldiers from groups that rose up against the regime found ways to defend their coethnics without defecting. According to one soldier, "I would never [shoot to kill] ... I'd shoot into the air, shoot everything but the fighters. A lot of people do that."[3] Of course, in more extreme circumstances, officers might turn their guns against the state. Enloe (1980, 98–99) cites an example of Bengali officers in the Pakistani police force engaging in mutiny when asked to suppress Bengali dissidents in 1971.

The police's visibility, discretion, and capacity for violence shape citizens' perceptions of how the police treat them on a day-to-day basis, an important but well-established outcome (Lasley 1994; Weitzer and Tuch 2004; Weitzer and Hasisi 2008; Mazerolle et al. 2013). I argue that in addition to shaping current perceptions, inclusive policing shapes citizens' expectations of how the state will treat them in the future. Inclusion in the police is costly for the state to reverse once it occurs. Sudden attempts to purge a particular group's officers may be met by armed resistance. After the US invasion of Iraq, purged members of Saddam Hussein's security forces took off their uniforms and went home, but they brought their weapons with them, equipping the insurgency (Dodge 2005; Hashim 2005; Spain and Turchie 2013). Globally, purges of police force are exceedingly rare (González 2019). Even if the government were able to purge all of a group's officers, doing so would leave a substantially understaffed police force, degrading its ability to deliver public safety and maintain order. Thus, citizens should expect that any effects of police inclusion on the way the police treat

[3] Khazan, Olga. "A defector's tale: Assad's reluctant army." *Washington Post* January 9, 2013, www.washingtonpost.com/news/worldviews/wp/2013/01/09/a-defectors-tale-assads-reluctant-army/?utm_term=.4dc7470f7876

them today will persist into the future. As such, inclusion allows the government to send a credible signal of its future behavior.

This credible signal of future behavior makes police inclusion a powerful response to the commitment problem which frequently plagues divided societies. Because it is more powerful, the state cannot commit to future treatment of a weaker group (Fearon 1995a; Lake and Rothchild 1996; Mattes and Savun 2009; Tezcür 2016). The resulting "security dilemma" (Posen 1993) provides the weaker group with an incentive to invest in its defenses and increases the likelihood that either side misinterprets the other's actions as aggressive. If the weaker group fears that its relative power will erode even further, perhaps due to government consolidation or divergent population trends, its members may take up arms in anticipation of becoming even more vulnerable in the future. The commitment problem is especially problematic in states with prior communal violence, where a history of negative interactions exacerbates mistrust. Asymmetric power across groups characterizes conflict between Shias and Sunnis in Iraq, Jews and Arabs in Israel, Protestants and Catholics in Northern Ireland, Turks and Kurds in Turkey, and dozens of other ethnic or religious groups in conflict across the globe.

While existing research deals primarily with the commitment problem in terms of threats to physical security, governments struggle to commit to future treatment of weaker groups on any number of dimensions, for example, providing public goods and services. Concerns about future mistreatment on these less extreme dimensions also affect citizens' behaviors. In Israel, the government is concerned not just with reducing the likelihood of suicide bombings but also with increasing Arab citizens' social and economic integration into the state (Levi and Suchi 2018). Arab-Israeli citizens who do not expect the police or other arms of government to provide them with adequate goods and services may look to tribal or informal justice systems, foreign donors, and political parties rather than to the government.

Heterogeneity and Credible Commitments

The extent to which inclusion in the police rank and file shapes expectations about police behavior depends not just on how many individuals are included but also on how those individuals are distributed within the police. The impact of the former is relatively straightforward: the greater a group's representation in an institution, the more influence that group likely has over the operations of the institution and its treatment of citizens. While there are certainly factors which can interrupt the link between representation and influence, for example, a "glass ceiling" preventing minorities from advancing beyond a certain rank, the discretion that rank-and-file officers hold over their treatment of citizens means that where group identity is salient, more representation in the rank and file should correlate with more power.

The impact of officers' distribution within the institution is less obvious. It would be natural to assume that a group with a history of marginalization at the hands of the state should wish to minimize contact with out-group police officers, implying a preference for in-group policing in which each group's officers serve only that group's citizens. It may also be that individuals prefer to be policed by coethnics out of intrinsic coethnic bias (Lyall et al. 2015) or to benefit from improved communication and shared norms (Habyarimana et al. 2007; Laitin 2007).

However, isolating officers in homogeneous units erodes some of their power. When officers serve in homogeneous units, the state can withhold equipment or information from certain identity groups by selectively providing those items to some units and not to others. Sunni police officers leading the charge to retake Iraq's Nineveh province from the Islamic State in January 2015 complained that the government dragged its feet in arming and equipping them. The Shia militias "have support, they have weapons, equipment and salaries from the government," said Lt. Hardan Khalaf, a Sunni police recruit. "We are the official security forces. We belong to the Ministry of Interior and are part of the state, but we get nothing."[4] It is much easier for the state to stratify equipment at the unit level than at the level of individual officers. Similarly, it would be extremely difficult to keep information secret from officers who patrol together. Local-level heterogeneity ensures that officers from the marginalized group receive the same equipment and access as their dominant-group colleagues.

Second, the distribution of officers determines whether dominant-group citizens rely on minority-group police officers for services. When

[4] Morris, Loveday (2015), "Iraqi police at Nineveh Liberation Camp aim to help free Mosul but lack food and guns." *The Washington Post*, January 15. www.washingtonpost.com/world/middle_east/these-iraqis-are-preparing-to-liberate-mosul–as-soon-as-they-have-guns-and-food/2015/01/14/297efc30-95be-11e4-8385-866293322c2f_story.html?noredirect=on&utm_term=.7564175935f5

officers are organized into heterogeneous patrols, minority officers can impose costs on the state by withholding participation or reducing their effort, leading to poorer service provision in dominant-group areas. The inability to provide policing services harms the state's legitimacy and weakens the regime in the eyes of its citizens (Akerlof and Yellen 1994). Officers may go on strike, significantly affecting the police's capacity to prevent crime or, in conflict zones, defend the government against rebel forces. In addition to the anecdote above about Syrian security forces shooting over the heads of rebels to avoid harming members of their own group, thousands of Sunni police officers and soldiers defected outright, dramatically cutting the strength of pro-regime forces.[5] In a less extreme measure, officers may engage in a "slowdown," coming to work but refusing to exert effort on certain types of tasks. In May 2015, police officers in Baltimore, Maryland, refused to carry out basic tasks like writing traffic tickets or responding to calls for service to protest the arrest of six of their fellow officers for their alleged involvement in the death of citizen Freddie Gray while in custody. Slowdowns harm both the regime and its citizens, with the government losing revenue from unwritten citations and citizens suffering from reduced service provision. In Baltimore, arrests dropped 43 percent and the city suffered its most violent month in more than thirty-five years.[6] Other public service providers also used strikes to impose costs on the state. In November 2015, Arab-Israeli employees of schools, municipal governments, and the trash collection agency went on strike to protest what they called a discriminatory action by Israel's cabinet, causing an interruption in public services.[7] Arab teachers went on a similar strike in response to Israel's management of the Temple Mount in October of the same year.[8] Officers who serve only in-group citizens do not have these opportunities, as withholding participation would primarily hurt

[5] Oweis, Khaled Yacoub. "Syrian secret police defect, Arab deadline passes." *Reuters* December 5, 2011, http://in.reuters.com/article/syria-idINDEE7B400B20111205

[6] Bouie, Jamelle. "Criminal neglect." *Slate.com* June 18, 2015. www.slate.com/articles/news_and_politics/politics/2015/06/baltimore_police_are_virtually_on_strike_the_city_deserves_something_better.html

[7] *Times of Israel*, November 19, 2015."High follow-up committee protests decision to outlaw northern branch of Islamist organization." http://www.timesofisrael.com/israeli-arabs-on-strike-after-islamic-movement-ban/

[8] Weiner, Stuart. *Times of Israel*, October 11, 2015. "Israeli Arabs to strike over move 'to keep Muslims from Temple Mount.'" www.timesofisrael.com/israeli-arabs-to-strike-over-move-to-keep-muslims-from-temple-mount

citizens from their own group. For similar reasons, patrol-level heterogeneity makes it more costly for the state to purge officers from the out-group, as doing so would damage the police's ability to maintain order and deliver services even in pro-government areas.

Next, patrol-level heterogeneity positions minority-group officers to monitor the behavior of dominant-group officers. Officers often patrol in pairs or groups, and multiple officers respond to calls for service. If the police use heterogeneous patrols, officers from multiple groups are likely to be present for most interactions. Coupled with institutional arrangements for reporting abuses or the possibility of external pressures via the media, monitoring can deter mistreatment of citizens (over-policing) or shirking (under-policing). While group-based autonomy over law enforcement would also prevent identity-motivated over- or under-policing, citizens in mixed neighborhoods would remain vulnerable, as would citizens traveling outside of their group's neighborhood. Ordinary citizens recognize this opportunity for monitoring. When asked how the police can ensure that officers from different ethnic and religious groups behave professionally toward all citizens, a Jewish Israeli focus group participant recommended, "Put the Arab police officer and the Jewish officer [together] in the same situation."[9]

Finally, while this book deals primarily with citizens' attitudes and resulting behavior, it bears mentioning that heterogeneity may influence the attitudes and behaviors of officers as well. Working for an integrated police force provides significant exposure to non-coethnics, first during training and then as colleagues and partners. These interactions occur in the context of equal-status individuals working together toward a common goal, conditions which "contact hypothesis" suggests will improve attitudes toward out-group members (Allport 1954; Zajonc 1968; Ball and Cantor 1974; Blair et al. 2016). In turn, officers who have more positive attitudes toward out-groups may be less likely to harass or withhold service from citizens based on their sectarian identity.

I refer to local-level heterogeneity among rank-and-file officers as *police integration*. Integration contrasts with *segregated inclusion* in which officers largely serve in homogeneous units and provide services in areas where their group is the majority. Regardless of whether these mechanisms actually change police officers' behaviors, I propose that citizens

[9] FG3J, Haifa, March 2019

from weaker or marginalized groups *expect* patrol-level heterogeneity to lead to better treatment for their group, both now and in the future. While marginalized groups may prefer segregated inclusion over exclusion, I argue that integration is more likely to lead to durable, long-term improvements in citizen–state relations because it makes citizens feel more secure in the long term.

ALTERNATIVE ARGUMENTS: OPPORTUNITIES FOR REBELLION AND CO-OPTATION OF OUT-GROUPS

Worryingly, the same characteristics of police integration which empower the weaker group to defend itself against mistreatment also empower would-be rebels to attack the state. A predominant strand of research on civil war proposes that a rebellion's likelihood of success is an important limiting factor in whether or not conflict occurs (Fearon and Laitin 2003; Collier and Hoeffler 2004). That is, there is always *someone* who holds grievances against the government or fears future mistreatment, but they only turn to violence when they believe that doing so is likely to advance their interests. By this argument, integrating a marginalized group into the police might actually increase the likelihood of conflict, as a group with access to weapons, equipment, and information would be more likely to prevail in an armed confrontation.

Violent conflict ends lives, destroys property, and diverts resources away from more productive uses. Rather than fighting, both sides would be better off agreeing to a settlement which avoids such destruction (Fearon 1995b). The costliness of sectarian violence suggests that marginalized groups prefer not to fight if negotiations can solve their underlying motives for fighting. Police integration improves a group's bargaining position and sends a clear, credible signal that the state intends to treat them fairly, creating space and trust for negotiation and peaceful political competition.

A second alternative argument suggests that police officers from the marginalized group will treat their coethnics worse than dominant-group officers treat them, further degrading relations between the marginalized group and the police. For example, the police may recruit only individuals who are most sympathetic to the government and identify least strongly with their identity group. I show in Chapter 4 that the Israel Police struggle with this perception. Arab officers are frequently accused of being collaborators rather than representatives of their community. A related possibility is that if the marginalized group hesitates to join the police, the police may recruit less-qualified individuals from that group, leading to lower-quality service provision.[10]

A final possibility is that in an effort to fit in with their colleagues, officers from the marginalized group treat their coethnics harshly to prove themselves when observed by officers from another group. In a study by Weitzer and Hasisi (2008), an Arab-Israeli citizen told an interviewer that he prefers to be policed by Jewish officers than by Arabs. "Next to each Arab officer there is a Jewish officer and then he has to prove [to the Jewish officer] that he is strong." Similarly, in Adida and Robinson's (2019) study on African immigrants in the United States, a Black subject told researchers, "You're lucky if you get a black police officer, but if he is with one white officer then he won't spare you either, because he doesn't want the other officer to think he is not giving you a ticket just because you are black. He makes a show of it." These anecdotes suggest that police departments and governments seeking to use police integration to improve relations with minority communities must be cognizant of the perception that officers treat the marginalized group more harshly when out-group officers are present than they otherwise would have.

These possible mechanisms suggest that integration might worsen citizen–police or citizen–state relations if citizens expect it to lead to worse treatment. The question will ultimately be settled empirically. Regarding the possibility that marginalized-group officers are lower quality, I describe the substantial lengths to which the Israel Police go to ensure that their Arab officers are highly qualified. If anything, Arab officers are likely to be better educated than their Jewish colleagues. For their part, the Iraqi police face an oversupply of qualified individuals from all groups wishing to join, so there is little reason to worry that minority officers will be substandard. Regarding branding of officers as collaborators rather than representatives, the quotes mentioned earlier flag a distinction between representation in numeric terms and perceptions of integration. Integration is more than just the likelihood of interacting with an officer who is a coethnic; it is the perception that a group is empowered to impact the police's treatment of citizens. It is unlikely that the Arab-Israeli citizen quoted above would

10 I point out in Chapter 2 that while plausible, this particular mechanism is far less dangerous for police integration than for integration of law-making institutions, which require more specialized skills and provide members with little to no training.

characterize the police as "integrated," even though the concept of interacting with an Arab officer is plausible to him.

Assumptions, Scope, and Case Selection

For these arguments to hold, group identities must be sticky enough that citizens cannot simply switch between groups as it suits them, and individuals must belong to a group that can be classified as either dominant or marginalized. I do not suggest that the political relevance of group identities cannot change, but if they change to the point of violating this assumption, then the case moves out of scope. More specifically, I do not suggest that Israeli Jews and Arabs or Iraqi Shias and Sunnis have always made up (or will always make up) the primary societal cleavage, only that these are the primary cleavages in the current conflict, and that in the short term, they are stable enough to be treated as static. While the theory allows for the existence of multiple marginalized groups, it only provides explicit treatment of interactions between the dominant group and a marginalized group.

Race, religion, ethnicity, and language differ in important ways, but they interact with politics through similar mechanisms. Their differences may become relevant at the margins. For instance, Jewish Israeli police officers who speak only Hebrew may have difficulty communicating with Arab citizens who speak primarily Arabic, while Arabic-speaking Shia and Sunni Iraqis do not have this problem. For the main argument, however, it is not these mechanical differences which matter for political behavior but rather the fact that group identity is costly to change, easily identifiable, and politically activated (Chandra 2001). To that end, when making general statements about group identity, I follow the convention of referring to all such conflicts as "ethnic" conflicts, even though they often occur between religious, racial, or linguistic groups. Similarly, references to "coethnics" should be read as "members of the same politically relevant identity group," not just those sharing heritable biological traits.

A second set of conditions refers to the state and its institutions. I assume that laws are created and enforced by a coherent state with relevant security institutions. If law enforcement institutions operate beyond the control of the state, then attitudes toward the institution are unlikely to be correlated with attitudes toward the state. Such a situation is particularly likely to occur when institutional control is subnational, as in the Kurdish region of Iraq (see Chapter 5), or in the

United States. As a general rule, the chain of command determines the appropriate level of government to which citizens link their attitudes toward the police.

No single book can provide a thorough treatment of the entire citizen–police relationship. I focus mainly on the way that integration affects citizens' attitudes and behaviors toward the police. Existing research provides a thorough treatment of other parts of the relationship, including police-on-citizen violence (Westley 1970; Weitzer 1995; Smith 2003; Weitzer and Tuch 2004; Jensen and Hapal 2018; Ben-Porat and Yuval 2019; Boudreau et al. 2019).

A final set of conditions deals with citizens' perceptions. Changing police demographics can only accomplish so much, especially in the short term. Citizens need not view the state's *actions* as desirable, but they must recognize the right of the state to govern, even if they are dissatisfied with its leaders or policies. Indeed, support for anti-state violence – the key outcome in Chapter 6 – does not stem directly from rejection of the regime's right to govern. Millions of people worldwide question their government's legitimacy, but only a tiny portion turn to violence. Violence is an extreme reaction to an imminent threat of personal or communal harm, coupled with the perception that nonviolent responses are unlikely to mitigate that threat. It is this perceived threat to safety, not merely a lack of government legitimacy, that police integration addresses.

In order to shift perceptions, group identity must be observable. In most divided societies, the relevant identity cleavage is demarcated by observable characteristics like skin color, clothing choice, or language, allowing citizens to easily form perceptions based on direct observations. Iraq is a difficult case because there is no inherent physical difference between Sunni and Shia Arab Iraqis. Yet, as is often true of religious groups, Sunni and Shia Muslims develop cultural differences which visibly demarcate group membership. Iraqis interviewed for this research suggested that they can determine sectarian affiliation using cues like an individual's name (which police officers display on their uniform), facial hair, accent, and manner of dress. Identity is somewhat more visible in Israel, as the Jewish, non-Jewish cleavage correlates with heritable ethnic divisions which manifest themselves in skin tone and facial structure. Other cues like names and accents also play a role. With some margin for error (i.e., mistaking Jews of Sephardic descent for non-Jewish Arabs), it is possible to distinguish Jewish and non-Jewish Israeli police officers by appearance.

With these scope conditions in mind, rank-and-file police integration is relevant in an unusually broad set of circumstances. In particular, the police provide a forum for inclusion even in nondemocracies. Even the most competent autocrat cannot govern without an effective police force, and civil servants' discretionary powers are just as strong under autocracy as they are under democracy. Additionally, as my focus on Iraq and Israel demonstrates, policing is highly relevant in both developing and advanced-industrialized countries. All modern societies depend on police to maintain security, regardless of their level of economic development, giving police integration broad relevance.

POLICING IN TWO DIVIDED SOCIETIES

I explore the effects of police integration in two very different divided societies, Iraq and Israel. In Iraq, I focus primarily on conflict between Shia and Sunni Arabs, while in Israel I explore the relationship between Jewish and non-Jewish citizens.[11] Both countries have deep social and political divisions, and intergroup conflict frequently devolves into violence. Both are democracies with a politically dominant ethno-religious majority, and each has a large, well-equipped national police force. While less obvious than some group divisions like race in the United States, I show later in this book that the relevant cleavages are observable in both countries, and that most citizens are reasonably confident in their ability to identify the group membership of police officers with whom they interact.

Iraq and Israel are cases of partial police integration. The level and configuration of inclusion varies over time and across regions. I leverage this subnational variation in my analysis. In Iraq, while initial rebuilding efforts failed to pay proper attention to the police, subsequent reforms fostered Sunni inclusion, first in 2008 due to pressure from the United States, and especially following the 2014 election of Haider al-Abadi, whose government sought rapprochement with Sunnis. Reforms faced challenges from regional politicians, leading to geographically uneven implementation. In Israel, the share of non-Jews

[11] I limit the Israeli case to territory governed by Israeli civil law. I do not study policing or institutions in Gaza or the West Bank, nor do I deal with Palestinians who are not Israeli citizens. While the discussion of Iraq does not ignore Kurds or other minorities entirely, the primary analysis is limited to interactions between the Shia Arab majority and the Sunni Arab minority.

in the police rose from only 10 percent in the early 2000s to more than 14 percent in 2014 due to a perception among police leadership that Arab officers could more effectively serve Arab communities. The police distribute Arab officers unevenly around the country, leading to some regions in which officers are highly diverse and others in which they are almost exclusively Jewish.

Iraq and Israel differ substantially on levels of violence, political institutionalization, and the stability of group power structures. Extreme violence dominates Iraq's narrative since 2003. Violence in Israel, while common enough to be relevant, does not match the levels seen in Iraq. Iraq has a short history of democratic rule, while Israel's spans seven decades. Iraq's institutions are young and weak, while Israel's are highly consolidated. The 2003 invasion of Iraq turned the country's power configuration on its head, with the Shia Arab majority taking control of the government after more than a century of political dominance by the Sunni Arab minority. In contrast, Jews have dominated Israeli politics since the creation of the state in 1948.[12] These differences demonstrate police integration's broad relevance. They vary not just in terms of context but also on the relevant dimensions of peace and security. In Iraq, I argue that improved citizen–police relations reduce the intensity of violent anti-government insurgency, while in Israel citizen–police cooperation improves crime prevention.

Iraq

The task of rebuilding Iraq's institutions following the 2003 regime change motivates this project. When troops from the United States, United Kingdom, Australia, and Poland made quick work of the Iraqi army in spring 2003, few predicted the extent of the state-building quagmire that would follow. For policy-makers from the United States and the thirty-five other countries involved in reconstruction, the task was to rebuild, or in many cases simply *build*, Iraq's institutions. The country had little preexisting framework for effective and inclusive governing institutions after decades of dictatorial rule (Dodge 2005), and its complex ethno-religious cleavages exacerbated the challenge. Both religious sect and ethnic identity play important roles in the way that Iraqi citizens organize socially and politically. Sunni Arabs, who make up about one-third of the Iraqi population, dominated the Baath Party, in power from 1968 to 2003, as well as the Ottoman-

[12] Israeli Jews are themselves subdivided into ethnic and religious factions, of course, but these divisions are outside the scope of this project.

and British-ruled governments before it (Dawisha 2009). Despite Shias' demographic majority, Iraq's twentieth-century governments largely excluded them from power. This exclusion, and the inferior conditions it generated, motivated violent uprisings against the Iraqi regime in 1991 and 1999. These conflicts were political, not religious, in nature (Lawrence 2009; Polk 2005), yet they proved the relevance of sectarian identity in political organization. Iraq's third-largest politically relevant group is distinguished not by religion but by ethnicity. Kurds, who make up about 20 percent of the Iraqi population, constitute a distinct identity group for the purposes of political organization despite most being Sunni Muslims (Lawrence 2009). Dozens of smaller religious and ethnic groups also dot Iraqi society.

In the wake of the 2003 invasion, policy-makers' attempts to design institutions capable of supporting Iraq's fragmented citizenry focused almost exclusively on law-making institutions like the legislature and executive branch. Meanwhile, "de-Baathification" allowed Shia militias and sectarian interests to co-opt the bureaucracy and security forces (Perito 2011). The Iraqi government gave in to pressure from the United States to utilize Sunni militias in the fight against al-Qaeda in 2008, and later integrated many of these fighters into the police. A second, more concerted round of Sunni integration began under the government of Prime Minister Haider al-Abadi in 2014. This process resulted in considerable variation in the makeup of officers serving in a given area. The incompleteness of Iraqi police integration allows citizens to have dramatically different experiences with the police and develop a range of expectations about future treatment.

Iraq's post-2003 experience illustrates a broader trend in which policy-makers view representation in law-making institutions as a panacea for identity pluralism while ignoring the institutions that enforce laws and distribute public goods. Iraq provides an opportunity to test the relationship between citizens' perceptions of police inclusion and their motives for conflict in precisely the setting in which those perceptions should matter most, a society whose politics are deeply divided along identity lines, and where the struggle to survive has become inextricably linked with both ascriptive identity and the behavior of the government.

Israel

Like Iraq, Israel's population is fragmented along both ethnic and religious lines. Non-Jews make up about 20 percent of the citizen population. The majority are Muslims, although the country has sizable populations of Christians and Druze as well. An overwhelming majority of non-Jews are ethnic Arabs, while only a tiny minority of the Jewish population is Arab, leading to the shorthand terminology of "Jews and Arabs" as all-encompassing and mutually exclusive categories.

Many of Israel's non-Jewish citizens are descendants of those living in British Mandatory Palestine when Israel declared independence in 1948. Others were living in the Golan Heights when Israel captured the territory from Syria in 1967. Israel offered citizenship to the Golan Heights residents when it placed the region under civilian rule in 1981, although only some accepted. Residents of Gaza and the West Bank also came under Israeli authority after these territories were taken from Egypt and Jordan, respectively, in the 1967 war. However, these individuals are not citizens and are outside the scope of this study. In Israel's early years, Arab citizens lived under martial law and had fewer rights than their Jewish countrymen. Since 1966, however, the law provides all citizens with the same legal rights and responsibilities, regardless of religious identity.[13] Despite Israel's self-proclaimed status as a Jewish state, non-Jewish citizens vote in elections, enjoy freedom of religion, and attend state-funded schools.

Despite the legal equality between Jews and non-Jews, non-Jewish citizens receive lower-quality goods and services from the state on most dimensions. Arab schools receive only a fraction of the funding that Jewish schools receive, leading to lower rates of matriculation and university enrollment (New Israel Fund 2005). Arab-majority towns have fewer (and more poorly maintained) roads, less access to public transportation, and lower rates of employment (Levi and Suchi 2018). The difference in services and human welfare is perhaps most stark when it comes to public safety and relations with the police. Arab-majority municipalities experience some of Israel's highest crime rates, particularly violent crime. Studies show that Arab-Israelis perceive public safety as worse than their Jewish neighbors (Ben-Porat and Yuval 2012; Saunders et al. 2013).

Perhaps due in part to the divergence in welfare and services between Jews and non-Jews, tensions periodically spill over into violence. The Temple Mount (*Haram ash-Sharif*) in Jerusalem is a frequent flashpoint for riots, leading to conflict between Muslim residents of Jerusalem and the almost-exclusively Jewish police force assigned to the area.

[13] There are a small number of exceptions, most notably that Jewish citizens are required to serve in the military, while Muslims and Christians are not.

In September 2009, Muslim worshipers attacked several non-Muslim tourists and police officers, injuring thirty-five.[14] Violence spilled into the surrounding neighborhoods, and clashes between Arab residents and the police continued for several weeks. Similar outbreaks of violence, which typically involved stone throwing by rioters and the use of tear gas and stun grenades by police, occurred in 2015 and 2016.[15] Conflict between Arab and Jewish citizens, and between Arabs and the police, is not limited to Jerusalem. In July 2014, Arab rioters in the town of Qalansawe attacked cars belonging to Jewish drivers, and protesters in the northern towns of Taibe, Tira, and Baqa al-Gharbiya clashed with police.[16] In the most extreme cases, masked men blocked a road with burning tires and demanded that drivers tell them their religion. The men dragged two drivers who responded in Hebrew from their cars and beat them. They also attacked a uniformed police officer.

MAIN FINDINGS

I test the effects of police integration on citizens' attitudes, expectations, and behaviors using a variety of sources, including interviews with citizens and police officers, data on the religious identity of police officers, and journalist accounts of violent conflict and citizen–police relations. The Data and Methods Appendix at the end of this book details each of the sources with an eye toward replicability, and describes how each source's strengths and weaknesses complement one another.

Overall, I find consistent evidence that minorities who perceive the police as more integrated are less likely to perceive service provision as biased, less likely to believe that their group is unfairly excluded from employment in the police, and less expectant of future harm at the

14 Weiss, Efratt. "35 lightly injured in Temple Mount riots." *Ynet News*, September 27, 2009. www.ynetnews.com/articles/0,7340,L-3782317,00.html

15 Eisenbud, Daniel K., Ben Hartman, Khaled Abu Toameh, and Yaakov Lapin. "Riots break out on Jerusalem's Temple Mount for third straight day." *Jerusalem Post*, September 15, 2015. www.jpost.com/Arab-Israeli-Conflict/Riots-breaks-out-on-Jerusalems-Temple-Mount-for-third-straight-day-416198. Also see Eisenbud, Daniel K. "Police temporarily close Temple Mount to non-Muslim visitors after rioting resumes." *Jerusalem Post*, June 28, 2016. www.jpost.com/Arab-Israeli-Conflict/Policec-temporarily-close-Temple-Mount-to-non-Muslim-visitors-457938

16 Yaakov, Yifa and Itamar Sharon. "Israelis attacked, car set on fire during riots in Arab Israeli towns." *Times of Israel*, July 5, 2014. www.timesofisrael.com/israelis-attacked-car-set-on-fire-during-riots-in-arab-israeli-towns/

hands of the police or government. In Iraq, Sunnis who received an experimental prime about police integration are significantly less willing to use violence against the government. In Israel, non-Jews who perceive the police as more integrated are more willing to report crimes to the police, and local increases in police integration are associated with lower crime rates.

The results yield several additional insights about institutional design in divided societies. First, perceptions of police integration differ between the local and national levels, and in many cases, these perceptions predict different outcomes. My surveys asked respondents about the extent to which they believe the police are integrated both nationwide and in their neighborhood. In Iraq, the correlation between responses to these two questions is only .27; in Israel, it is .17. Differences in perceptions at different levels of government have important implications for citizen–state relations. Citizens are typically able to identify the demographic makeup of the police in their neighborhood or town, but perceptions of integration at the *national* level have the most explanatory power on outcomes like trust and expectations of mistreatment. Integration is not simply a story about the identity of the officers citizens interact with personally, but rather the way that institutional structures signal the government's intentions.

Second, dominant-group civilians do not stand in the way of police integration. One might reasonably assume that since members of the dominant group benefit from the status quo, they should oppose integration. In reality, very few of the Iraqi Shias and Israeli Jews I surveyed said that they oppose integration for fear of lost employment opportunities. An overwhelming majority of these individuals said that integration "allows [minorities] to do their part in contributing to society," while less than one in five worry that including them in the police "might allow them to disrupt the government." Rank-and-file police integration avoids the zero-sum attitudes which frequently characterize group-based competition for influence within law-making institutions. Opposition to integration comes not from ordinary citizens but from political elites. In Iraq, local politicians distribute jobs in the police as political patronage and resist moves which would erode their autonomy over hiring. In Israel, Arab political leaders worry that integration of the police and other areas of society will normalize the status quo and reduce pressure for Palestinian statehood.

Third, local-level officer heterogeneity, but not segregated inclusion, increases feelings of security and decreases expectations of mistreatment. Minorities who believe the police are heterogeneous, that is, integrated, are significantly less afraid of police and government repression, and are more likely to believe that the police and government distribute services fairly, compared to those who believe police officers are mainly out-groups. However, there is little or no difference between those who perceive officers as mostly coethnics and those who perceive officers as mostly out-groups.

Finally, improvements in crime prevention from integrated policing benefit all members of a community, regardless of their personal relationship with the police. In Israel, integration is associated with increased information sharing by Arab citizens but has no apparent effect – positive or negative – on Jewish citizens. In turn, integration is associated with a measurable decrease in crime in areas with large Arab populations, precisely the areas where it leads to greater information-sharing. Within those areas, both Arab and Jewish citizens report experiencing less crime. As its name implies, public safety is a pseudo-public good. Typical crime prevention techniques benefit all members of a community. An increase in police efficiency gives members of the dominant group reason to support integration and makes integration of the police a plausible first step toward broader reforms.

PLAN OF THE BOOK

The book proceeds as follows. Chapter 2 begins with an overview of the patterns of police integration worldwide. Nearly 40 percent of modern peace agreements include police reforms, and the makeup of the police rank and file is often central to these reforms. Despite this central role of the police in peace-building, existing literature on power sharing pays little attention to law enforcement (Lijphart 1969; McGarry 2005; Roeder and Rothchild 2005; Strøm et al. 2017). I place police power sharing in the context of this broader literature on institutions in divided societies. I argue that in divided societies, the police rank and file's unique combination of three characteristics – visibility, discretion, and capacity for violence – makes it especially influential in shaping citizen–state relations. The final section of the chapter details potential causal mechanisms, linking police integration with citizens' attitudes and expectations.

Chapters 3 and 4 introduce the independent variable, police integration, in Iraq and Israel. Chapter 3 explores the development of the Iraqi police in post-Saddam Iraq. After an initial purge of Sunnis from the security forces in 2003, the government faced intense pressures to reintegrate Sunnis into the police as a counterinsurgency measure. In Anbar and parts of Baghdad, these pressures led to substantial inclusion of Sunnis in the police. In other areas, local politicians resisted Sunni integration so they could instead distribute police jobs as political patronage. Drawing on interviews with Iraqi citizens, I show just how salient the police's makeup is to ordinary citizens' relationships with the state. Citizens view police jobs as a path toward empowerment and self-preservation. They also perceive that shared identity smooths interactions between citizens and the police.

In Israel, many Arab Israelis express skepticism that participation in the criminal justice system will improve services, worrying that Arab officers will instead be used as collaborators in anti-Arab repression. Interviews with police officers paint a picture of an institution that wishes to provide better services to minorities but struggles to do so due to a lack of citizen buy-in. I explore detailed panel data on police officers' religious identities and the processes through which the police assign officers from different groups to different locations.

Chapter 5 tests two intermediate links in the chain connecting police integration and citizens' behavior. First, how do citizens form perceptions of police integration? Interviews and focus groups reveal that citizens use a variety of cues like accents, names, and facial hair styles to determine an officer's group identity. Citizens' perceptions correlate closely with local integration, validating the confidence they express in their ability to identify officers' identities. After establishing this link between reality and perceptions, I turn to testing the relationship between perceptions of the police and perceptions of the government more broadly. Using Arab Barometer survey data from twelve countries, I show that citizens' attitudes toward the police are closely linked with their attitudes toward the government.

Chapters 6 and 7 explore the impacts of police integration on two relevant outcomes, anti-state violence in Iraq and crime prevention in Israel. The implementation of democracy in Iraq in 2004 shifted the balance of power between Sunnis and Shias, creating a security dilemma in which the Shia-dominated state struggled to credibly commit to positive future treatment of the newly weakened Sunnis (Dodge 2005). Police integration addresses this commitment problem by improving citizens' perceptions of how they are treated now and how they will be treated in the future. I first show that Iraqi Sunnis who believe the police are integrated interpret service provision as fairer, perceive that their group has better access to government jobs, and expect less future repression from the police or the government. These outcomes map onto commonly identified motives for conflict, including horizontal grievances (Gurr 1970; Wood 2003; Østby 2008; Cederman et al. 2011), unemployment (Miguel et al. 2004; Dube and Vargas 2013), and the commitment problem (Posen 1993; Fearon 1995a; Lake and Rothchild 1996). Indeed, Sunnis exposed to an experimental cue that the police are integrated are significantly less likely to support anti-state violence.

Chapter 7 asks how police integration affects the quality and distribution of crime prevention, a major concern for marginalized communities in Israel. I find that Arab citizens who perceive the police as more integrated are more willing to report crimes to the police, information the police can use to allocate resources more efficiently. Because public safety is locally non-excludable, improvements in crime prevention through this information mechanism benefit both Arab and Jewish citizens. Using panel data on officer demographics and a nationwide crime victimization survey, I show that within a given location, increases in the religious diversity of officers are associated with decreases in crime.

Chapter 8 explores potential barriers to police integration in the form of opposition from individuals privileged by the status quo. Survey data show that an overwhelming majority of Iraqi Shias and Israeli Jews support police integration. Instead, variation in police integration results from opposition by elites. In Iraq, local politicians resist sectarian integration for fear that it will limit their opportunities to distribute jobs in the police as patronage in return for political support. In Israel, Arab community leaders and politicians portray participation in the police as collaboration with the enemy, discouraging citizens from joining.

The concluding chapter highlights key findings and proposes a path forward for the implementation of police integration in power-sharing and post-conflict agreements. I specify policy recommendations based on my findings and lay out several questions for future research on policing and institutional representation in divided societies.

2

POWER SHARING, POLICING, AND PEACE

The police play a central role in shaping citizens' relationships with the state. Nowhere is this role more evident than peace-building in divided societies. Dozens of modern peace agreements call for police reforms, including changes to the makeup of rank-and-file officers. From the Philippines to Northern Ireland, and Burundi to Bosnia, peace-builders saw an inclusive police rank and file as critical to fostering peaceful and productive interactions between citizens and the state.

Despite the prevalence of police reforms that focus on officers' demographic makeup, we have an incomplete understanding of the mechanisms through which these reforms affect citizen–state relations. Many studies consider the effects of police demographics on service provision (Meier and Nicholson-Crotty 2006; Weitzer and Hasisi 2008; Ben-Porat and Yuval 2012; Kennedy et al. 2017), but we know less about how the makeup of the police affects broader political attitudes and behaviors. A related line of research asks whether inclusive governing institutions foster peaceful coexistence in divided societies but mentions the police only in passing (Lijphart 1969; McGarry 2005; Roeder and Rothchild 2005; Roeder 2007; Norris 2008; Strøm et al. 2017).

This chapter sets the stage for later microanalyses of Iraq and Israel with a discussion of police power sharing worldwide. Rank-and-file integration is common in attempts to end group-based conflict. Nearly one in five peace agreements signed between 1975 and 2011 explicitly refers to the composition of the police rank and file (Ansorg et al. 2016). Police integration is also relevant in societies that do not suffer from outright civil war; police departments in the United States, Israel, and Canada explicitly recruit minority officers under the expectation that an integrated force will foster better relations with citizens.

The second section situates policing within the broader literature on institutions in divided societies. I draw on the lessons of legislative and executive institution-building and especially military power sharing (Enloe 1980; Hoddie and Hartzell 2003; Toft 2009; Krebs and Licklider 2016). I argue that police integration provides many similar benefits to legislative and military power sharing, but that rank-and-file officers' unique combination of visibility, discretion, and capacity for violence makes their demographic makeup an especially strong signal of future behavior by the state. Police integration functions similarly to third-party enforcement of peace agreements, tying the powerful government's hands and credibly committing it to positive future treatment (Walter 1997; Fortna 2004; Mattes and Savun 2009).

The final section explores the specific mechanisms through which demographic inclusion in the police affects citizens' well-being. I focus on three outcomes in particular: the quality and distribution of policing services, access to employment, and assurance of physical safety. Integration signals the government's intention to treat marginalized groups positively on these dimensions, improving citizen–state relations.

POLICE INTEGRATION AND PEACE WORLDWIDE

From 1969 to 1998, conflict in Northern Ireland between those wishing to remain part of the United Kingdom and those seeking independence or a union with Ireland claimed 3,532 lives (Sutton N.D.). Most Catholics advocated independence, while most Protestants preferred loyalty to the British Crown. In 1998, the major parties to the conflict signed the Good Friday Agreement, a comprehensive peace accord that redesigned Northern Ireland's institutions and conferred a path to peaceful secession at a future date. Police reforms made up a significant part of the agreement. Prior to 1998, the Royal Ulster Constabulary (RUC) had very few Catholic officers, and many Catholics perceived it as a tool of Protestant oppression rather than a service-providing institution (Weitzer 1995; McGarry 2000). The agreement called for a dramatic increase in the proportion of Catholic officers via recruitment in Catholic neighborhoods and generous retirement incentives for Protestant officers (Bayley 2008). In 2015, the renamed Police Services of Northern Ireland (PSNI) had about 30 percent Catholics, up from 10 percent in the RUC in the mid-1990s. At the same time, Northern

Ireland experienced a dramatic reduction in violence. Notably, neither the police reforms nor the larger political agreement presented a permanent solution to Northern Ireland's political fate. Many Northern Irish Catholics still support independence from Great Britain.[1] However, peaceful political participation has replaced violent insurgency as the preferred method of competition.

The Good Friday Agreement is not unique in its use of police integration to address violent civil conflict. Of the 196 peace agreements signed between 1975 and 2011, 39.8 percent included provisions for police reforms, including 17.4 percent that specified a target or strategy for altering the composition of officers (Ansorg et al. 2016). Beyond Northern Ireland, agreements specifically mention the composition of the rank and file in countries as diverse as the Philippines, Bosnia–Herzegovina, Burundi, and Sudan. Most call for an institutionalized process by which members of the group associated with the opposition will be hired into the police, often specifying numbers or quotas.

The 1996 Mindanao Final Agreement between the Philippine government and the Moro National Liberation Front (MNLF) provides another example. The MNLF and other groups had been fighting against government forces in Mindanao, a Muslim-majority island in the overwhelmingly Catholic country, for decades. The agreement includes the following clause:

> During the transitional phase (Phase I), there shall be a program or process to allow the joining of MNLF elements into the PNP [Philippine National Police] and to be part of the PNP in accordance with guidelines and procedures under existing laws. The Philippine Government shall allocate one thousand five hundred (1,500) PNP vacancies for this purpose to be filled up by MNLF elements during the transition period, and another two hundred fifty (250) items for special or auxiliary services.[2]

In July 1998, the first group of 496 former MNLF fighters completed their police training and were assigned to PNP units. A further 979 new recruits underwent training in 1999, dramatically increasing the representation of Muslims in the PNP in Mindanao.

[1] *Belfast Telegram*, September 29, 2014. www.belfasttelegraph.co.uk/news/northern-ireland/northern-ireland-says-yes-to-a-border-poll-but-a-firm-no-to-united-ireland-30622987.html

[2] Peace Accords Matrix, Kroc Institute for International Peace Studies, University of Notre Dame. https://peaceaccords.nd.edu/provision/police-reform-mindanao-final-agreement

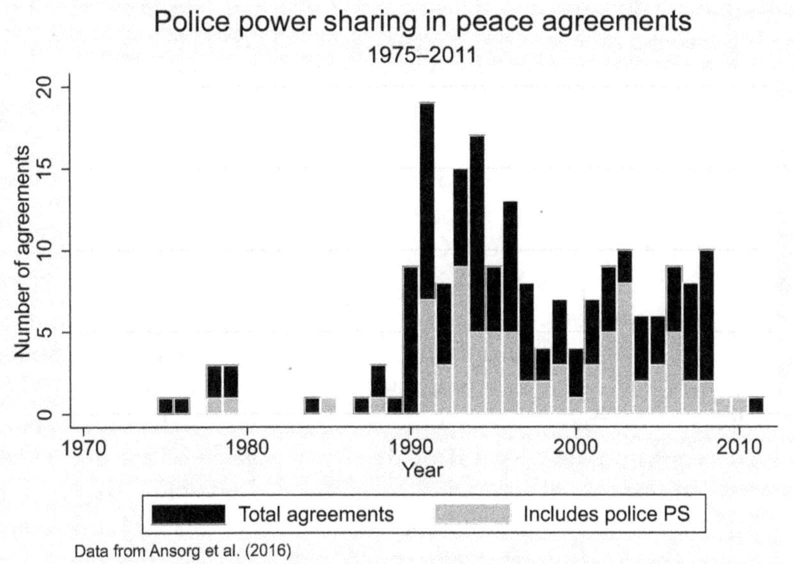

FIGURE 2.1 Police power sharing in peace agreements

Figure 2.1 shows that the proportion of peace agreements that include police power sharing has remained stable over the past four decades. Preliminary analysis suggests that these provisions prevent conflict recurrence, with agreements that include political provisions for police reform less likely to fail than agreements that do not include such provisions (Ansorg et al. 2016).

Countries not experiencing outright civil war also frequently employ police integration in hopes of improving security. In the United States, forces ranging from the Chicago Police Department to the Louisiana State Police have attempted to increase the hiring of racial or ethnic minorities in hopes that doing so will help them provide public safety more effectively (Skogan and Hartnett 1997; Lott 2000). In Norfolk, Virginia, where only 16 percent of officers are Black compared to 43 percent of the population, the police advertise in newspapers with large African American readership, and officers make regular recruiting visits to historically Black colleges and a gospel music radio station. The department also updated its entrance exam to correct for a disproportionate failure rate among minority test-takers. According to Chief Michael Goldsmith, "The problem is if you don't have a diverse and inclusive workforce, you end up not making good decisions because you don't have everybody's perspective at the table."[3]

Nationwide, US police departments implement integration through a number of channels, including recruitment drives like the ones in Norfolk, quotas, preferential hiring for minorities, which uses identity as a tie-breaker among similarly qualified applicants, and increased compensation (McCoy 1984). While departments typically enact these measures of their own volition, occasionally courts require them to take action to increase minority representation. In 1974, a federal judge ordered the Boston, Massachusetts, Police Department to implement procedures that would correct for "gross imbalances" in the department's racial makeup.[4] The department implemented a policy of hiring one new Black officer for every new White officer. Neighboring Cambridge, Massachusetts, as well as departments in Philadelphia, Pennsylvania, and Montgomery, Alabama, operated under similar court orders for decades (McCrary 2006).

Many departments in the United States require that their officers live in or within a certain distance of their jurisdiction. These "residency requirements" increase departments' racial representation (the extent to which officers' demographics match citizens' demographics) by restricting the recruiting pool to one that reflects the jurisdiction's civilian population. In previous coauthored research (Kennedy et al. 2017), I find a significant positive correlation between residency requirements and the extent to which departments racially represent their jurisdiction in large US cities. It is noteworthy, then, that residency requirements are losing popularity across the United States. In 1993, 54 of the 100 largest departments in the United States had residency requirements; by 2013, only twenty departments imposed such restrictions. Critics argue that these requirements prevent departments from hiring the most qualified officers. Police officers themselves are often the most vocal opponents, noting that residency requirements may force them into unaffordable or unappealing neighborhoods.

[3] Botti, David. "Why is it so hard to hire Black police officers?" BBC, www.bbc.com/news/av/magazine-33681160/why-is-it-so-hard-to-hire-black-police-officers

[4] Estes, Andrea. "Suit seeks to end hiring quotas." *The Boston Globe*, September 17, 2004. http://archive.boston.com/news/local/articles/2004/09/17/suit_seeks_end_to_police_hiring_quotas/

INSTITUTIONS IN DIVIDED SOCIETIES

Despite the frequent implementation of police integration globally, the police are largely absent from political science research on institutional solutions to group-based conflict (Horowitz 1985; Hartzell and Hoddie 2003; Collier and Hoeffler 2004; Roeder and Rothchild 2005; Laitin 2007; Cederman et al. 2010). Much of this research focuses on the way that political institutions affect citizens through legislation. It proposes that majoritarian democratic processes are inappropriate for societies with congealed intergroup divisions because they permanently exclude minorities from the decision-making process (Lijphart 1969). Ensuring that each relevant group is represented in law-making institutions will produce laws that all view as acceptable and legitimate (Lijphart 1984; Norris 2008). For example, the Taif Agreement, which ended Lebanon's bloody civil war in 1989, mandates a 1:1 ratio of Christian and Muslim members of parliament and divides power between the Sunni-held prime ministerial position and the Christian-held presidency. This agreement followed a similar arrangement in place since 1943, which called for a 6:5 Christian-to-Muslim ratio in parliament, and allocated key executive positions across religious confessions. In Iraq, following Saddam Hussein's removal in 2003, the Transitional Administrative Law (TAL) divided the executive branch into three positions and distributed one to each of the country's largest politically relevant sects: Shias, Sunnis, and Kurds.

The overwhelming majority of research on institutions in divided societies deals with legislatures and executives (Norris 2008; Strøm et al. 2017). Power sharing in these policy-making institutions distributes power at the elite level, implying that the concerns of the masses can be addressed by inclusiveness across ethnic elites (Nordlinger 1972). While a branch of this work discusses the military and bureaucracy, the police are almost completely absent.[5]

I argue that rank-and-file police officers are unique among government representatives in their combination of three characteristics: visibility, discretion, and capacity for violence. While members of other state institutions may hold one or two of these characteristics, no other institution empowers its members with all three. This combination makes police officers unusually influential in shaping citizens' expectations of the state.

[5] For notable exceptions, see Enloe (1980); Blair et al. (2016); Karim and Beardsley (2017)

Visibility

Police officers patrolling streets, issuing traffic tickets, and investigating crimes do so in the public eye. Compared to legislators, cabinet members, and soldiers, police officers interact far more frequently with civilians. They require citizens' cooperation to carry out these jobs effectively (Becker 1968; Skogan 1986; Weitzer and Tuch 2006; Nanes 2020), giving officers reason to seek out interactions even with citizens who have not broken the law. Citizens may go years without seeing their congressperson, but it is unlikely that they would go more than a few days without observing a police officer. Of Israeli citizens surveyed for this project, 34 percent reported that they "interact[ed] directly with a uniformed police officer" in the last year (30.5 percent of Jews, 38.2 percent of non-Jews). In their study of public safety in the Philippines, Haim et al. (2019) find that more than 84 percent of survey respondents encounter a public safety officer at least once per day. Contact with police officers constitutes citizens' most direct interaction with state authority: "The police are not only a regime's first line of defense; they are also the ordinary citizen's first line of trust – or distrust. For police are the extension of state authority with which citizens have most day-to-day contact" (Enloe 1980, 87). Virtually every citizen interviewed for this project in both Iraq and Israel reported seeing police officers daily.

Visibility provides citizens with direct, personally relevant information about the police that informs their perceptions of the institution, through both personal encounters (Tyler 2003, 2004; Murphy 2009; Mazerolle et al. 2013; Saunders et al. 2013) and stories from friends and family about their own experiences (Weitzer and Tuch 2006; Warren 2011). Given that politically salient group identities tend to be observable through skin color, language, accent, hair style, clothing style, or the name printed on an officer's uniform, visibility means that in divided societies citizens are aware of the demographic makeup of the police. Information about officer demographics is not just available to citizens who actively seek it out, as it may be with other government institutions; it is placed in front of them on a regular basis as they go through daily life. I show in Chapter 5 that Israeli citizens are well aware of the demographic makeup of the police officers in their city.

The importance of visibility is evident in debates over symbolism as well. During reforms to the Royal Ulster Constabulary (RUC), now the Police Services of Northern Ireland (PSNI), during the late 1990s, policy-makers on both sides of the conflict fiercely debated the police's use of nationalist symbols like the royal crown in the police logo. According to the Patten Report on potential reforms:

> The problem is that the name of the RUC, and to some extent the badge and the uniform too, have become politicised – one community effectively claiming ownership of the name of "our" police force, and the other community taking the position that the name is symbolic of a relationship between the police and unionism and the British state. (p. 99)

As a result, the RUC's metamorphosis into the PSNI involved removing nearly all symbols associated with the British government and monarchy (Smyth 2002).

Discretion

Frequent interactions between police officers and citizens also provide opportunities for officers to affect citizens' lives. Rank-and-file police officers hold enormous discretion over the way they enforce laws (Lipsky 1980). No law can anticipate every possible contingency, and the officers tasked with enforcement will inevitably encounter situations in which they must apply their judgment. The impossibility of providing sufficient police capacity to enforce every law 100 percent of the time means that officers must decide how to allocate their time and effort. Police officers are not just permitted but *expected* to overlook minor infractions much of the time. When officers engage with a citizen who has committed an infraction, they have discretion over the punishment, for example, choosing to give a verbal warning rather than a citation.

This discretion creates opportunities to differentiate services based on a citizen's identity. Even when the government passes laws that provide the same rights to all citizens, it is relatively easy for police officers to enforce those laws selectively. If the police systematically use their discretion to treat some groups differently than others, citizens who are treated more harshly may become frustrated with the government. In extreme cases, this frustration spills over into violence. In July 2016, an African American man in Dallas, Texas, shot and killed five White police officers in retaliation for what he perceived to be institutionalized violence by police against African American civilians.[6] As is the case throughout this volume, when it comes to citizens' reactions to police treatment, all that matters is that citizens *perceive* that the police engage in biased treatment. Not only does officers' discretion allow them to engage in bias, but the understanding that police officers have such discretion allows citizens to imagine that any negative treatment is due to officers' biases.

These two characteristics of the police, visibility and discretion, appear among other bureaucratic institutions like public works, education, healthcare, and social services. There is no shortage of evidence that bureaucratic representation matters for citizen–state relations in divided societies. Looking at courts in Israel, Shayo and Zussman (2011) find that legal claims are more likely to be accepted when the claimant is from the same ethnic group as the judge, while Grossman et al. (2015) show that Arab defendants receive more lenient sentences when there is at least one Arab judge on an appeals panel. Literature on "representative bureaucracy" (Kingsley 1944) generally argues that bureaucracies whose demographics match those of the population they serve administer public policy more responsively. Representation is important for symbolic reasons, as inclusion reflects equal access to power and confers legitimacy to bureaucratic institutions (Selden 1997). Perhaps more importantly, it affects the way that government institutions provide goods and services. Schools with more teachers and administrators from racial minorities make policies about student groupings that are more favorable for minority students (Meier and Stewart Jr. 1992). Rocha and Hawes (2009) find that an increase in teachers from minority groups leads to better educational outcomes for citizens from *all* groups, a result that I partially replicate with regard to police representation and crime in Israel (Chapter 7). While there is no conclusive evidence on why bureaucracies that demographically match the civilian population provide higher-quality services, most explanations focus on bureaucrats' discretion in implementation as the key mechanism (Lipsky 1980; Kennedy et al. 2017).

Capacity for Violence

The police diverge from bureaucratic and law-making institutions in their third characteristic, the capacity for violence. Police officers are

[6] Fernandez, Manny, Richard Perez-Pena, and Jonah Engel Bromwich. "Five Dallas officers were killed as payback, chief says." *New York Times*, July 8, 2016. www.nytimes.com/2016/07/09/us/dallas-police-shooting.html

equipped and expected to use violence to enforce laws. To the extent that the state has a monopoly on the legitimate use of violence (Weber 1919), the police execute this violence. The physical capacity and legal authority to use violence against civilians raises the stakes in the design of the police and ensures that in divided societies, citizens should care deeply about the extent to which the police include their group.

The police's capacity for violence affects citizens' relationships with the state through a number of channels. Most obviously, it affects citizens' physical security. The police do not always use their capacity for violence to protect citizens; they also use it to control them (Westley 1970; Willis 2015). The police's role in providing security and protecting the rule of law is also central to the state's raison d'etre (Olson 1993). Crime prevention clearly falls into this category, as does combating rebels or organized violence in countries where such problems exist. Finally, the police's capacity for violence makes it difficult for the government to purge the police, and therefore makes inclusion of the police a credible signal of *future* behavior. Once police officers have been armed and provided access to sensitive information, it is difficult to take their weapons and information away.

The police are not the only armed state institution. A related body of research asks whether identity-based inclusion in the military mitigates conflict (Enloe 1980; Toft 2009; Hoddie and Hartzell 2003; Wilkinson 2015; Krebs and Licklider 2016). Military power sharing is concerned first and foremost with ensuring the physical security of each group. An inclusive military contributes to the security of weaker groups much in the same way as an inclusive police force: by arming and organizing members of the group, and by making the state's security dependent on the participation of that group. Aside from the obvious possibility of turning their guns against the state, disgruntled security forces may refuse to protect the regime (Hassan 2017). When Irish soldiers serving in colonial India received news about the suffering of the Irish under the British "Black and Tan" police back home, they protested by refusing to report for duty despite the regiment's 200-year history of "loyal combat on behalf of the British Crown" (Enloe 1980, 47).

An integrated military in which soldiers serve alongside out-group members may also affect the attitudes and behaviors of the soldiers toward out-groups. Enloe (1980) notes that the military is a highly structured environment within which soldiers of all backgrounds are equals working toward a common goal.

> Men (rarely women, which may be a critical flaw in the concept) fighting together in the trenches against a common enemy sharing the same tinned food and grievances against drill sergeants, will learn to communicate across allegedly superficial cultural barriers and come to appreciate their common allegiances to a supra-ethnic sates. Eventually, if complemented by other integrative trends in society, universal military service may make ethnic categories quite irrelevant even to security-conscious state elites. (202)

Indeed, evidence from the militaries in Burundi (Samii 2013) and Malaysia (Ostwald 2013) suggests that increased ethnic representation decreases prejudicial behavior against non-coethnics and increases expressions of civic identity.

Whereas the military shares the police's capacity for violence, soldiers do not have the same level of visibility as police officers. Shaping citizens' attitudes depends not just on the makeup of the institution but on citizens being able to observe its makeup (or at least *believe* they can observe it). Soldiers typically serve outside of the public eye, fighting on the battlefield and residing in barracks. In the rare situations in which soldiers interact regularly with civilians, the security situation has likely already deteriorated to the point that peace is unlikely in the near term.

Finally, the police and military differ in the discretion they allow their members. Whereas police officers have wide berth to interpret policies and implement them as they see fit (Lipsky 1980), soldiers are expected to follow orders in all but the most extreme circumstances. While soldiers can certainly affect citizens' lives, under normal circumstances police officers have greater opportunities to do so thanks to their discretion and more frequent interactions.

Shaping Future Expectations

The police's capacity for violence does not just allow officers to harm or protect civilians today; it also empowers included groups to resist any attempts to backtrack on inclusion in the future. While a powerful leader can ignore or remove out-group cabinet members with relative ease, attempts to fire all police officers from a particular identity group *en masse* could spur armed resistance by those very officers. Similarly, minority-group members of parliament have little recourse if they are suddenly relieved of their duties, or if the government simply ignores their votes. Magaloni (2008, 716) applies this weakness to dictators attempting to solve a commitment problem with their rivals, pointing out that "once a rival gives up his intention to rebel by entering the legislature, what prevents the dictator from reneging by simply ignoring the rival's policy demands or by taking his seat away?" Boix and Svolik (2013) note that such arrangements can only remain credible when they coincide with a balance in power between the involved parties. Power sharing in the police and military diverges from power sharing in most other institutions because the capacity for violence makes it more difficulty for the state to renege on inclusion.

Iraq's experience with legislative power sharing in the early 2000s, before integrating the police, illustrates the problematic reversibility of conventional power sharing. The Iraqi Governing Council, in power from July 2003 to June 2004, consisted of tribal and political leaders roughly in proportion to each sect's population share: thirteen Shias, five Sunnis, five Kurds, one Turkmen, and one Assyrian, all hand-picked by US leaders to represent their sect. The Transitional Government that followed was similarly fragmented, with a prime minister, president, two vice presidents, and three deputy prime ministers carefully allocated across Shia, Sunni, and Kurdish leaders. The country's constitution, drafted and ratified in 2005, shares executive power among the prime minister, president, and three vice presidents, with convention dictating that the positions be distributed to representatives of each main sect. In the legislature, a parliamentary system with multimember districts privileges smaller groups and leads to a proliferation of parties, and eight seats are reserved for the country's smallest religious minorities (United States Commission on International Religious Freedom 2013). In short, law-making positions throughout the government included members of all salient ethnic and religious groups.

As soon as the United States began to draw down its troops in 2011, the Shia-dominated government began to backtrack in this inclusiveness. Prime Minister Nouri al-Maliki, a Shia, ordered the arrest of Sunni Vice President Tariq al-Hashemi. A year later, the government arrested the bodyguards of Sunni Minister of Finance Rafi al-Essawi, causing him to flee Baghdad for Sunni-majority Ramadi.[7] According to al-Essawi, "All the commitments that Maliki gave to the politicians ... nothing from that agreement was fulfilled or implemented.

[7] Boghani, Priyanka (2014), "In their own words: Sunnis on their treatment in Maliki's Iraq." *PBS Frontline*, October 28. www.pbs.org/wgbh/frontline/article/in-their-own-words-sunnis-on-their-treatment-in-malikis-iraq/

Maliki – he had to get rid of all Sunni politicians who were capable of saying 'no' to him, his policies or his behavior."[8] Shia politicians forced out Sunni rivals using the Shia-dominated security forces when necessary. Former Vice President Hashemi tried to convince Sunni insurgents to lay down their weapons in spite of the violence and participate in elections. Their response: "You remember in 2008 when you convinced us to join you in the political process? This is the result? Now you are not able to protect yourself? [There's] no way that we are going to participate in the political process."[9] Power sharing in Iraq's legislative and executive institutions failed to prevent powerful leaders from reneging on their promises and returning to exclusionary, repressive policies. In turn, minorities who feared for their future eschewed the democratic process and turned to violence.

On the other hand, purges of the police are extremely rare, and reforms tend not to involve the wholesale replacement of personnel. In São Paulo and Buenos Aires, the police used their capacity for violence to prevent major changes sought by the government (González 2019), while policing institutions in post-Soviet Russia proved to be even more durable than the regime itself (Taylor 2014). True purges occur only in extreme circumstances, for example, during regime change accompanied by massive shifts in the balance of power between groups. Once such instance occurred with the end of White rule in modern-day Zimbabwe, then Rhodesia, in June 1979. Abel Muzorewa replaced Ian Smith as the country's first Black prime minister and immediately appointed twelve new Black Rhodesians to his cabinet. Yet, Zimbabwe's armed institutions were not purged; the White military and police leadership initially retained their positions.[10] It was only after the total collapse of the previous regime and Robert Mugabe's election the following year that the police gradually began to "Africanize" through early retirements for White police officers (Lohman and MacPherson 1983). Even then, compared to the tidal wave of change in most other spheres of politics and society, the removal of White police officers occurred relatively gradually.

The difficulty of reversing police integration allows it to play a similar role to third-party enforcement in peace agreements. Walter (2002)

[8] Boghani 2014

[9] Borghani 2014

[10] BBC, "1979: End of White rule in Rhodesia" http://news.bbc.co.uk/onthisday/hi/dates/stories/june/1/newsid_2492000/2492915.stm

argues that power sharing alone is insufficient to solve the commitment problem, and that peace agreements between formerly warring parties can only survive if they contain third-party guarantees. Under such an arrangement, a powerful outside actor, perhaps another state or an international organization, commits to intervening in the event that either side breaks the agreement (Walter 1997, 2002; Mattes and Savun 2009). These third-party guarantees may require an indefinite peacekeeping presence (Fortna 2004), a costly prospect.

To the extent that security forces integration balances power *and* is expected to retain that balance indefinitely into the future, it reduces the need for third-party enforcement. Security forces power sharing reduces expectations that any side will renege on its agreement by positioning the opposing side to defend itself in such an event. Just as the threat of third-party enforcement should prevent the more powerful side from harming the weaker side, placing weapons in the hands of minority police officers and making security dependent on their participation similarly deters attempts to renege on any agreement. Security forces power sharing provides an appealing alternative to requiring an outside enforcer to bear the military, financial, and political costs of indefinite involvement.

EXPECTATIONS: SERVICE PROVISION, EMPLOYMENT, AND PHYSICAL SECURITY

Police integration affects minority citizens' well-being in a number ways. In this section, I explore three categories of outcomes: the quality and distribution of police services, access to desirable employment, and assurance of physical security. In Chapter 6, I draw on the civil conflict literature to link deficiencies in these outcomes with participation in anti-state violence. In many cases, the mechanisms I describe affect citizens' actual well-being, for example by reducing over-policing or providing fair consideration for employment. Yet, it is the *perception* of these outcomes that drives citizens' behavior, and I note several instances in which perceptions may deviate from reality.

Quality and Distribution of Policing Services

First, police inclusion may influence the quality and distribution of police service provision. Language abilities often coincide with politically relevant cleavages. In Israel, most Jewish citizens' first language is Hebrew, while most Arab citizens' first language is Arabic. Officers and citizens who are fluent in the same language can communicate more effectively, avoiding misunderstandings, fostering cooperation, and improving service delivery. According to First Sergeant Zohar Subash, "Being an Arabic speaker is a real asset. Having someone understand me, having us understand each other, will make [the citizen] feel more secure speaking to someone in his own language. He'll feel more secure speaking to me in my own language."[11] Subash's statement highlights that language or even accent can affect citizens' *feelings* about an interaction regardless of their functional impact. In Israel, most Arab citizens speak sufficient Hebrew to communicate effectively with Hebrew-speaking police officers, yet they might feel more confident about their interaction if they conduct it in Arabic. In Iraq, where Sunni and Shia police officers and citizens all speak native Arabic, citizens frequently point to regional accents as an obvious signal of an officer's sect, making it likely that these accents color their perceptions of how the officer treats them as well. Shared culture between officers and civilians might have a similar effect, providing common heuristics which guide behavior in unfamiliar situations (Habyarimana et al. 2007).

While shared language and culture suggest that "in-group policing" will maximize perceptions of the quality of service delivery, patrol-level heterogeneity may reduce identity-motivated biases in officers' behaviors through a separate set of mechanisms. First, integration may reduce officers' cognitive bias against out-group civilians. In divided societies, individuals often have limited interaction with non-coethnics and form attitudes toward out-groups based on stereotypes and received wisdom. Contact hypothesis (Allport 1954) specifies that regular contact with out-groups should increase an individual's preference for that out-group when the individuals in question are of equal status, cooperate with one another, pursue common goals, and acknowledge a common authority. By forcing these types of interactions between non-coethnics, police integration may replace negative stereotypes with positive personal experiences as the basis for attitudes toward out-groups.

The Israel Police attempted to leverage the positive effects of contact hypothesis by centralizing training for all officers in a single academy starting in 2015. According to one of the designers of the training program, during training Jewish officers get to know minority officers as

11 Yanovsky, Roi (2016), "Arab police officers urge young Arabs to join force." *Ynet News* October 30, www.ynetnews.com/articles/0,7340,L-4872271,00.html

people and as representatives of their community. This exposure helps break stereotypes, so that by the time officers begin working they have professional acquaintances from all backgrounds.[12]

There is some concern that minority officers may learn to identify more with the police than with civilians from their own group (Weitzer 2000), preventing integration from improving police treatment of minorities. But the same mechanism of learned police identity could also lead members of the dominant group to become more objective, reducing their mistreatment of out-group citizens.

Even if interactions between out-group officers do not shift officers' attitudes toward out-groups, integration may reduce biased behavior by constraining officers' actions. When one officer treats a citizen poorly based on his or her identity, other officers can intervene. Biased treatment is often subconscious, allowing the mere presence of a coethnic officer to reduce mistreatment even without having to threaten sanctions. During an informal conversation, a Jewish volunteer police officer who works near Hebron expressed to me that he holds great respect for his Arab police partners and defers to their authority on certain professional issues:

> **MN:** Is there a difference in the way that Jewish and Arab police officers treat people? Do officers tend to treat people who are like them differently? Or is ethnicity totally irrelevant?
>
> **Officer:** There are some offenses that I will ticket you for no matter what. Things related to safety. If you're talking on the phone while driving, or if you're not wearing a seat belt, you know you're not supposed to do that. I write them a ticket.
>
> But there are other things that are different. Like if someone has a headlight out, if they're Jewish I'll probably give them a pass. If they're a Jew, you know they're probably going to go get it fixed. But Arabs, they'll just let the car fall apart. So I give them a fine or else they won't get it fixed.
>
> [pause] But if I have an Arab officer with me I won't. I won't stop them unless the other guy [the Arab officer] says to, and then I will.[13]

[12] Author interview, July 24, 2014

[13] Author interview, July 31, 2014

This anecdote suggests that the presence of an Arab officer alongside this Jewish officer decreases the likelihood that Arabs will be over-policed.

Regardless of officers' actual behavior, changes in citizens' perceptions can improve public safety by increasing cooperation with the police. The police rely heavily on information from citizens about problems in the community to allocate their resources for crime prevention (Weitzer and Tuch 2006; Skolnick and Bayley 1988; Akerlof and Yellen 1994). Existing research, both from my own work (Haim et al. 2019; Nanes 2020) and from other studies (Lyall et al. 2015), suggests that citizens are most likely to cooperate with state security forces when they come from the same identity group or have other personal ties to them. In turn, the police are able to provide citizens with better services. In Chapter 7, I find that local increases over time in police integration are associated with decreases in minor crimes like petty thefts, as citizens are increasingly willing to report information that the police use to address crime.

Employment

Many governments employ large swaths of their population, with jobs in education, healthcare, infrastructure management, and law enforcement providing paychecks for many citizens. The Israeli government employs about 6.5 percent of its population, nearly 15 percent of the workforce,[14] many of whom are police officers. In Iraq, a staggering 60 percent of full-time workers and 12.5 percent of the population worked for the state in 2013. The security sector alone employs close to a million of Iraq's thirty-five million residents (al-Ali 2014). Because of its visibility, police integration provides a strong source of information to citizens about opportunities for employment in the government. Where group identity is salient and exclusion along group lines is common, seeing large numbers of officers from one's own group reassures citizens that the police offer a viable avenue for employment.

In many developed countries, policing is a public-minded service that citizens do for their community, often for less money than they

14 "Size of the public sector: Government wage bill and employment." *The World Bank* February 17, 2016. www.worldbank.org/en/topic/governance/brief/size-of-the-public-sector-government-wage-bill-and-employment

could earn elsewhere. I argue in Chapter 4 that one of the main impositions to Arabs joining the Israeli police is the feeling that working as a police officer provides a service to the state that the state has not earned. Yet in other settings, employment as a police officer is highly desirable for the stable paycheck it provides compared to other options. Particularly in less-developed countries like Iraq, government jobs provide an unusually stable income. A former administrator at the Jordan International Police Training Center, an academy outside of Amman that trained tens of thousands of Iraqi police recruits during the mid-2000s, recounts that one day trainers noticed a group of recruits gathered around one of the trainees. One of the trainers asked what was going on. A recruit said to him, "You don't know who this is, do you? This guy is one of the most famous comedians in Iraq!" Following the collapse of the government and the outbreak of civil war, there was little demand for professional comedians, making employment in the police attractive for this out-of-work celebrity.[15] Employment in the police also conveys authority and power, both officially and through opportunities for corruption. Thus, citizens should care whether their group has fair access to government jobs, and police officers' visibility sends a strong signal of this access.

Physical Security

Finally, police integration bolsters the physical security of included groups. Inclusion provides members of the included group with access to weapons, vehicles, and communications equipment, which enhance the group's ability to defend itself. It brings together fighting-age men and women, aiding coordination and solving a barrier to participation in conflict. Assigning officers to serve civilians from all groups, not just from their own group, provides an additional layer of security by making service provision contingent on the participation of officers from the marginalized group.

The physical security that inclusion in the police confers did not go unnoticed by Iraqis during the early period of postwar reconstruction. The international trainers who staffed one of the largest training academies quipped that they were "training the future veterans of the

[15] Author interview with Sam Juett, a former administrator at the Jordan International Police Training Center. February 22, 2016

great Iraq civil war," as a large number of recruits joined not just to become police officers but to jockey for position in anticipation of the fighting they expected to come.[16] These recruits knew that if fighting were to break out, their membership in the police would help them protect themselves and their families. Civilians, too, understood the variety of ways in which participating in the police could secure their families and communities. "[Sunnis in Ramadi] felt safe when their men could join the police force and secure their areas by themselves. Joining the police and working in their own local areas were also a way to avoid being targeted by the Americans" (Al-Jabouri and Jensen 2010, 11).

CONCLUSION

Peace agreements aimed at halting violence between warring groups in divided societies regularly call for greater inclusiveness in the state security services. At the same time, police departments in developed countries worldwide are increasingly concerned with the demographic makeup of their force. In both cases, policy-makers and political leaders expect that greater inclusiveness in the police will decrease conflict and improve service provision. Yet, the causal pathways linking inclusiveness with security outcomes remain understudied. Despite a rich political science literature on institutions in divided societies and research from criminology linking identity-group representation with police service provision, these bodies of work rarely speak to one another. As such, we know little about the specific mechanism through which police integration in divided societies can improve citizen–state relations.

While the makeup of legislatures, cabinets, and courts is undoubtedly important for these relations, I argue that rank-and-file police officers' unique combination of visibility, discretion, and capacity for violence sets them apart from all other government institutions and positions them to impact citizens' attitudes and expectations to a greater extent than any other institution. I identify a number of mechanisms through which integration shapes these relations: by impacting perceptions of the quality and distribution of policing services, access to government jobs and their associated benefits, and expectations of physical security.

[16] Author interview with Sam Juett. February 22, 2016

I return to these mechanisms in Chapter 6, where I map them onto common motives for participating in anti-state violence.

Ultimately, the linchpin of my argument rests on citizens' ability to recognize police integration and its resulting effects on their attitudes and expectations. The police's critical role in fostering security, whether by reducing insurgent violence in war-torn Baghdad or mitigating petty theft in Tel Aviv, depends on citizens' expectations about how the government and its representatives will treat them. Nowhere does demographic integration shape these expectations more than it does in the police.

3

SECTARIANISM AND CONFLICT IN THE IRAQI POLICE

In late 2006, sectarian violence in Iraq reached a fevered pitch. Since the start of the war three and a half years earlier, more than 650,000 individuals had been killed in fighting, and the frequency of fatal violence was increasing at an alarming rate. Some of the fiercest fighting occurred in Anbar and Diyala provinces north of Baghdad, home to large Sunni populations. In a desperate effort to regain order, the international coalition combating the insurgency recruited nearly 75,000 fighters from Sunni tribes (Dodge 2012, 98). They initially organized these fighters into militias which fought alongside foreign troops. The following year, however, Prime Minister Nouri al-Maliki expanded the size of Anbar's police force to absorb about 12,000 of the Sunni militia members, significantly increasing the proportion of Sunnis serving in the government's forces in Anbar. "Acceptance of a substantial number of volunteers [into the police] would convince many Sunnis that there was a place for them in the system, and the many safeguards [for screening recruits] would reassure the government" of the fighters' loyalty (Robinson 2009, 254). Around the same time, the government also offered jobs or pensions to 46,800 former members of Saddam's army who had lost their posts after the invasion (Robinson 2009, 335). Many found their way back to the police in Anbar.

Yet, elsewhere in Iraq, the ranks of the police remained filled almost exclusively by Shias. "De-Baathification" purged Sunnis from the security forces in 2003, and in many places local politicians prevented their reintegration even after the coalition forces warmed to the idea. In 2016, entire neighborhoods of Baghdad were policed exclusively by Shias. Southern Iraq's police also remain overwhelmingly Shia, as the police tend not to send Sunni officers recruited from northern provinces to the predominantly Shia southern provinces. Thus, Iraq exhibits incomplete police integration, with geographic variation in the extent to which the police include minorities.

This chapter explores the causes and patterns of this variation. The absence of systematic data on officer demographics in Iraq makes this task challenging, but I piece together a picture of regional trends using media reports and survey data. I then ask where these patterns came from. I first argue that despite sectarian tensions and violence since 1990, Iraqi history provides substantial precedent for sectarian cooperation and institutional integration. For most of the country's history, peaceful coexistence characterized the relationship between Sunni and Shia Arabs, and governments intentionally designed bureaucratic agencies to emphasize national rather than sectarian identity. The post-2003 hyper-relevance of sectarian identity emerged not from "ancient hatreds" of out-groups but from fears of violent mistreatment by the government, insurgent militias, and foreign forces.

Today's pattern of police integration results from foreign forces' purge of the security forces in 2003, followed by substantial incentives for leaders to consolidate personal political support. In this environment, Shia politicians – in power thanks to their demographic majority – traded positions in the police to clerics and leaders of social movements in return for votes and support. As violence worsened, some leaders recognized that they could not restore order in primarily Sunni areas without the participation of the Sunni population. Other leaders responded to conflict by doubling down on favoritism and sectarianism, resisting integration for fear it would hamper their ability to trade jobs for support. These leaders undermined police integration not just by refusing to include Sunnis outright, but by isolating Sunni officers in homogeneous units that serve predominantly Sunni areas, and by under-equipping and failing to pay officers in those units.

The final section explores citizens' attitudes toward police integration. Surveys and interviews with Iraqi citizens show that an overwhelming majority of Iraqis believe they would be better off under an integrated police force. For example, interviewees worry that prejudices cause out-group officers to be skeptical of their statements or concerns when they go to the police for help. Regardless of whether officers actually behave differently based on sect, it is clear that citizens *believe* that they do so, with several interviewees recounting anecdotes in which they think their identity affected the way a police officer treated them.

Three formal scope conditions delineate the Iraqi security institutions discussed here. First, the institution must be controlled by the central government. Second, it must have only a *domestic* security mandate. Lastly, the institution's officers must regularly interact with ordinary citizens. Consequently, my analysis excludes the military, as well as the Kurdish Peshmerga and other ethnic militias whose chain of command does not run through Baghdad. I include the Local Police (who despite their name fall under the authority of the Ministry of Interior), the Federal Police, and paramilitary forces under the government's direct command (referred to here as "domestic security forces").

IDENTITY, CONFLICT, AND COOPERATION

Sectarian identity in Iraq, and especially the relationship between the approximately 50 percent Shia Arab majority and the 25 percent Sunni Arab minority,[1] is both omnipresent and taboo. While Iraqis consider explicit references to sect offensive in everyday discourse, Iraqi politics has been organized around sect in some capacity since Ottoman rule. Sunni and Shia designations are more relevant as cultural group identities than as religious demarcations. There are, of course, real differences in religious practices between followers of the two sects, but these theological differences are rarely relevant to ordinary citizens (Haddad 2011, 24–25).

The sudden elimination of the Baath regime in 2003 left a political power vacuum. In the absence of strong state institutions, civic and political associations organized along sectarian lines were the most developed institutions. Iraqis turned to them for services and, increasingly, security (Robinson 2009). Militias, many associated with sectarian organizations like the Supreme Council for the Islamic Revolution in Iraq (SCIRI) or cleric Muqtada as-Sadr's *Jaish al-Mahdi* (Mahdi Army, or JAM), took on increasing roles in national politics.

[1] These figures are contested and imprecise. While it is clear that there are far more Shia Arabs than Sunni Arabs, Shias' absolute majority of the population is not universally accepted. Collection of accurate figures is further complicated by Iraq's cross-cutting ethnic and religious cleavages; virtually, all ethnic Kurds are either Sunni or Shia Muslims, but from a political perspective they are distinct from the Sunni and Shia Arab "sects" which make up sociopolitical groups. The numbers I present conform to most independent estimates of the Iraqi population's religious demographics but are not based on any new evidence and should not be viewed as authoritative.

Simultaneously, Shias dominated the newly elected government thanks to their demographic majority and the "de-Baathification" policy, which purged many Sunni members of the previous regime from government (Robinson 2009; Spain and Turchie 2013).

This coalescing of society around identity alongside the sudden shakeup of each group's relative power created a security dilemma. Haddad (2011, 184) describes a "mini arms race" in which antagonistic group relations spiraled out of control due to uncertainty over future distributions of power. Many of the militias that surfaced in 2003 had a history of violence along identity lines. For example, during the Iran-Iraq war of the 1980s, SCIRI's military wing fought on the Iranian side of the conflict and committed violence against Sunni Iraqis. SCIRI's reemergence in 2003 caused considerable fear and uncertainty among Sunnis (al-Ali 2014, 41). Political elites further stoked Sunnis' fears of insecurity through fiery rhetoric. Adnan al-Dulaimi, an MP from one of the Sunni parliamentary blocs, proclaimed in a speech in December 2006, "It is a sectarian war! It is a sectarian struggle that aims to eradicate the Sunni ... Your [Sunni] brothers in Iraq and especially in Baghdad will be destroyed. They will be trampled under the feet of the Shia. They will be exterminated" (al-Ali 2014, 115). The United States' withdrawal in 2011 and uncertainty over its willingness to intervene in future violence further eroded Sunnis' expectations of security.

Today's citizen–police relations are influenced by police complicity in sectarianism in the early post-invasion years. In some cases, the overwhelmingly Shia force neglected Sunni neighborhoods. In the upper-class, mixed-sect Baghdad neighborhood of Mansour, citizens felt the predominantly Shia police force never left their station to patrol or provide services (Robinson 2009). Other sectarianism was more overt. In August 2005, police officers dragged thirty-six men from their homes in the Huriya neighborhood of Baghdad, tortured them, and dumped their bodies near the Iranian border (Perito 2011). In a separate incident, police units associated with the Badr Organization were accused of acting as death squads against Sunnis. "Men dressed as police commandos kidnapped men from Sunni neighborhoods. These men later turned up dead, often from a bullet to the back of the head" (Cole 2007, 116). There are numerous reports of Shia imagery and slogans posted at police checkpoints and around police stations.[2]

[2] Damon, Arwa. "Iraq at crossroads as bombs explode." *CNN*, April 30, 2013. http://edition.cnn.com/2013/04/30/world/meast/iraq-violence-qa/

US soldier James Danley recounts his own observations of policing in the predominantly Sunni Baghdad suburb of Dora, circa 2005:

> The national police were sectarian murderers. They were there to kill people who lived [in Dora]. You had what could only be described as liquidation missions in which they would go into a Sunni neighborhood like ours and this National Police Unit would simply shoot everything they could. They would simply fire in every direction. (Dodge 2012, 64)

After Sunni insurgents bombed the Samarra mosque, an important Shia site, in February 2006, "police units in the city had a direct role in pushing hundreds of thousands of Sunnis out of mixed-sect neighborhoods, especially on the west side of the city" (Rayburn 2014, 81). In Basra, the largest city in southern Iraq, the police chief "admitted that much of his force was of dubious loyalty and mainly oriented to militias and religious parties" (Cole 2007, 116). US Lieutenant Colonel Joel Rayburn refers to the Iraqi police by their partisan militia affiliation: "The Badr officers who took command of much of the Ministry of Interior in 2005 unleashed the police machinery on the population of greater Baghdad" (Rayburn 2014, 81).

The police also made attractive targets for insurgents, especially those seeking to undermine the legitimacy of the new regime or retaliate for sectarian attacks (Rayburn 2014). In a particularly bloody incident in September 2004, a car bomb outside the Al-Karkh police station killed forty-seven people, primarily police officers and recruits (Hashim 2005, 39). Insurgents attacked four police stations in January 2005 alone.[3]

Sectarian behavior by the police began to subside in mid-2006. New Interior Minister Jawad al-Bolani purged the most egregious sectarian actors from the Federal Police, including more than 60,000 officers, seven of the nine commanders of National Police brigades, and seventeen of twenty-seven heads of National Police battalions (Dodge 2012, 125). The reforms halted the most egregious abuses, paving the way for integration and improved citizen–police relations that I describe later in this chapter.

While the police's overt complicity in sectarianism has declined dramatically since the early post-Saddam years, negative perceptions of the

[3] January 10, in southern Baghdad; January 11 in Tikrit; January 26 in Riyadh; January 28 in Dora, Baghdad. *MIPT Terrorism Knowledge Base*. Accessed May 2, 2018, https://web.archive.org/web/20061007163729/http://tkb.org/Incident.jsp?incID=21477

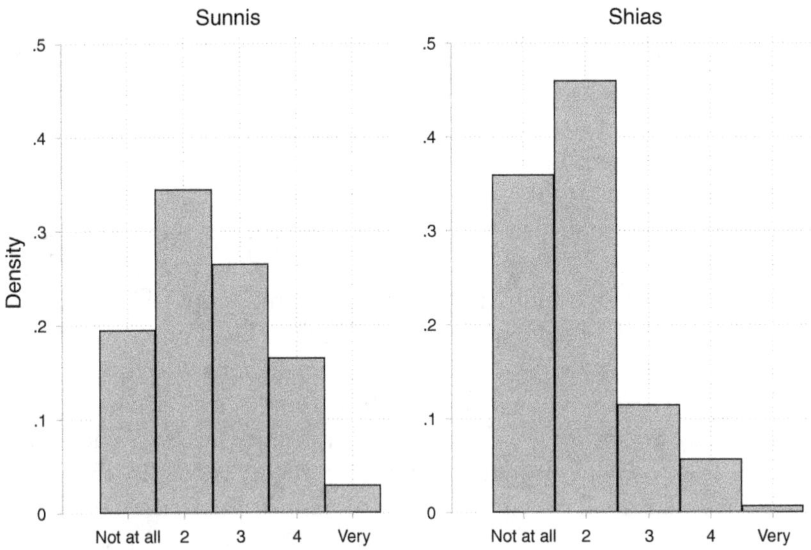

FIGURE 3.1 Responses to the question, "Do you ever feel afraid of the Iraqi Police?"

force linger. Among respondents to my survey of Baghdad residents, Sunnis were much more fearful of the police than Shias on average (Figure 3.1). While the difference between Sunnis and Shias is striking, the fact that 18 percent of Shias and 46 percent of Sunnis report being at least somewhat afraid of the police is troubling in its own right.

The police's poor performance in defending Iraq in June 2014 further shaped perceptions of the institution. The Islamic State invaded the northern border with Syria and quickly overran Iraqi police and military forces, taking several major cities including Mosul. Tens of thousands of soldiers and police officers abandoned their positions as opposition fighters approached.[4] Analysts blamed the Iraqi forces' poor performance on corruption and politicization, arguing that the recruitment and promotion of soldiers and officers based on political loyalties undermined morale.[5] The latter half of 2014 through early

[4] Sly, Liz and Ahmed Ramadan (2014), "Insurgents seize Iraq city of Mosul as security forces flee." *The Washington Post*, June 10. www.washingtonpost.com/world/insurgents-seize-iraqi-city-of-mosul-as-troops-flee/2014/06/10/21061e87-8fcd-4ed3-bc94-0e309af0a674_story.html?noredirect=on&utm_term=.63faa63b6078

[5] Fraiman, Keren, Austin Long, and Caitlin Talmadge (2014), "Why the Iraqi army collapsed (and what can be done about it)." *The Washington Post: Monkey Cage*, June 13. www.washingtonpost.com/news/monkey-cage/wp/2014/06/13/why-the-iraqi-army-collapsed-and-what-can-be-done-about-it/?utm_term=.18a1c3a16a56

2016 witnessed intense fighting as Iraqi forces regrouped to retake territory. As they did, reports of sectarian retaliation reemerged. In 2015, the government launched an investigation over accusations that security forces had executed eighty unarmed civilians who they suspected of sympathizing with IS.[6]

Still, many Iraqis believe that the police's qualifications have improved substantially since the height of the civil war. Selda, a Christian resident of Baghdad, points out that as recently as 2004 most police officers could not even read and write, whereas now they are required to have a university degree.[7] The consensus among interviewees is that while the police remain fraught with corruption, they are nowhere near as bad in 2019 as they were a decade earlier, nor are they as corrupt as other Iraqi security institutions. "The police are the least corrupted, [but] corruption is everywhere, in the army, the police, Hashd al-Shaabi [pro-government militias associated with political parties], but the police are the least corrupt because they're among the people."[8]

POLICING POST-INVASION IRAQ

In May 2003, the US Department of Justice (DOJ) sent a team of twenty-five civilian contractors to Iraq to evaluate the state of the Iraqi criminal justice system. Upon their arrival, the team realized that there was not much to assess. When the invasion began the previous month, the vast majority of police officers simply removed their uniforms and went home. Police stations and municipal buildings were looted, records and databases destroyed, and service weapons stolen, sold, or kept for personal use. In the words of Gerald Burke, a former Major in the Massachusetts State Police and member of the DOJ team, the report could be summarized in three words: "They need everything."[9]

The United States never intended to rebuild the Iraqi police from scratch. According to National Security Advisor Condoleezza Rice,

[6] Arraf, Jane. 2015. "Iraq PM orders urgent probe into military 'massacre.'" *al-Jazeera*, January 29. www.aljazeera.com/news/2015/01/iraq-pm-orders-urgent-probe-military-massacre-150129132719377.html

[7] IIACSS interview 01CF, February 2019

[8] IIACSS interview 02SM, February 2019

[9] Author interview January 22, 2016

"the concept was that we would defeat the army, but the institutions would hold, everything from ministries to police forces" (Dodge 2005, xxiii). In practice, when the Baath regime fell in April, 2003, fears of subversion by Baath loyalists prompted the United States and its allies to fire all members of the regime's security forces. Officers and soldiers were simply told to turn in their weapons and go home, purging the ranks of a police force already decimated by desertion.[10] "De-Baathification" created as many as 120,000 newly unemployed individuals and removed any notion of institutional memory in the security sector (Dodge 2012, 38–39). To make matters worse, while police officers followed orders to go home, they generally ignored the part about turning in their weapons, flooding Baghdad with firearms. In June, 2003, the United States partially reversed course, forcibly retiring all officers who held a rank of colonel or higher but telling rank-and-file officers to return to work, but the damage had been done. Ted Spain, a US Army Military Police Colonel whose troops played a role in rebuilding the Baghad police in 2003–2004, says of the decision to disband the Iraqi police: "The removal of senior levels of the Baath party resulted in a loss of manpower of the high level leaders within the Iraqi police. Although they had served under Saddam, most did so out of necessity to avoid losing their heads. They would have been loyal to a more independent Iraqi state when Saddam was overthrown and extremely helpful in rebuilding the police force" (Spain and Turchie 2013, 169). As for the returning patrol officers, looting in police stations and government offices destroyed most police records, making it virtually impossible to determine who was a legitimate police officer (and at what rank), who was unqualified but saw an opportunity to claim a job with a stable paycheck, and who sought to infiltrate the police for nefarious purposes (DePue 2007). As a result, at the end of 2003, what was left of Iraq's police force was overwhelmingly Shia, and recruiters were forced to view all Sunnis claiming to be officers as potential threats. Thus, post-Saddam Iraq's starting point was a Shia-dominated police force, with future efforts to integrate the police requiring a substantial deviation from this reality.

10 Gerald Burke, working in 2003 as a police trainer in Baghdad, notes that under the Baath regime soldiers and police officers often wore the same uniforms, differentiated only by a removable patch. An Iraqi could move seamlessly between police and army as needed by the regime, or as the individual in question saw fit. Thus, the lack of differentiation between army and police by the initial US policy may not have been so absurd. (Author interview, January 22, 2016)

Structures of Policing

Post-2003 Iraq divides its domestic security forces into several branches under the authority of the Ministry of Interior (MOI). The Iraqi Police Service, sometimes called the "local police," is responsible for ordinary policing tasks like enforcing traffic laws, preventing crime, and conducting investigations. Local police officers are assigned to a specific station and are responsible for the surrounding community. The local police are comparable to a municipal police force in the United States, except that they fall under the federal government's jurisdiction.

The Federal Police, the largest branch of the domestic security forces, are a national police force responsible for everything from ordinary policing to counterinsurgency. The government established the institution in 2004 as the Special Police, a small force responsible for assisting the military in security operations. Over time, the force's role expanded to include criminal investigations as well. It became the National Police in 2006 and took its current name in 2009. The Federal Police is divided into brigades responsible for specific geographic areas. Compared to police in most developed countries, the training and expertise of the Federal Police is skewed toward security and gendarmerie-style policing. Most Federal Police units use civilian-style police cars, but some are equipped with light-armored vehicles like those used by American SWAT units. Whereas in most of Iraq the Federal Police supplement the local police primarily on security issues or investigations requiring enhanced resources, in Baghdad they are a full-service police force, blurring the lines between the two groups. The Federal Police's blue camouflage uniforms reflect the emphasis of their mission, which straddles the line between ordinary policing and counterinsurgency.

A handful of other law enforcement agencies operate under the MOI. The Prison Service runs and maintains the country's detention facilities. The Department of Border Enforcement guards international borders and points of entry against nonmilitary threats, while the Facilities Protection Service guards embassies and government buildings. Finally, the Iraqi National Intelligence Services, a force of about 12,000 officers, collects information about domestic threats to national security.[11] I do not deal directly with these ancillary agencies as they provide highly specialized services and rarely interact with citizens.

[11] *GlobalSecurity.org*, "Iraq Police Service (IPS)." www.globalsecurity.org/intell/world/iraq/ips .htm

Iraq distributes police officers across more than 1,200 stations.[12] When Prime Minister Haider al-Abadi took office in 2014, the Ministry of Interior employed seven million Iraqis, including 660,000 police officers.[13] This figure, which represents one officer for every fifty-three Iraqis, was inflated by rampant corruption, with thousands of officers who never came to work remaining on the roster and drawing a paycheck. Interior Minister Mohammed al-Ghabban slimmed the ranks of the police to a smaller but more effective force; between 2014 and 2016, he cut the number of Brigadier Generals from 230 to 110 and froze hiring of patrol officers.[14] Even so, the ranks remain bloated with thousands of "ghost officers." Pinpointing the precise strength of the force is difficult, but even a conservative estimate suggests a massive force that employs a large portion of the population. One in every eight respondents to my survey says someone in their household is a current or former police officer, and nearly every Iraqi interviewed for this project in Baghdad and Mosul report seeing police officers every time they leave home.

Officers' demographic makeup varies considerably from one location to another. The Iraqi government intentionally avoids collecting systematic information on officer demographics. No doubt local commanders know to which groups their officers belong, but neither the police nor the MOI aggregate this data nationwide. The US military also failed to keep such statistics during its involvement in police training. Asked about the sectarian makeup of the Iraqi security forces during a briefing in 2005, General David Petraeus replied, "I don't have a breakdown like that. We don't keep one" (Sharp 2005).

Still, news reports and survey data paint a picture of a police force that includes minorities in some areas but not others. As I described earlier, many Sunnis who fought in the Sons of Iraq program were later integrated into the police in Anbar province. Reports reference Sunnis in Ramadi, Anbar's capital, joining the police to protect their families from al-Qaeda (Al-Jabouri and Jensen 2010). In neighboring Diyala province, the government attempted to reduce al-Qaeda's potential

12 ibid

13 Cockburn, Patrick. "Iraq's Interior Minister on why state corruption is helping the murderous campaign of Isis." *The Independent* March 1, 2016, www.independent.co.uk/news/world/middle-east/war-with-isis-iraq-s-interior-minister-on-why-his-country-is-impotent-against-the-militants-a6905941.html

14 ibid

recruiting pool by offering police jobs to fighting-age men. "The main promise these recruits were given was a chance to rejoin the provincial police force, which had been purged of Sunnis by a police chief affiliated to the ISCI [Islamic Supreme Council of Iraq, a Shia Islamist political party]" (Dodge 2012, 99–100).[15]

Integration does not occur only through foreign initiatives. As early as 2004, before the United States emphasized recruiting Sunnis, the 202nd Battalion in Falluja was made up primarily of Sunni Arabs (Hashim 2005, 311). Security forces in Tal Afar, a town about seventy-five kilometers west of Mosul with a religiously and ethnically mixed population, were primarily Kurdish, along with some Sunni Arabs. Long after the US forces departed, mixed Sunni Arab and Kurdish police units took on a high-profile role in combating the Islamic State (IS), especially in Nineveh province.[16] In Kirkuk, a report from 2014 describes the city's police force as ethnically mixed, citing 40 percent Kurds, 27 percent Arabs, 25 percent Turkmen, and the rest from other minority groups among the city's 5,000 officers.[17] Integration of the Kirkuk police is not just a matter of numbers; the local chief created a training program to encourage officers to "think like policemen, not as members of a certain ethnic community."[18]

On the other hand, integration in other northern and central cities was sporadic, and there is hardly any mention of Sunni officers serving in the southern half of the country where most citizens are Shias. The same report that recounts substantial police integration in Ramadi notes that the police excluded Sunnis in parts of Salah al-Din, Diyala, and Baghdad (Al-Jabouri and Jensen 2010). A survey of Iraqis throughout the country found that residents of Baghdad were the least likely to believe the police fairly represent minorities (Chapman 2012, 6).

15 Reports provide conflicting information about the extent of police integration in Diyala province, suggesting that perhaps the police are integrated in some towns but not others

16 Morris, Loveday. 2015. "Iraqi police at Nineveh Liberation Camp aim to help free Mosul but lack food and guns." *Washington Post*, January 15. www.washingtonpost.com/world/middle_east/these-iraqis-are-preparing-to-liberate-mosul–as-soon-as-they-have-guns-and-food/2015/01/14/297efc30-95be-11e4-8385-866293322c2f_story.html

17 Unknown Author. "Kirkuk police can't escape from Iraqi politics." *Washington Post*, June 14. www.washingtonpost.com/wp-dyn/articles/A40219-2004Jun14_2.html?sections=http://www.washingtonpost.com/wp-dyn/world. It is not clear how the article arrived at these figures

18 ibid

Even within Baghdad, the makeup of the police varies from one neighborhood to the next. In some areas Sunnis perceive that "police officers are mainly Shiites who are not interested in helping Sunnis. Reporting an offense is perceived to be a waste of time, or even dangerous. Sunnis are afraid to draw attention to themselves, or afraid to report a crime. They are afraid that the militia will seek revenge if they find out that a crime has been reported." In other areas, "people say they have reported crimes and the police have investigated them."[19] A resident of the Saydiya neighborhood believes almost all officers are Shia.[20]

Chapman (2012) identifies a disconnect between the mere presence of Sunni officers and their inclusion in sufficient numbers to be considered "fair." While 87 percent of surveyed Sunnis say there are "members of [their] ethnic/religious community in the security forces in [their] location," only 40 percent agree that "their numbers [are] fair and representative." My survey shows substantial variation in citizens' perceptions of how integrated the police are across different neighborhoods of Baghdad (see Chapter 5). Variation coincides far more with political boundaries than with demographic ones; in Sadr City, a stronghold for supporters of Shia cleric Muqtada al-Sadr, citizens believe the police to be almost entirely Shia. In the adjacent Jamila neighborhood, whose population is similarly Shia but where support for Sadr's populist bloc is much lower, citizens believe the police are quite integrated.

Sectarian Identity and Cooperation

One possible explanation for the police's incomplete integration is that Sunnis and Shias have no basis for cooperation or co-governance. Such fears of incompatibility spurred Western suggestions that Iraq be divided into self-governing regions for each group (Biden and Gelb 2006). Yet, Iraq's history reveals more cooperation than antagonism between sects. Before the Baath party's antagonism against Kurds and Shias in 1991, large-scale sectarian violence in Iraq was exceedingly rare and always spurred by outside invasions (al-Ali 2014). Even while Sunnis dominated high-level government positions for much

19 Finnish Immigration Service, "Security situation in Baghdad – The Shia militias." April 29, 2015, p. 21. https://migri.fi/documents/5202425/5914056/61225_Security_Situation_in_Baghdad_-_The_Shia_Militias_29.4.2015.pdf/00c75e2d-9ff7-4894-a851-39228b5a3c5e/61225_Security_Situation_in_Baghdad_-_The_Shia_Militias_29.4.2015.pdf.pdf

20 IIACSS interview 09NM, February 2019

of the twentieth century, Iraqi society was comparatively integrated. For example, under British rule in the 1920s, religious celebrations were attended by members of both groups. Sunnis and Shias celebrated religious events together,

> symbolizing a unity of purpose against the outsider ... During the holy month of Ramadan, a large procession would leave the Baghdad Shiite neighborhood of Kadhmiya and go to the Sunni neighborhood of A'dhamiya, which lay on the opposite side of the Tigris river, where the senior clerics of the two communities would embrace to signal their unity in Islam, and the two communities would pray together. The following week, the same would happen, this time in reverse direction. (Dawisha 2009, 77)

Similar events occurred on the anniversaries of the Shia martyrs Ali and Husayn, with Sunni Iraqis emulating their Shia countrymen in mourning their deaths.

This societal integration extended to the bureaucracy as well. Sati al-Husri, charged with reforming Iraq's education system in the 1920s, located all of the teacher training colleges in Baghdad to help build a national identity. He placed them in the capital "where students from all parts of the country can attend together to develop a spirit of community, or national, rather than parochial, identity" (Dawisha 2009, 86).

Saddam Hussein, a Sunni Arab, stacked his regime with individuals whose backgrounds made them seem trustworthy: first people from his hometown of Tikrit, then members of his tribe, and finally Sunni Arabs. Even so, many Baath Party members were Shias, while most Sunnis had little to do with the regime (Blaydes 2013). In the midst of Saddam's ascension to power in 1978, Farouk-Sluglett and Sluglett (84) wrote, "It seems almost unnecessary to point out that, given the shaky social basis of the regime, the fact that most of the members of the Revolutionary Command Council came from [Sunni western Iraq] is because they are the friends and kin of those already there, rather than because they attend the same mosque ... Baathist ministers and technocrats, while acknowledging the importance of [connections], would be astounded at any suggestion that they owned their position to their sectarian affiliation."[21] Several citizens I interviewed for this

[21] Farouk-Sluglett, Marion and Peter Sluglett (1978), "Some reflections on the Sunni/Shia question in Iraq." *The Bulletin of the British Society for Middle Eastern Studies*, vol. 5, no.2

project expressed similar beliefs that sectarian preferences are simply a byproduct of favoritism on other cleavages. Nasim, a Sunni and former police officer under Saddam Hussein's regime, says that enrolling more Sunni police officers "will benefit [officers'] relatives" first and foremost, meaning that Sunnis to whom the officers are not related may or may not benefit.[22]

The upshot of this discussion is that there is precedent for integrating service-oriented state institutions in Iraq. The post-2003 conflict, like previous sectarian conflicts in Iraq, resulted from a sudden and dramatic change in conditions spurred by foreign intervention. There is no reason to believe that Sunni and Shia police officers are incapable of serving side by side, or that citizens would reject the services of an integrated police force composed of officers from all groups.

Supply-Side: Sunnis' Attitudes on Participation

Integration requires a supply of citizens willing to join the police. In Iraq, the prospect of a stable paycheck motivates many new recruits (Deflem and Sutphin 2006; DePue 2007). The Baath regime used state employment as a form of control, making families reliant on their government jobs for income. From 1958 to 1977, the number of Iraqis employed by the civilian organs of the state increased from 20,000 to 580,000, with an additional 430,000 employed in the army and security services. Immediately following the 1991 Gulf War, the civilian arm of the state employed 21 percent of the working population, and 40 percent of Iraqi households directly depended on government payments (Dodge 2005). By 2012, the security forces had 930,000 employees, two-thirds in the Ministry of Interior and one-third in the ministry of defense (Dodge 2012, 120). In a return to Baath-era reliance on state employment, these figures constituted 8 percent of Iraq's total workforce. While the rest of Iraq's economy languished, foreign support for statebuilding providing massive growth in the public sector. From 2005 to 2009, the MOD budget grew by 28 percent, while the MOI benefited from a 45 percent budget increase. Even after international troops departed, the police continued to offer lucrative jobs in an otherwise desolate economic landscape.

Typical pay for a patrol officer is 1 million to 1.5 million dinar, about 1,000 USD.[23] With an unemployment rate around 15 percent and more

22 IIACSS interview 12NM, Baghdad, February 2019

23 Interview with Iraqi citizen living in Baghdad, January 2019. IIACSS 05CM

than 40 percent of the population living below the poverty line, there is no shortage of Iraqis from any religious or ethnic group who could improve their economic situation with such a salary. A former soldier under the Baath regime said upon joining the new security forces, "I am coming back for the money of course. There are no other jobs, and I don't know how I will feed my family" (Hashim 2005, 302).[24] After a particularly brutal bombing on an Iraqi police station in al-Karkh, a witness expressed consternation over insurgents' attacks on the security forces. "Why are these people targeting Iraqi police recruits? They just want to get a salary because they are unemployed" (Hashim 2005, 39). Speaking in early 2019, a woman in Mosul told an interviewer:

> Everyone wants to join [the police], not just Sunni or Shia. They want to join to get a better income. Most people lost their businesses and homes after the war, so they want anything, especially the young men who didn't complete their studies and have high school or middle school degrees, so their chances of getting employed are low. They go and serve the country and at the same time they get a good income.[25]

Other recruits join to ensure their own safety, both because of the status that comes from being a police officer and because it provides access to a weapon.[26] Bayda, a college-educated Sunni living in Baghdad, feels that if there were more Sunnis in the police, Sunnis would be "not just stronger, they would be able to protect themselves and their sect."[27] Foreign police trainers picked up on this mentality as well. Sam Juett, an administrator at one of the largest police training academies from 2004 to 2007, said there was a sense among his colleagues that many Iraqis signed up to receive a gun and training they could use to defend their families.[28]

These motives for joining the police suggest that citizens who are wealthier or live in safer locations are less likely to join the police, which does not correspond with the country's geographic patterns of police integration. The relatively safer provinces in southern Iraq are home mainly to Shias, so any reticence by this portion of the

[24] Also see Daniszewski, John, "Hundreds line up to join new Iraqi army." *Los Angeles Times* 22 July 2003, http://articles.latimes.com/2003/jul/22/world/fg-recruits22

[25] IIACSS intervew 10SF

[26] Sam Juett, Author interview February 22, 2016

[27] IIACSS interview 8NF, January 2019

[28] Author interview February 22, 2016

population to join would not explain shortages of Sunni officers. Unemployment and low wages are widespread throughout the country. The Iraqi police face a surplus of willing applicants from all sects, making the supply of recruits relatively unimportant in explaining levels of integration.

Demand-Side: Recruitment Policies and Strategies

Officially, provincial governors make most hiring and firing decisions (Pfaff 2008). Political parties, sheikhs, and tribal leaders play an important role in recruitment by encouraging members of their community to join the police, often providing governors with lists of men and women they should hire. After vetting applicants, the Ministry of Interior sends recruits to one of several police academies around the country. The reliance on local politicians to nominate officer candidates has a predictable, negative impact on officer quality. "[Political] parties bring [officers] without education, knowing nothing at all and they don't even know how to read or write. They don't even go to the military academy or the police academy."[29]

Politicians view the police as a tool for pursuing their personal ambitions as they jockey for power. This politicization of the police makes officers' sectarian demographics relevant. When democracy was introduced in 2004, Iraqis fell back on communal ties that often coincided with sect (Wimmer 2003). Shia politicians' success in the 2005 elections allowed them to recruit heavily from party strongholds and Shia militias (Cole 2007; Rayburn 2014). According to Ali Allawi, one of the leaders of the United Iraqi Alliance (UIA, a coalition of the major Shia parties), the "security file" was the most important ministry, and the UIA called for a "thorough spring-cleaning of the security forces and asked that elements from outside, obviously meaning the [Shia] Badr Organization, join the security forces en-masse" (Dodge 2012, 63). Bayan Jabr, a former officer in the military wing of Shia party Supreme Council for the Islamic Revolution in Iraq (SCIRI), became Minister of Interior in April 2005. Jabr gained infamy for employing Shia militiamen in the Special Police and allowing them to carry out sectarian violence (Perito 2011). In 2009, political parties nominated 1,500 police recruits, indicating the extent of political interference in the composition of the security forces. Because most influential politicians

29 IIACSS interview 09NM, February 2019

are Shias, Sunnis struggle to win jobs in the police. According to Bayda, a Baghdad resident, "It's like a chain. If there was 50% Shia and 50% Sunni in the government, everything else would follow, like the police and the army."[30]

Local politicians also use their influence to give police positions to family members, friends, and politically connected individuals as a form of patronage. One sheikh asked coalition forces to set up a police force of 200 officers in his town of 3,000 residents – a police–civilian ratio fifteen times higher than normal. The sheikh's goal was clearly not to use the police to maintain order but to provide "employment, salaries and brand new Glock pistols to the young men of his tribe" (Hashim 2005, 106). The political value that governors and other local elites enjoy from their discretion over officer appointments makes it difficult for national-level politicians to affect large-scale institutional change. The administration in Baghdad faces immense resistance at the local level when it attempts to influence officer recruitment (i.e., for the purposes of integration) not because governors necessarily oppose integration, but because they oppose any measure that reduces their ability to use police positions as patronage. These systems of favoritism become self-perpetuating, as officers who received their jobs through connections pass along the favor. One former officer told an interviewer, "Everything depends on [connections] and how many people you know in the Iraqi Police Service, you know. My officer friends promised to recruit my son into the police service once he graduates from high school."[31]

Officers have little say on their first posting, but with experience and promotions they can influence their future assignments. Burke estimates that most officers prefer to serve close to home,[32] and in the early 2000s the few minority police officers that existed tended to serve in the same area from which they were recruited (O'Leary et al. 2007). By the end of the decade, however, official policy required officers to serve a two- to three-year period outside of their home towns. While this policy leads to more thorough integration, with citizens relying on officers from all groups to provide security, it also pulls minority officers away from their coethnic citizens, leading to complaints of insufficient representation. In 2006, the federal government hired 700 Christian officers

30 IIACSS interview 08NF, February 2019

31 IIACSS interview 12NM, February 2019

32 Author interview January 22, 2016

from the Nineveh Plains. Rather than posting them to communities with large Christian populations, the local governor sent them to Mosul to join the fight against al-Qaeda (Chapman 2012).

Citizens note the isolation of non-Shia officers, whose units are often sent to the least desirable posts. "[The government] makes [Sunni officers] work in distant locations, and that's why most of the Sunnis quit, because it's dangerous. That's how they [the government] fight them."[33] "If the officer of the regiment is Shia then he won't allow more than 5% Sunni [police officers]. If he was Sunni then he would allow as many [Sunnis] as possible, but 90% of the [ranking] officers are Shias and they won't allow Sunnis. If they want to bring Christians or other religions [into the police], there would be a different force just for them. We haven't seen Christians or Yazidis in the federal police force in ages [in Mosul] because they all have their own units."[34]

ATTITUDES TOWARD POLICE INTEGRATION

The sensitivity of sectarian identity makes it difficult to take an accurate pulse of Iraqis' true attitudes about police integration. When first asked, most interviewees claimed that an officer's sect is unimportant to them. However, when the question was reworded to focus not on interviewees' preferences but on officers' behaviors, many citizens revealed that they believe sect does influence the way that officers treat them and others. According to a Shia from Mosul's Jaza'er neighborhood, "If the two of you belong to the same sect, [the officer] will be more understanding . . . we have a different mentality, our doctrines are different, our sayings are different, so I would prefer that he belongs to the same sect."[35] A Sunni from Mosul concurs with this assessment: "If he belongs to the same sect, that would be better, just a little bit . . . [people] have an impression about other provinces or other doctrines or colors, they have a bad impression about us [Sunnis], that we're with [the Islamic State] and so on, but people from Mosul or other [war-torn] provinces know our suffering more, so they treat us more smoothly."[36] Citizens' expectations often center around a police officer's willingness to take them at their word. "My sect can understand me. It is possible to

33 IIACSS interview 06SF, February 2019

34 IIACSS interview 02SM, February 2019

35 IIACSS interview 02SM, February 2019

36 IIACSS interview 04NM, February 2019

excuse me. They can understand my words. I can swear to them, while the other sect won't believe me."[37]

Sometimes, shared sect between a citizen and an officer can smooth over disagreements or prevent mistreatment. Mohamad, a Shia, got in a car accident with a Shia officer in the predominantly Sunni city of Mosul. The officer initially tried to extort him. However, when Mohamad told him he was also a Shia, the officer

> immediately turned into a different person. You wouldn't believe that he's the same person that was fighting and arguing with me a minute ago. He said, "that's it, you fix your car and I fix mine." . . . Why? Because we belong to the same sect. If not, it would be a big deal and we'd go to police stations and courts, and it would take a long time.[38]

Interviewees are just as concerned about under-policing as they are about overt harassment or mistreatment. Ahmad, a Shia from Mosul, does not expect officers from other sects to assist him in the event of a problem. "If we belong to the same sect he would help me, and if we do not belong to the same sect . . . he wouldn't help."[39] Similarly, Ali, a Taxi driver in Baghdad, says that if he goes into a dangerous neighborhood and the police at a checkpoint see that he has a Shia name, a Shia officer would warn him about any dangers ahead, but a Sunni officer would not.[40]

Notably, interviewees do not necessarily prefer to be policed only by coethnics, but express a desire for balance in the police. When asked whether more Sunnis joining the police would be a good thing, a Sunni woman from Mosul replied, "I think this [would be] comforting. We don't want the Shiite to be the majority, and of course we don't want the Sunni to be the majority. Anyone who wants to join should be accepted whether he was Sunni or Shiite."[41] Similarly, a Shia housewife from Baghdad expressed, "There must be equality. Like I told you, my husband is Sunni. Me being Shiite doesn't mean that I'm with them. My husband is Sunni, my children are Sunni and tomorrow they will grow up. We're living together in Iraq, and we're marrying each other, there must be equality so there can be security and people can be

[37] IIACSS interview 07SM, February 2019
[38] IIACSS interview 02SM, February 2019
[39] IIACSS interview 02SM, February 2019
[40] IIACSS interview 07SM, February 2019
[41] IIACSS interview 03NF, February 2019

reassured."[42] According to Ahmed, a clothing salesman from Baghdad, "there must be a mixture of sects" in the police.[43]

These anecdotes are consistent with existing evidence that most Iraqis support integrating minorities into the police. In one 2011 survey, a plurality of respondents said that "recruit[ing] more minorities into the police/army" would be "very likely to improve security," with only about 1/4 suggesting that such recruitment might be harmful (Chapman 2012, 9). In the same survey, 63 percent said that recruiting members of their community would improve their security. The respondents also drew a clear distinction between integrating minorities into the state security forces, which they expected to improve security, and allowing minorities to set up their own militias to protect themselves, which they expected to make security worse.

My survey of 800 Baghdad residents asks respondents whether they think integrating the police would make them better or worse off. Responses are overwhelmingly positive toward inclusiveness. Just under two-thirds of respondents believe that integration would make people like them better off, while fewer than 10 percent believe that integration would make people like them worse off. Interestingly, responses varied little between Sunnis and Shias. Figure 3.2 shows that despite being the politically dominant group, Shia Iraqis give little indication that they would oppose a change to the status quo. I expect that two factors drive the high levels of support for integration among Shias. First, despite being a demographic minority, Sunnis dominated the government for centuries. It was only after significant foreign military intervention that Shias took on their current role as the politically dominant group. Shias, then, may view integration as a safeguard against future changes in the balance of power. Second, Sunnis and Shias alike experienced considerable harm during Iraq's sectarian civil war. Hundreds of thousands of civilians from both groups lost their lives in the fighting, and millions suffered injury, lost family, and experienced economic ruin. Police integration signals a rejection of the sectarian politics and squabbling which caused so much damage and loss of life since 2003. I return to Shias' motives for supporting police integration in Chapter 8.

42 IIACSS interview 06SF, February 2019

43 IIACSS interview 09NM, February 2019

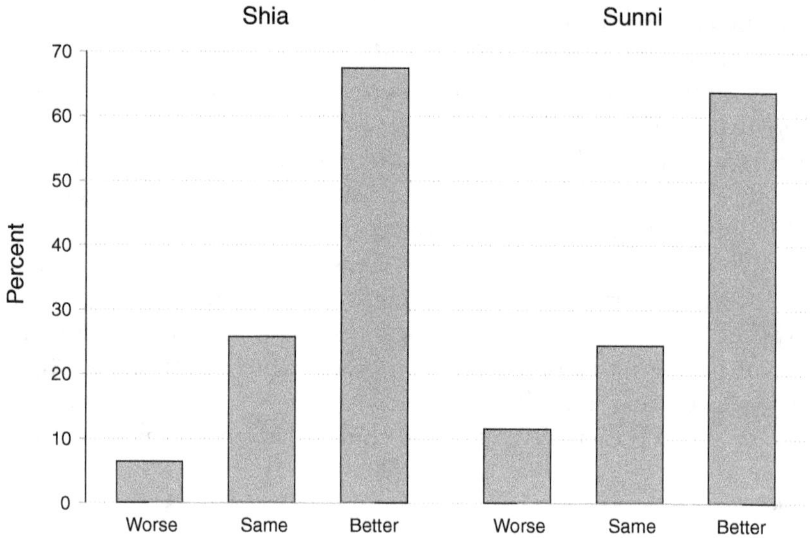

FIGURE 3.2 Do you think that greater sectarian integration of the Iraqi Police Services would make citizens like you better off, worse off, or about the same?

Integration and the Police Work Environment

Civilians are not the only people potentially influenced by police integration. Changing the force's demographic makeup, and especially forcing members of different sects to serve side-by-side in mixed units, likely impacts officers' attitudes and behaviors as well. The Federal Police's training emphasizes professionalization and reinforces identity as police officers. According to a former high-level administrator at a training center, "One of the philosophical issues we tried to teach them was you're a police officer . . . you're going to live together, or you're going to die together if you don't support each other."[44] Beyond active training measures, the mere circumstances of training often forced officers to identify with one another. Many recruits come from small villages and have never been away from home before being thrown into their new environment. They often do not know anyone in the area aside from other police officers. Naturally, they socialize together. Perhaps as a result of this socialization and identification as police officers, interviewees noted a conspicuous absence of sectarian conflict between

[44] Author interview, April 12, 2016

officers during training. "In general, you had these guys acting very nationalist," that is, emphasizing their Iraqi identity over their sect.[45]

CONCLUSION

In February 2009, video footage emerged of Iraqi security forces taunting and berating a blindfolded detainee in Mosul. There is nothing inherently sectarian in the video. The treatment of the detainee is reprehensible, but there is no objective reason to believe that identity has anything to do with it (Haddad 2011). However, the video has been used by sectarian anti-government groups as evidence of anti-Sunni treatment by government forces, who are assumed to be Shia because of the way they treat the Sunni detainee. An article posted along with the video reads, "Dancing and chants reveal their ugly sectarian faces. Look at the 'pagan guard' [referring to Shias' religious practices] and their reprehensible actions with an elderly detainee in the city of Mosul" (162). This episode sums up Sunni Arab Iraqis' relationships with the police and security forces, and the importance of sectarian inclusion in shaping the way civilians interpret the officers' behaviors. The complicity of the Iraqi security forces in sectarian violence during the early years of the conflict created enormous mistrust of the institutions and the perception that officers' actions are motivated by sectarian identity.

The sectarian co-optation of the state's security forces during the 2003–2007 period resulted not from ancient hatred between groups battling over religious practices but from political leaders using identity and state institutions to consolidate their personal power. When the state collapsed, powerful elites commanded militias which, thanks to prior instrumental uses of tribal and sectarian identity under the British mandate and Baath regime, happened to be organized along sectarian lines. Political leaders who did not command a personal militia sought to transform the state security forces into one. De-Baathification's wholesale exclusion of the Sunni rank and file from the police further exacerbated sectarian overtones and cleared the way for political elites to fill the ranks as they saw fit. It should come as little surprise that rank-and-file officers showed loyalty first and foremost to their political patrons and terrorized members of other groups competing for political influence.

45 Sam Juett, Author interview February 22, 2016

Despite opposition from some political elites, the Iraqi police are integrated in many areas. In Anbar Province, home to a large Sunni population, the government integrated tens of thousands of former Sons of Iraq militia members into the official security forces. Elsewhere, efforts were more organic, with Sunni citizens applying for positions in the police to acquire a stable paycheck and to protect their families from insurgents. The localized processes of recruitment and officer distribution resulted in a checkerboard pattern of integration, with some areas served by diverse police forces and others remaining dominated by Shias, depending on the incentives of local political elites.

ADDENDUM: OFFICER TRAINING

Many of today's procedures for recruitment and training were shaped by the international coalition's efforts during reconstruction. A 2003 report by the US Department of Justice called for as many as 6,000 foreign trainers, but the State Department cut that number to 1,500 due to budget concerns. Budget issues also caused planners to reduce the training course from sixteen to eight weeks, four for classroom training and four for "hard skills" like firearms training.[46] According to one trainer, recruits regularly received insufficient weapons and ammunition, or even the wrong type of ammunition for the weapons that they had.[47] The US agencies responsible for training were unprepared to operate in Iraq. The agencies responsible for training, International Criminal Investigative Training Assistance Program (ICITAP) and International Law and Narcotics (INL), reused training materials from previous operations in Kosovo and failed to fully adapt them to the Iraqi context. PowerPoint slides occasionally contained location and agency labels from the Kosovo mission.[48] Virtually none of the trainers spoke Arabic, nor did the training force include enough translators. Instead, Iraqi recruits who happened to speak English translated. Kurdish recruits often required a double translation from English to Arabic, and then from Arabic to Kurdish, with the predictable loss in accuracy. Training content focused almost exclusively on security and counterinsurgency, with little attention to ordinary crime fighting or service-oriented

[46] Author interviews, Gerald Burke (January 22, 2016) and Sam Juett (February 22, 2016)

[47] Gerald Burke, Author interview January 22, 2016

[48] Sam Juett, Author interview February 22, 2016

policing. Juett notes the absurdity of creating law enforcement under a situation in which there were no laws (the Iraqi constitution was not approved until 2005, and even the Transitional Administrative Law was not drafted until after police training had begun). He says that the new officers were essentially "trigger pullers," providing armed men capable of combating threats to the state but little else.

Training in Baghdad was impossible because the existing facility was too small, while insecurity made training in other parts of Iraq unappealing. An initial plan to train Iraqi police recruits in Hungary fell apart due to political disagreements. Instead, the Jordanian government built a large training center just outside the capital of Amman in November 2003. The Jordan International Police Training Center (JIPTC) became one of the most important police academies for the first several years of rebuilding. In total, about 53,000 Iraqi police officers graduated from the JIPTC training course between the end of 2003 and the end of 2007. For comparison, as of October 2005, 67,500 officers in total had been trained between JIPTC, the Baghdad Police College, and a handful of regional police academies (Deflem and Sutphin 2006).

While only some Iraqi police officers completed their training at JIPTC, its operations provide a window into the procedures at all US-supported police academies. After selection and vetting, new recruits arrived at JIPTC in classes of 1,500. With one class completing classroom lessons and a second learning hands-on skills, approximately 3,000 trainees resided at the academy at any given time. Trainers distributed these recruits randomly into platoons of fifty officers each. According to Sam Juett, who filled a registrar-type role at JIPTC, it was literally a case of "you go this way, you go that way." Thus, while there was no explicit policy at the center that led to a mixing of recruits from different backgrounds or sects, the process resulted in considerable interaction between members of different groups. Recruits lived and trained with individuals from other tribes and different parts of the country for eight weeks, during which they got to know one another as members of a team.[49] They socialized primarily with other members of their platoon, if for no other reason than because they did not know anyone else.[50]

[49] Gerald Burke, Author interview January 22, 2016
[50] Author interview April 12, 2016

Command-level Iraqi police officers, including Sunnis, Shias, and Kurds, oversaw operations at the training center.[51] Conflicts among trainees on the basis of sectarian affiliation were rare; laziness was a much larger issue, perhaps the result of recruiting classes filled with individuals only interested in a paycheck.[52] JIPTC trainers took basic measures to prevent sectarian discord like disallowing recruits from hanging sectarian posters in the barracks (pictures of Sadr, for example), but for the most part there was little tension. The general theme that emerges from conversations with former trainers and administrators is that sectarianism was not a first-order issue. "In general you had these guys acting very nationalist."[53] Just as the 1920s government conducted all teacher training in Baghdad to minimize the role of regional and sectarian identity among teachers, it seems likely that this centralized training for police officers in Jordan helped socialize trainees into a nationalist identity and reduced the salience of sectarianism.

[51] Author interview April 12, 2016

[52] Gerald Burke, Author interview January 22, 2016

[53] Sam Juett, Author interview February 22, 2016

4

IDENTITY AND INCLUSION IN THE ISRAELI POLICE

Since winning independence in 1948, Israel's government has faced a constant challenge over how to govern its non-Jewish population. Arab-Israeli citizens suffer from social and political marginalization on nearly every measurable dimension, including crime. Minorities express a deep skepticism of the police and its officers. Arabs, who make up 20–25 percent of the citizen population, perceive the Israel Police more negatively than Jewish citizens on most dimensions, including trust, fairness, and expectations of police abuse. These negative attitudes frequently spill over into protests, strikes, and riots, and feed back into the police's inability to efficiently serve minority communities. The Israel Police have historically underrepresented non-Jews, with Arabs' share of officers accounting for less than half of their share of the civilian population for much of the country's history (Weitzer and Hasisi 2008). The number of non-Jewish officers has increased substantially since 2008 thanks to explicit attempts by police leadership to increase recruitment in Arab, and especially Muslim, towns. Yet, the police and government face an uphill battle in convincing non-Jews to engage with the state based on promises of future service provision.

This chapter begins by framing citizen–police relations in the context of grievances about broader political marginalization. It then explores geographic and temporal variation in minority participation in the police. In addition to evidence from interviews with high-ranking Israel Police officers, I provide an overview of new data on the religious identity of every Israeli police officer assigned to a station between 2008 and 2014. These figures show remarkable variation in local-level integration. The police's focus on recruitment in non-Jewish neighborhoods appears to be working, with a marked increase in the number of Arab officers on the force since 2008. The police proactively account for societal inequalities which would otherwise make minority inclusion difficult, for example, by counting university completion among Arab recruits similarly to the way they prioritize military combat service among Jewish recruits. Yet, many Arab Israelis express skepticism over the prudence of joining the police, fearing that the government will use them as instruments of control over Arab communities. As a result, integration remains spotty, with some stations including many non-Jewish officers while others include few or none. The degree of inclusion also varies across groups. Some minorities like Druze are overrepresented, while Muslims remain significantly underrepresented.

The relationship between officer identity and citizen perceptions is shaped by decades of police–citizen interactions. Mistreatment, whether perceived, real, or a bit of both, in a setting dominated politically by one religious group has taken a toll on intergroup and minority–state relations. Good intentions by all sides are met with skepticism and doubt. Such a history of negative relations between the police and Arab citizens proves difficult to overcome. Attempts by the police to boost inclusion and improve relations with minority communities face major challenges, making Israel a particularly difficult case for police integration as a solution to conflict.

A preface on scope is required. First, I deal only with Israeli citizens. Noncitizen Palestinians remain outside the scope of analysis because of the different laws and security institutions which govern them. Although Palestinian nationalism motivates much of the tension I discuss, this chapter is not an analysis of the "Israeli–Palestinian conflict" but of the social and political marginalization of large segments of Israeli society. Second, I focus on the ordinary "blue" police.[1] I do not include in my analysis the green-uniformed Border Guard, a civilian (nonmilitary) force whose primary goal is to combat violence and terrorism. The Border Guard are associated almost exclusively with combating Palestinian nationalist violence, which means that the services citizens expect to receive from them vary dramatically based on citizens' ethno-religious affiliation and location of residence.

[1] The institution earned this designation from the light blue uniforms worn by officers for most of its history. In late 2016, most units switched to black uniforms, but the nickname survives.

While the analyses in this book focus primarily on variation *within* Iraq and Israel, the two cases provide for a useful comparison. Both exhibit highly salient identity group cleavages. They share a history of British colonialism, high levels of international involvement in their political affairs, and a national police force under the authority of the central government. Israel exhibits two dramatic differences from Iraq which speak to the theory's generalizability. First, relative power between Jews and non-Jews in Israel is much more stable than the balance between Shia and Sunni Arabs in Iraq. Israel's Jewish majority has dominated politics since 1948, and it is difficult to imagine a reversal of this balance. Second, while violent conflict along identity lines in Israel is substantial, claiming several thousand lives since the start of the First Intifada in 1987, it does not compare to the hundreds of thousands of Iraqis killed and millions displaced following the 2003 invasion. To this end, the future treatment of Arab citizens to which the Israeli state struggles to commit has less to do with physical security and more with service provision and political marginalization.

IDENTITY AND MARGINALIZATION IN ISRAELI SOCIETY

Israeli society is divided both ethnically and religiously. Religiously, the population of approximately 8.7 million citizens includes Jews (75 percent), Muslims (18 percent), Christians (2 percent), Druze (1.5 percent), and a handful of smaller religious groups.[2] These religions are themselves subdivided on both sect and religiosity. Israeli Jews are also divided between Ashkenazim (Eastern European descent), Sephardim (Spanish descent), and Mizrahim (Middle Eastern or African descent). Each of these cleavages takes political relevance at times, with ethnic and religious groups making up distinct partisan blocs.[3] Ben-Porat and Yuval (2019) provide an excellent treatment of the Israel Police's relationship with four politically relevant minorities, Arabs, Eastern European immigrants, Ethiopian-Israelis, and ultra-orthodox Jews. In this book, I focus on the broadest and arguably most salient of these

[2] These demographic figures are rough estimates derived by triangulating from multiple publicly available sources. They should not be read as precise or definitive measures.

[3] For example, the right bloc of parties garners most of its support from Ashkenazi Jews, the so-called "Arab" bloc is supported almost exclusively by Arab citizens, while Haredi Jews support a number of "religious" parties.

cleavages, the division between Jewish and non-Jewish, primarily Arab, citizens, and between Arab citizens and the Jewish-dominated state. Nearly all Israeli non-Jews are ethnic Arabs, while only a small minority of Israeli Jews are ethnic Arabs, leading to the shorthand distinction between "Jews and Arabs."

Non-Jewish Israelis suffer from societal and political marginalization at all levels of government. Arab-bloc parties have never been included in any of Israel's governments despite often holding more than 10 percent of seats in parliament. This exclusion is not for a lack of desire – 83 percent of Arab respondents to a 2018 survey want Arab parties included in the government.[4] Perhaps as a consequence of this exclusion, voter turnout among Arab-Israelis is low: 49 percent in the April 2019 election compared to 68.5 percent turnout in the overall population.[5] Marginalization extends to government service provision as well. Arab localities receive 40 percent of the public transportation services present in comparable Jewish localities (Levi and Suchi 2018, 17). A report from 2005 showed that the Israeli government spent the equivalent of $192 US per year on each Arab student, compared to $1,100 for each Jewish student (New Israel Fund 2005). While the gap has narrowed since then, it remains substantial.

These differences in government service provision coincide with low levels of educational attainment and economic development in the Arab sector. Fifth-grade Arab students achieve standardized test scores 4–9 percent lower than their Jewish classmates, and Jews are more than twice as likely to pursue education beyond high school. Arabs are less likely to hold employment than Jews. The gap is especially pronounced among women; approximately 30 percent of Arab women are employed compared to 80 percent of Jewish women (Levi and Suchi 2018). All of these gaps contribute to poverty. While Israel's overall poverty rate of 21.2 percent is already the highest among OECD countries, an even higher 49.2 percent of Arab families lives below the poverty line.[6]

[4] 65 percent "very much want it," 18 percent "moderately want it." 2018 Peace Index, Guttman Center for Public Policy and Opinion Research.

[5] Associated Press, "Right-wing alliance, Arab bloc formed ahead of Israeli vote." *The Washington Post* July 29, 2019, www.washingtonpost.com/world/middle_east/israels-arab-parties-unite-to-make-gains-in-upcoming-vote/2019/07/29/9f3a383a-b1e9-11e9-acc8-1d847bacca73_story.html?noredirect=on&utm_term=.326668b25af5

[6] Einhorn, Alon. "21.2% of Israeli population live below the poverty line – New report. *Jerusalem Post* December 31, 2018, www.jpost.com/Israel-News/212-percent-of-Israeli-population-lives-below-the-poverty-line-new-report-575883

The Arab community is underserved when it comes to public safety as well. Victimization rates cannot be easily compared across populations due to differences in reporting levels, a challenge I address in Chapter 7. Notably, however, the Israel Police report that 55.6 percent of murders, 43.7 percent of robberies, and 37.9 percent of assaults were perpetrated by Arabs, who make up only 21 percent of the population (Levi and Suchi 2018).

Police Service Provision

By most objective measures, the Israel Police prevent crime effectively compared to the police in other developed countries (Saunders et al. 2013). Israel's murder rate of about 20.5 per 100,000 is similar to Finland, Jordan, and the Czech Republic, and measurably better than South Korea, Argentina, and the United States.[7] While Israel experiences high rates of motor vehicle thefts, robbery rates are relatively low.[8] The criminal justice system boasts conviction rates similar to those in Denmark, Iceland, and Poland.[9]

Despite the police's competence on objective measures, they have a poor relationship with citizens, who express less trust in their police than do citizens in countries with similarly effective police forces (Yogev 2010; Saunders et al. 2013). Focus group participants from all religious backgrounds and walks of life voiced complaints about police service provision. Many complain of police inaction. "I had an accident and I called 100 [the emergency number]. They asked me if there were any injured people. I said there weren't, so they didn't come." According to another participant in the same group, "Regarding home burglaries, they do nothing. They only ask if there is insurance or if someone is injured."[10] Even when there is an imminent threat to safety, citizens are unsure whether the police will respond. A Jewish resident of Tel Aviv recounted a particularly troubling experience:

> I heard violence, screaming, in the building next to me so I called the police and then I tried to direct them to the destination. They were a little stupid. They did not arrive quickly and they also took a while to figure out where [the problem was], and I had to

7 United Nations Office on Drugs and Crime, www.unodc.org/

8 www.unodc.org/documents/data-and-analysis/Crime-statistics/International_Statistics_on_Crime_and_Justice.pdf

9 ibid

10 FG1J, Tel Aviv, March 2019

> show them otherwise they would simply turn around and leave. So I insisted that they go and check what is happening to the woman screaming there, to the stuff that is being thrown around the house. Maybe the fact that I appreciate them even arriving shows what I think of the Israeli police, that it is not obvious that they will come. This is the level we've come to.[11]

Other citizens feel more confident in the police. A clerk who works at a shop in a crime-ridden neighborhood on the outskirts of Tel Aviv says he regularly has to call the police when customers become aggressive. Often, simply the threat of calling resolves the situation, implying that people do expect the police to respond. When the threat has not been sufficient, the clerk is satisfied with the responding officers' behavior. "I really witnessed patience, here. I am happy to find something positive, the manner [the officers] patiently and kindly figured out [the problem] . . . and solved it without anyone getting harmed."[12]

Many complaints focus on what citizens perceive as inefficiency, for example the over-enforcement of traffic laws while more serious problems go ignored. "When you see, day after day, a police officer with speed gun, at the bottom of a hill where no one drives and nothing is going on, and at the same time eight people get killed in a car accident on Edom road, then you realize [police resources are] a zero-sum game."[13] Despite their complaints, most Jewish subjects anticipate improvements in service provision if police presence is increased. They expect "fewer car accidents," "safer driving," "less crime," and that "[the police] will catch more criminals."[14]

Arabs and Jews voice remarkably similar complaints about a lack of urgency in the police's responses. An Arab resident of Jaffa says, "I had four cases of burglaries, and I caught the thief. [The police] let the thief go and did nothing to him! They don't do their work."[15] One hundred kilometers to the north, a Jewish resident of Haifa recounts a similar episode:

> I had a burglary at my home, and fortunately I caught the thief. And I called the police, I said, "guys, there is a burglar in the house, come and get him." They told me "Okay, we are on the way." I waited for 10 minutes, 15 minutes, 20 minutes. I called

[11] FG1J, Tel Aviv, March 2019
[12] FG1J, Tel Aviv, March 2019
[13] FG3J, Haifa, March 2019
[14] FG1J, Tel Aviv, March 2019
[15] Focus Group FG2A, Jaffa, March 2019

> them again, I said "the burglar is dying here. I am strangling him and he is soon to die here." In 10 minutes I had four police cars here.[16]

Some citizens express more serious concerns. An Arab resident of Jaffa, a port city of 435,000 next to Tel Aviv, says, "What we have today, we live in a small place like Jaffa, it's like Syria. We are almost living in Syria. Do you know how many people are murdered every year? And without solutions. Not one person was found guilty."[17] In Holon, just south-east of Jaffa, a Jewish Israeli expresses similar concerns. "In my neighborhood there have been several occasions where someone was killed while sitting in his car. [Criminals] shot him... I don't feel so protected in my own city. I don't know when someone is going to get crazy and start shooting. And I don't know what the police are doing in order to protect us."[18]

A Jewish resident of Haifa tells a joke that sums up the general attitude toward the police in his neighborhood.

> A teacher asked her students what their parents do, and one student said "my father is a pimp." So the teacher called the father and told him "You know, today in the classroom your son told everyone you are a pimp." He told her, "This is very serious, I will handle it." So he asks his son, and his son said "I was embarrassed to say that you are a police officer."[19]

Although these anecdotes show that both Jews and non-Jews have negative experiences with the police, systematic data reveals marked differences in the way Jewish and non-Jewish citizens evaluate the police as an institution. Non-Jewish citizens tend to have less trust in the police than their Jewish counterparts (Saunders et al. 2013; Ben-Porat and Yuval 2012). In the 2018 Israel Democracy Index Survey, 17.9 percent of non-Jews say they trust the police "quite a lot" or "very much," compared to 52.3 percent among Jews.[20] On my survey, non-Jewish respondents rated the police nearly a full point lower in fairness compared to Jewish respondents (5-point scale), and were also significantly more likely to fear mistreatment by the police. These differential

[16] FG3J, Haiffa, March 2019

[17] FG3A, Jaffa, March 2019

[18] FG1J, Tel Aviv, March 2019

[19] FG3J, Haifa, March 2019

[20] Guttman Institute for Public Policy Research. Similar gaps appear in evaluations of the Parliament, President, Government, and military.

rates of trust have real implications for police–community cooperation. In one survey carried out in 2008, 70.1 percent of Jews said they would call the police if they witnessed a crime, compared to 50.6 percent of non-Jews (Hasisi and Weisburd 2014). Arab-Israelis sense that the police treat them worse because of their identity. "[We want] equal rights. Treat us like they treat the Jews. When they see that you are an Arab they start talking with you differently."[21] "Arab citizens' reluctance to cooperate is not necessarily about 'political' considerations and the lack of moral alignment, but rather because they do not trust police to act in their interests or to protect them if they cooperate" (Ben-Porat and Yuval 2019, 100). Jewish citizens also believe that the police treat citizens differently depending on group identity. A Jewish citizen from Haifa was out drinking with his friends. On his drive home, an officer stopped him at a DUI checkpoint. The driver initially denied drinking, and the officer was about to let him go.

> I told him, "check me," and he said "these tests cost me money. Go, go." Why [didn't he stop me]? Is it because I am an Ashkenazi [Jew of European descent]? . . . He was courteous and kind. And he was searching, as I saw, for certain stereotypes. . . . You can assume that had he encountered a young Ethiopian he would treat him differently.[22]

Many Arab citizens perceive that the police intentionally neglect Arab population centers (Ben-Porat and Yuval 2012). Following a spike in violent crime in their town in 2012, residents of the predominantly Arab village of Tira demanded a greater police presence.[23] "There's no other solution anymore," Mayor Mamoun Abdul Hai said. "We can't handle it anymore. We don't have the money and resources to do it ourselves."[24] At a 2013 conference on policing held in the Knesset (Parliament), Arab Member of the Knesset Esawi Freij said, "In terms of [policing] results, the Arab sector lags behind. There is a gap and distance between the Arab citizen and the police. Violence and illegal firearms are extensive, and personal security is deteriorating. The police take action, but not enough" (Abraham Fund Initiatives 2013, 1). "The

21 FG2A, Jaffa, March 2019

22 FG3J, Haifa, March 2019

23 Sanders, Edumund. "Arab citizens in Israel bemoan lack of policing." *Los Angeles Times*. October 29, 2012 http://articles.latimes.com/2012/oct/29/world/la-fg-israel-police-arabs-20121024

24 ibid

police don't care for Arabs," said Amneh Freij, the mayor's wife. The couple's twenty-four-year-old son was murdered in January 2015, and his killer was never caught. Amneh believes the police did not try hard enough. Had the victim been Jewish, she says, "[the police] would pluck him from between the eyelashes of the townspeople."[25] According to Salim Salibi, head of the predominantly Arab town Majd al-Krum's local council, "When there is violence or fighting in the village, we wait hours for the police but they don't arrive. But when a company comes to collect debts, it is accompanied by police officers from the Special Patrol Unit. This creates a lack of trust with the police." Arab Israelis are simultaneously concerned about under-policing, or neglect, and over-policing, or harassment. Salem Abu Ayash, mayor of the predominantly Arab town of Laqiya, says, "When they demolish a home or a shack, we see a whole convoy of police cars – two or three hundred, you can't see the end of the convoy. When there is a fight in the village, they barely send a patrol car."[26] This desire for an increase in police involvement in their communities conflicts with the stereotype that Arab citizens would prefer that the police simply leave them alone.

Some research attributes Arab-Israelis' negative relations with the police to the police's role in combating Palestinian nationalism (Hasisi and Weisburd 2014). The police assisted the military in securing the Arab population following independence in 1948 and officially took over responsibility from the army for domestic security and counterterrorism in 1974. While the police's role in domestic security is hardly unique among police forces in the developed world, the fact that most threats against Israel's security come from individuals of a particular identity group contributes to perceptions of the police as a participant in the Israeli-Palestinian conflict and harms its ability to provide ordinary policing services for Arab citizens.

Perhaps the most formative event in the relationship between Israeli Arabs and the police occurred in October 2000. Arabs in northern Israel rioted in response to a series of deaths caused by police, including the killing of five Arab protesters in Jerusalem on September 29 and the accidental shooting of thirteen-year-old Muhammad al-Durrah the following day. Police responded to the riots using tear gas and live

25 Hadid 2016

26 While the claim of "two or three hundred" patrol cars is hyperbole, I observed a line of several dozen police cars entering an Arab town in Northern Israel to oversee an eviction. I was informed by a (Jewish) local that such a show of force for evictions or home demolitions in Arab towns is quite common.

ammunition, drawing claims from citizens of excessive force.[27] Jewish Israelis living in nearby towns participated in violent counter-riots. By the time the riots subsided, thirteen Arabs – twelve of them Israeli citizens – had been shot and killed by the police.[28] A Jewish citizen was also killed when a rock thrown by protesters struck her car. The events heavily influenced Arab relations not just with the police but with the government more generally, which many citizens viewed as responsible for the heavy-handed police tactics. One journalist covering the events writes, "The scale and consistency of the brutality also made it clear that high-ranking Israeli officials were responsible for sanctioning the police's methods, including the use of sniper fire."[29] A report released in 2003 following an official inquiry criticized the police for being unprepared for the riots and for using excessive force to quell them.[30] Although a number of police officers received disciplinary sanctions, the inquiry did not lead to any significant structural changes in the way that the Israel Police interacts with Arab citizens. Years later, Arabs frequently point to the October 2000 events as a prime example of heavy-handed police tactics against the non-Jewish population.[31]

Similar, though less deadly, clashes between police and Arab protesters occur periodically. In October 2015, protests by Arab citizens in Jaffa resulted in confrontations with the police and left several officers injured.[32] In May 2016, bystanders used cellphone cameras to record a plainclothes border guard officer beating an Arab citizen in the heart of one of Tel Aviv's most cosmopolitan neighborhoods. Although a non-uniformed officer initiated the attack, on-duty officers soon joined, and the injured citizen was eventually taken away in a marked police car.[33] The citizen's only crime, according to police, was that he refused to provide identification when the plainclothes officer

27 www.haaretz.com/the-or-inquiry-summary-of-events-1.291940

28 Iraqi, Amjad. "Thirteen killed, no one punished: Remembering October 2000." 972mag.com, October 4, 2015 http://972mag.com/thirteen-killed-no-one-punished-remembering-october-2000/112266/

29 ibid

30 "Official Summary of the Or Commission Report." Accessed 11 March 2017 via www.jewishvirtuallibrary.org/the-official-summation-of-the-or-commission-report-september-2003

31 Amjad (2015)

32 Hartman, Ben. "Morning after violent riots, Jaffa residents take stock." *Jerusalem Post*, October 8, 2015. www.jpost.com/Arab-Israeli-Conflict/Morning-after-violent-riots-Jaffa-residents-take-stock-421227

33 Zonszein, Mairav. "Border police assault Arab supermarket employee in central Tel Aviv." *972 Magazine*. May 22, 2016, https://972mag.com/plainclothes-border-policemen-beat-arab-worker-in-central-tel-aviv/119492/

demanded it. Finally, Arab Israelis are not the only minority group with a poor relationship with the Israel Police. Jews of Ethiopian descent, who make up about 1.2 percent of the citizen population, also complain of systematic mistreatment by the police. In April 2015, a police officer attacked a soldier of Ethiopian descent on leave in Holon, just outside of Tel Aviv. A security camera captured the officer hitting and kicking the soldier repeatedly after the soldier allegedly refused an order to disperse. Protests in Tel Aviv over the incident injured fifty-seven officers and at least twelve protesters.

STRUCTURES OF THE ISRAEL POLICE

The Israel Police is a national department under the jurisdiction of the Ministry of Public Security. The country is divided into six policing districts: Central, which includes the coastal and plains areas around Tel Aviv; Southern, including the desert and Eilat; Northern, including Haifa, Nazareth, and the Golan Heights; Tel Aviv; Jerusalem; and Judea and Samaria. The Judea and Samaria district covers the West Bank, where the Israel Police share authority with the military as well as the Palestinian security forces. Because the legal and security situations in the West Bank are so different from the rest of the country, I exclude the Judea and Samaria district from this analysis.

Officers handle traffic enforcement, organized crime, and counterterrorism in addition to ordinary crime prevention. Approximately 28,000 full-time sworn officers are supported by more than 30,000 volunteers.[34] About one-quarter of the full-time officers are short-term recruits who elect to perform their mandatory national service in the police rather than in the military (Saunders et al. 2013). An overlapping one quarter of officers are members of the Border Guard, leaving a force of about 21,000 "ordinary" officers distributed across seventy police stations to serve eight million citizens.[35] Like police in the United States and Iraq, but unlike in many European departments, all officers are armed.

Officer Demographics: Inclusion and Distribution

In general, the Israel Police overrepresent Jews and underrepresent non-Jews. In 2014, the most recent year for which data was available at

[34] www.police.gov.il/GraphSkifout.aspx?mid=67

[35] At the time of data collection for this project in early 2016, there were fifty-two police stations across Israel. The number has subsequently grown as the police adopt a "community policing" model that emphasizes personal interactions between officers and citizens.

the time of the study, about 14 percent of all officers were non-Jewish, compared to about 20 percent of the general population. This figure represents a small increase in representation for non-Jews compared to most of the institution's history; in 1967 10.3 percent of officers were Arabs, and by 2003 the figure had crept up only marginally to 10.5 percent (Weitzer and Hasisi 2008). According to figures provided by the Israel Police, it was not until 2011 that the proportion of non-Jewish officers began edging upward. Thus, in terms of the Jewish–non-Jewish division, the police are somewhat uninclusive, although the extent of the malapportionment has decreased in the recent years.

The police attach between about one-third and two-thirds of officers to a specific station and distribute the rest throughout the country as needed on short-term assignments. The Israel Police provided me with data on the number of officers from each religious group assigned to each station for the years 2008–2009 and 2011–2014. Among permanently located officers, the proportion who are Jewish decreased from 92 percent in 2008 to 83 percent in 2014. Compared with the publicly available figures for the force as a whole, non-Jewish officers are slightly more likely than Jewish officers to be permanently attached to a station.

At the leadership level, every Minister of Police (the position's title until 1992) and Minister of Public Security (the current title) since independence has been Jewish. The minister responsible for the Arab recruitment drives described above, Gilad Erdan, is a member of the center-right Likud party led by Prime Minister Benyamin Netanyahu. Like all of his predecessors, the current police chief, Roni Alsheikh, is Jewish. Before being appointed as chief in 2015, Alsheikh was the deputy director of the Shin Bet, Israel's domestic intelligence agency, feeding perceptions of the police as an agent of state control rather than a service-providing institution. In June 2011, the police promoted Arab officer Jamal Hakroush to Deputy Inspector, making him the first Muslim to attain such a rank.[36] Now a Deputy Commissioner, Hakrush oversees a unit formed in 2017 to combat crime in Arab communities.[37] Despite this noteworthy exception, the leadership of the Israel Police remains almost exclusively Jewish.

[36] Efraim, Omri (2011), "Muslim police officer ascends to new heights." *Ynet News* June 15, www.ynetnews.com/articles/0,7340,L-4082782,00.html

[37] Gancman, Lee (2016), "Israel Police to appoint first Muslim Deputy Commissioner." *The Times of Israel* February 11, www.timesofisrael.com/israel-police-to-appoint-first-muslim-deputy-commissioner/

Regional and Subgroup Variation

Of the country's seventy police stations, a handful are small substations with only a few officers like the Bialik station in Tel Aviv, the French Hill station near Hebrew University's Mount Scopus campus in Jerusalem, and the Mount of Olives station overlooking the Old City of Jerusalem. Most stations have between 50 and 450 officers assigned to them. The largest stations are Haifa, Ayalon (in Holon), Dan (in the Tel Aviv suburb of Bnei Brak), and Yiftah (near Jaffah), each of which has more than 300 officers. Larger stations like these tend to include a higher proportion of administrative officers in addition to full-time patrol officers. However, administrative specialists are sworn officers and periodically conduct beat patrols, making them relevant for this research. Figure 4.1 shows the location of each station, along with the proportion of officers assigned to that station who are Jewish.

Police data classifies officers as either Jewish, Christian, Muslim, Druze, or "other." To measure integration, or the extent to which officers from different groups serve side by side at the local level, I calculate officer fractionalization using the Herfindahl–Hirschman formula. Frequently used by political scientists to calculate ethno-religious fractionalization, the formula produces a figure ranging from zero to one that indicates the probability that two randomly selected officers would come from different groups. A measure of 1.00 on *Officer Fractionalization* indicates that all officers are from different religious groups, while a measure of 0.00 means that all officers are from the same group. Applied to the station level, *Officer Fractionalization* provides a reasonable measure of the extent to which officers of all groups are included and distributed so that officers from different groups serve together. Station-level officer fractionalization ranges from 0.00 to 0.74, with a mean of 0.27.

Officer fractionalization varies widely from station to station. Figure 4.2 shows that fractionalization is skewed toward the low end of the scale, meaning that there are more stations with low levels of integration than with high levels of integration. The most diverse stations are Um al-Faham, David (central Jerusalem), East Jerusalem Downtown, Mishgav (east of Haifa), and Nazareth, all of which are within easy commuting distance of Israel's main Arab population centers. At the opposite end of the spectrum are stations in the southern coastal cities of Ashkelon and Ashdod, the desert city of Sderot, and the Tel Aviv

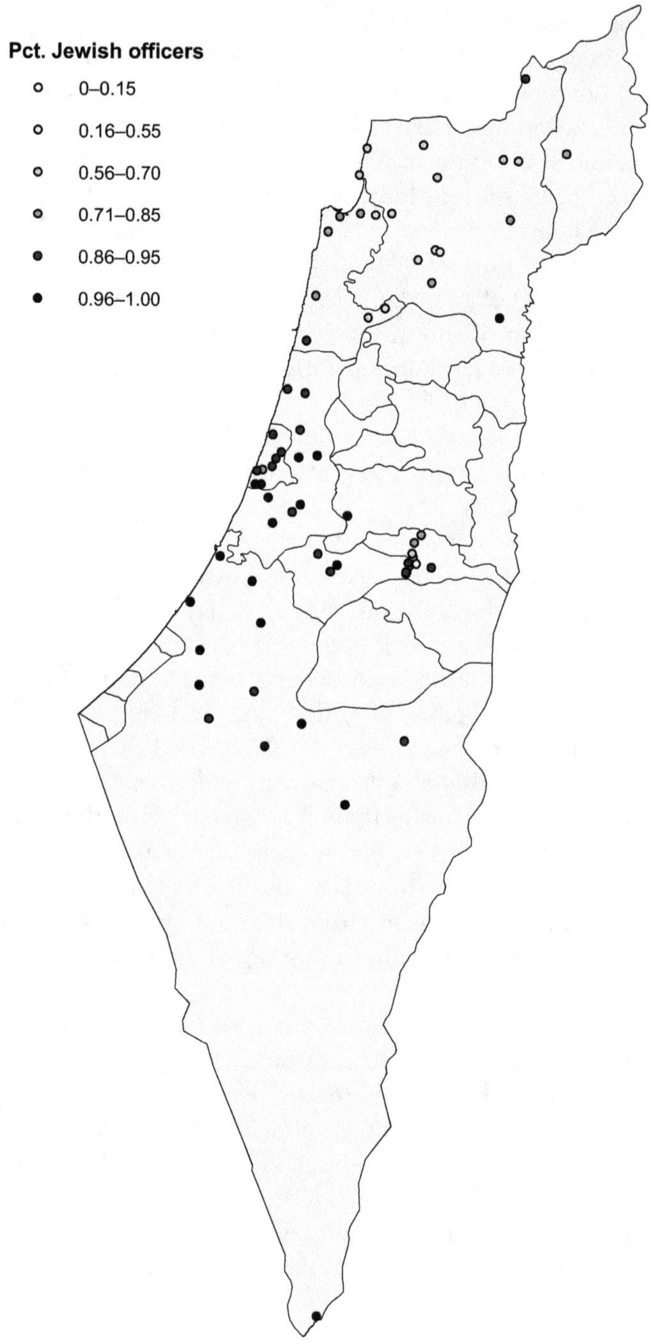

FIGURE 4.1 Police stations and officer demographics – 2014

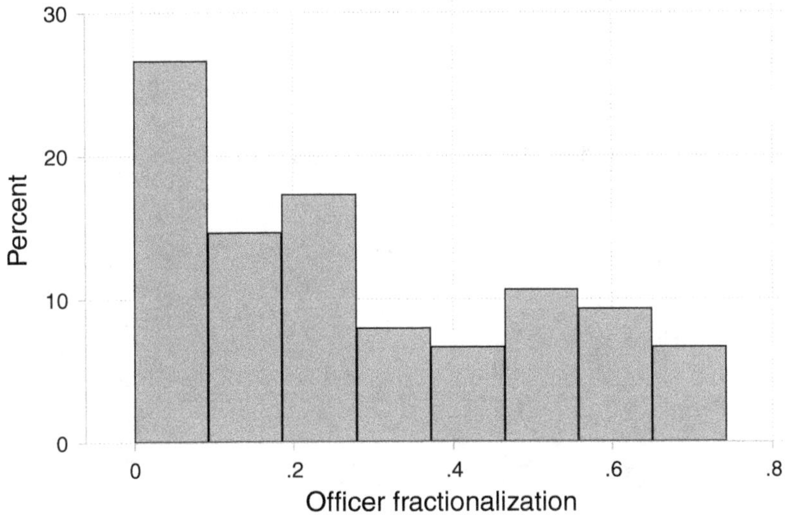

FIGURE 4.2 Station-level officer fractionalization

suburbs of Rishon Letzion and Rehovot, all of which have very low officer fractionalization. The location of the most and least diverse police stations makes sense given that a large proportion of non-Jewish officers are Druze. The majority of Israeli Druze live in the north, near the Nazareth, Mishgav, and Um al-Faham stations. In contrast, the non-Jews who live near the least integrated stations tend to be Muslims, a group with hardly any representation in the police. Table 4.1 lists officer demographics and the fractionalization measure by subdistrict. The northern subdistricts of Akko, Jezreel, and Kineret have the most diverse police officers.

The factors which determine these patterns are important not only for understanding the Israel Police but also for drawing valid inferences about the effects of police inclusion on outcomes like crime. For instance, if the police systematically assign minority officers to areas where the state has a better relationship with the community, it might appear as though integration is reducing crime when in reality the relationship is spurious.

According to a high-ranking officer in the Israel Police, there are no blanket policies on officer assignment and distribution with regard to identity. Rather, one of the most important criteria for locating officers

TABLE 4.1 *Officer demographics by subdistrict (2014)*

Subdistrict	Fract.	Other	Bedouin	Druze	Jewish	Muslim	Christian	Circassian	Total
Akko	0.51	7	4	61	168	6	10	0	256
Ashkelon	0.02	3	0	0	531	1	2	0	537
Beer Sheva	0.09	3	24	4	906	6	8	0	951
Golan	0.32	0	0	12	48	0	0	0	60
Hadera	0.45	13	36	33	370	19	30	3	504
Haifa	0.34	9	16	66	565	11	34	1	702
Jerusalem	0.46	53	32	176	885	48	34	1	1229
Jezreel	0.59	15	31	105	457	65	76	3	752
Kineret	0.51	9	8	80	308	17	32	5	459
Petah Tikva	0.08	3	0	3	274	2	3	0	285
Ramleh	0.08	12	0	4	469	0	4	0	489
Rehovot	0.05	2	0	0	251	1	3	0	257
Sharon	0.17	13	0	24	608	20	5	0	670
Tel Aviv	0.17	35	11	90	1706	11	22	0	1875
Tzfat	0.51	1	1	34	97	1	5	8	147
Yehuda and Shamron	0.15	4	0	8	216	6	1	0	235

is to assign them close to, but not in, their hometown.[38] Assigning officers close to home saves commuting and relocation expenses and allows officers to live with their families. At the same time, the police try to avoid assigning officers directly in their hometowns to avoid corruption. The police are concerned that officers working too close to home might be susceptible to extortion or tempted to look the other way if someone they know commits a crime. Thus, the area in which a new officer is likely to be assigned is a doughnut shape surrounding his or her hometown, with low probability inside the hole or outside of the ring. According to the officer I interviewed, the police split up minority officers so that any given interaction is likely to have "at least one real policeman," that is, a full-time Jewish male officer with experience.[39] The police's concern is not with the abilities of minority or female officers, who they view as just as capable as any other officer, but with the way that citizens react to them.

There are several notable exceptions to these practices. According to an academic who has worked as a consultant for the Israel Police, although the Old City of Jerusalem has entire neighborhoods in which the population is non-Jewish, only Jewish officers are assigned there as a political show of control.[40] I was unable to confirm that this policy exists. However, in many, many hours of wandering all four quarters of the Old City, I never noticed an officer who appeared to be non-Jewish. For the most part, the assignment criteria discussed here are standard practices but not official policies, and there is considerable flexibility for command-level officers to distribute their personnel as needed.[41] The upshot is that while officer assignment is far from random and the police do consider officer demographics when making assignments, there is no evidence that the police systematically integrate (or avoid integrating) officers in areas that are more or less susceptible to crime or violence.

The question of inclusion becomes more complicated when we break the non-Jewish category into its constituent religious groups. Some groups are significantly overrepresented, while others are underrepresented. Most notably, in 2014 Muslims made up about 4 percent of

[38] Author interview, July 24, 2014. Also see Ratner, David. "Civil Guard bridges Arab community police gap." *Haaretz*, November 1, 2004 www.haaretz.com/print-edition/news/civil-guard-bridges-arab-community-police-gap-1.138924

[39] Author interview, July 24, 2014.

[40] Author interview, July 1, 2014.

[41] Author interview with a former Israeli police officer, July 21, 2014

full-time officers despite being more than 17 percent of the population. Druze, on the other hand, are overrepresented with 7.4 percent of police officers compared to only 1.6 percent of the population. Druze are ethnic Arabs who follow a religion similar to, but distinct from, Islam. Their overrepresentation in the police is consistent with their broader political standing. Israeli Jews often consider Druze to be a "model minority," one that is more politically integrated than others. As a community, the Druze have largely accepted the Israeli government as legitimate and participate widely in state institutions. Unlike other Arabs, the Druze serve in the military in large numbers, including in combat units. Yet, despite their political attachment to the state, the Druze community remains culturally distinct from Jewish Israelis and mixed Druze-Jewish towns are exceedingly uncommon. While the overall proportion of non-Jewish officers increased by several percentage points from 2008 to 2014, the changes were driven disproportionately by increases in the number of Druze officers, the same population that was already included in the police and holds the most positive relationship with the police and the government.

DETERMINANTS OF INCLUSION

Minority inclusion in the police depends on two factors: (1) demand from the police for minority recruits and (2) a supply of minorities interested in joining the police. The theory laid out in Chapters 1 and 2 assumes that there is a surplus of minorities who desire to join the police, and that the limiting factor for inclusion is the state's or the police's willingness to hire those individuals. In Iraq, this assumption certainly holds, and Chapter 3 describes how the political incentives of governors and other politicians creates resistance to integration in some areas. Israel's situation is murkier. There is considerable demand for Arab police officers among police leadership, and the police have held several recruitment drives in Arab neighborhoods since 2011. However, a supply of willing Arab Muslim and Christian recruits cannot be taken for granted. Many Israeli Arabs, especially community leaders and politicians, express reservations about members of their community joining what they view as a repressive security institution, and worry that too much integration will normalize the status quo and prevent future movement toward Palestinian statehood. The steady increase in non-Jewish officers since 2008 demonstrates that there is some level of desire by Christian, Muslim, and Druze citizens to join the police.

However, for police integration to succeed in Israel, the state must convince its Arab citizens that it is genuinely committed to providing services in their communities and that it is not including Arabs in the police as a means of control.

Demand-Side: Recruiting Tomorrow's Israel Police

For most of Israel's history, the police only recruited officers who had previously served in the military, essentially excluding Muslims and Christians. Beginning in the 1980s, however, those restrictions were eased, and by the 2010s the police actively sought to increase the number of non-Jewish officers (Ben-Porat and Yuval 2019). The police carried out a series of recruiting programs in non-Jewish towns and neighborhoods between 2011 and 2019.[42] Speaking in 2014, Police Commissioner Yohanan Danino told a conference of Arab mayors, "I urge the Arab leadership to call on [Arab citizens] in every possible forum to join the Israel Police" (Kubovich 2007).[43] The police launched a third drive specifically targeting Muslims in 2016. These drives represent an explicit attempt by the police leadership to diversify the institution's rank and file based on the belief that minority citizens respond more positively to officers from their own community, eliciting greater cooperation and consequently providing the police with better information (Nanes 2020). A high-ranking officer I interviewed gave the example that Ashkenazi Jewish officers may not be as in-touch with minority communities as their minority colleagues. The officer specifically cited cultural barriers between Ethiopian immigrants and nonimmigrant police officers. If there is a problem in an Ethiopian neighborhood, the police try to respond with at least one Ethiopian officer to help facilitate the interaction, not because of any practical limitations but because the presence of an Ethiopian officer reminds citizens of Ethiopian descent that the police are there to serve them and are interested in hearing their side of the story.[44]

In addition to holding recruitment drives, the police try to increase the number of Arabs in the police by tailoring hiring standards to

[42] Hadida, Diaa (2016), "Israel seeking police recruits: Eager, and Arab." *New York Times* September 3. www.nytimes.com/2016/09/04/world/middleeast/israeli-police-recruiting-arabs-to-join-the-force-not-resist-it.html?_r=0

[43] Nahmias, Roee. "Police recruit Arabs to boost equality." *Ynetnews*. December 23, 2005 www.ynetnews.com/articles/0,7340,L-3189198,00.html

[44] Author interview, July 24, 2014

accommodate societal inequalities which might otherwise disadvantage non-Jewish applicants. For instance, the standard hiring process privileges those with military combat experience, which virtually no Muslim or Christian citizens hold. Recognizing this inequity, the police make frequent exceptions to the policy for non-Jews, accepting minority applicants without combat experience so long as they are otherwise highly qualified. When I asked the officer referenced earlier about the relevance of combat experience to policing, he explained that it signals a "higher level of maturity." To approximate the same screening mechanism for non-Jewish applicants, the police recruit Arabs with university degrees, which they view as a signal that the applicant is able to follow through on tasks and will thrive in a competitive environment.[45] The police are careful to make changes to recruiting criteria only in areas that they can correct during training. For instance, all recruits receive firearms training, so the university graduate's relative lack of weapons experience compared to the former combat soldier does not mean that he will graduate from the academy without adequate firearms ability.

Police recruiting drives occur in the broader context of government efforts to integrate Arab citizens into Israeli society, especially the workforce. Government Resolution 922, passed by parliament in December 2015, committed to increase funding for the Arab sector by fifteen billion NIS (four billion USD) over the next five years through a combination of new programs and redistribution of existing resources (Levi and Suchi 2018). The resolution, a recognition that Arab and other minorities' lack of integration into the workforce would damage Israel's economy if left unchecked, focused on key areas such as education, transportation infrastructure, housing, and public safety. The police's recent efforts to recruit Arab officers and open more stations in Arab towns fit neatly within these reforms.

Supply-Side: Arabs' Attitudes on Participation

As the preceding section shows, while the number of Arabs included in the police has increased noticeably, the proportion of Arab police officers remains lower than their share of the population, and lower than the police's stated goals. One contributing factor is that the mere perception that police hiring discriminates against Arabs discourages Arabs from applying. A 2003 survey found that 31 percent of Israeli

[45] Author interview, July 24, 2014

Arabs believed that Arabs were prevented from joining the police because of their ethnic background (Hasisi and Weitzer 2007). One Arab focus group participant in Jaffa thinks the police assume Muslims would not join the police, so the police do not even try to recruit them. When the moderator informed him that the police actually make considerable efforts to recruit Muslims, the participant remained skeptical. "It still doesn't solve the problem. It is just make-believe."[46] This perspective is likely shaped by the lack of Arab officers in Jaffa; participants estimated that about 2 percent of Israel Police officers are non-Jewish, an accurate depiction of officers in the Jaffa-Tel Aviv area but substantially off from the 14 percent nationwide figure.

This belief is part of a larger atmosphere of lukewarm support for joining the police among Arabs. One common argument against joining is that the system discriminates against Arabs, so Arabs should not become part of the system (Ben-Porat and Yuval 2012). Unlike Iraq, where a job in the police represents a desirable opportunity for a stable paycheck, Israelis view working as a police officer as a public service. Some Arab Israelis therefore view integration as an undue burden on their community. Perhaps the most damning accusation against the Israel Police by Arab citizens is that Arab officers are collaborators with an enemy force rather than representatives of their community. "The police can try to recruit but nobody will sign up. Why? Because they know that they will be called informants, snitches."[47] On the other hand, another Arab focus group participant suggests that increased participation might counteract the perception that Arab officers are collaborators. "Of course it is good [to have Arabs serve in the police]. People will start seeing that good people enter the police, not just informants."

Much of the Arab community's opposition to joining the police comes from politicians and community leaders (Ben-Porat and Yuval 2019). Abed Anbatawi, a spokesman for an Arab-Israeli political action committee, said that Arabs should object to any attempts to tie the receipt of public goods with their participation in Israeli institutions, including the police. As long as Arabs receive substandard services, he says, they should not feel obligated to serve.[48] Others worry that joining the police will lead to undesired assimilation. Chapter 2 suggests

[46] FG2A, Jaffa, March 2019

[47] FG2A, Jaffa, March 2019

[48] Nahmias 2005

that repeated interactions between officers from different groups should break down stereotypes and lead to greater understanding between communities with limited prior interaction. The opposite side of this argument is that individuals, and especially politicians who take a hard line on the Palestinian peace process, may prefer to avoid breaking down these communal differences. A number of Arab members of parliament, mayors of Arab towns, and NGOs opposed Government Resolution 922 on this basis (Levi and Suchi 2018, 36). A reporter speaking to Arab politicians about attempts to recruit more Arab officers sums up their perspective: "The sight of an Arab in an Israeli police uniform is, still, visual shorthand for a collaborator."[49]

Among citizens, however, there appears to be sufficient willingness to participate. A survey of Arabs in Northern Israel finds that 60 percent of respondents support recruiting Arab police officers. Twenty-nine percent say that they would consider taking a job with the police if they were looking for a job. Considering the challenges of a career in policing regardless of identity, this response seems quite positive. Only one quarter of respondents surveyed would object to a family member joining the police (Ben-Porat and Yuval 2012). A survey by the Abraham Fund, an Israeli NGO, found that 72 percent of Arab citizens support recruiting Arab police officers and 77 percent would like to have a police station in their neighborhood (Abraham Fund Initiatives 2018). While the employment benefits of policing may be relatively less appealing in Israel than in Iraq, the poverty and unemployment figures cited earlier should lead to relatively *more* interest in joining the police among Arabs, who are on average economically worse off.

Ultimately, the proof is in the proverbial pudding. In 2016, the police met their goal of hiring 2,000 new recruits, 14 percent of whom were religious minorities.[50] Over the course of a multiyear effort, the police hired 1,200 Arab recruits, allowing them to open ten new police stations in Arab communities.[51] With each new recruiting class, the proportion of minority officers in the police inches toward parity with the civilian population. While support for joining the police is mixed,

[49] Hadid 2016

[50] Kamisher, Eliyahu (2016), "Police hit goal of 2,000 recruits in 2016." *Jerusalem Post* December 29. www.jpost.com/Israel-News/Police-hit-goal-of-2000-recruits-in-2016-476940

[51] Yanovsky, Roi (2016), "Arab police officers urge young Arabs to join force." *Ynet News* October 30, www.ynetnews.com/articles/0,7340,L-4872271,00.html

there seems to be a sufficient supply of recruits to make integration possible.

CITIZENS' EVALUATIONS OF POLICE INTEGRATION

Globally, significant police reforms tend to be galvanized by public opinion and demand from the masses (González 2019). Widespread popular demand for police reforms creates space for reform-minded leaders to defy proponents of the status quo, whether in the police or the government, and implement reforms. Thus, citizens' preferences for integrated policing are important not only because they shape their responses to the police but because they influence the police's ability to reform despite institutional resistance to change.

Many Israelis I interviewed for this project, whether in informal conversation or in structured focus groups, believe that police integration will improve citizen–police interactions for minority citizens. The most common explanation surrounds communication and cultural understanding. An Arab resident of Jaffa recalls a dispute between relatives:

> A Druze (Arab) officer responded. I suggested we talk to the [accused] and not pass it forward [to the formal judicial system]. We brought the person, sat with him, and settled it. It was good treatment [by the police]. I was satisfied . . . a Jewish officer would have said "I don't care" and forwarded the complaint. In this case, since [the officer] was an Arab, he brought them together, did "Sulh" (informal conflict mediation), and it was solved.

Unlike in Iraq, where both Sunnis and Shias speak Arabic, language differences may give Arab officers an advantage over their Jewish colleagues in communicating with Arab citizens. While all Arab police officers speak fluent Hebrew, most Jewish officers speak little or no Arabic. Many Arab citizens are less comfortable communicating in Hebrew than in Arabic, which may prevent an Arabic-speaking citizen from seeking assistance from the police. The police recognize the importance of language, of course. Master Sergeant Ahed Shibli, a precinct officer in Jerusalem, says, "You can arrive at the scene of an incident speaking in Hebrew and understand something completely different [than what has happened]. But if you come speaking [the Arab citizen's] language and understanding what he's saying, you'll know how to solve the problem."[52]

There is some concern among Arab citizens that Arab officers may treat them more harshly for fear of being accused of favoritism (Weitzer and Hasisi 2008). Yet, while Jewish officers may be more likely to show mercy and bend the rules, the consensus is that Arab officers are less likely to abuse them, more willing to take the time to understand their problem, and more likely to put in effort to address those problems. Overall, most Arab focus group participants say they would prefer to be policed by Arab officers.[53] In my survey of Arabs in nine cities, the majority of Arab respondents say they would be neither better nor worse off if more Arabs joined the police, but 27.5 percent say they would be better off, compared to 17.8 percent who say they would be worse off. Among Christians, many more respondents support police integration than oppose it (37 percent compared to 8 percent). Support among Muslims is lower, with 24 percent saying they would be better off and 22 percent saying they would be worse off. In both cases, however, the modal answer is "about the same." Thus, while demand for police integration among religious minorities in Israel is far from unanimous, neither do Arab Israelis systematically oppose integration.

CONCLUSION

This chapter presents new insights into the religious makeup of the Israel Police using previously unexplored data on officer demographics. I show that while the police's level of minority inclusion remained constant for much of the state's history, recruitment policies which targeted Arab neighborhoods over the last decade resulted in a considerable increase in the proportion of officers from religious minority groups. I also note that when it comes to police inclusiveness in Israel, the Jewish–non-Jewish dichotomy that pervades discussions of identity-based conflict is misleading. Druze Arabs are dramatically overrepresented in the police while Muslims and Christians are underrepresented. This nuance is represented in the geographical distribution of non-Jewish Israeli police officers. In northern Israel, where most

52 Yanovsky, Roi (2016), "Arab police officers urge young Arabs to join force." *Ynet News* October 30, www.ynetnews.com/articles/0,7340,L-4872271,00.html

53 FG2A, Jaffa, March 2019

Druze live, the rank and file of the police is very diverse. In contrast, in the southern part of the country where most non-Jews are Muslims, the police tend to be almost exclusively Jewish.

In anticipation of later chapters' uses of regional variation in police integration as a predictor of attitudes and experiences, I explore the criteria that the police use to distribute officers across the country. If the police explicitly consider both officer identity and the "toughness" of policing as a criteria for assignment, any observed relationships may be spurious. Through interviews with several police officers involved in the assignment process, I demonstrate that while officer distribution is certainly nonrandom with regard to identity, there is little reason to think that it is also correlated with crime or citizens' attitudes about violence.

The long history of underrepresentation, mistreatment, and neglect by the police toward certain segments of society, and the highly entrenched attitudes and perceptions that result from this seventy-year history, provide an important contrast to the fluidity of attitudes in Iraq. Public safety institutions in Israel are highly consolidated. They underwent few structural changes during the twentieth century, and while the police today make considerable efforts to include underrepresented groups, these efforts are relatively new. This consistency contrasts with the Iraqi Police Service's short history, the dramatic changes in structure and composition experienced by the police since its formation, and the abrupt change in Iraq's sectarian power configuration in 2003. These structural differences between the two cases suggest that attitudes and perceptions should be much more entrenched in Israel than in Iraq. It follows that efforts at reform in Israel, including the Arab and Muslim recruitment drives of the past fifteen years, are likely to be met with skepticism by members of those communities. Changing attitudes is likely to be a slow process, and policy-makers seeking reform face an uphill battle.

5

PERCEPTIONS

The link between police integration and citizens' engagement with the state hinges on two intermediate steps. First, citizens form perceptions of the police, including the institution's degree of demographic inclusion. Strictly speaking, citizens' behavior depends not on the actual demographic makeup of the police but on the extent to which they *perceive* that the police include members of their group. Yet, police integration is not simply a matter of public relations, as officers' visibility allows citizens to form reasonably accurate perceptions. Second, citizens must translate their perceptions of the police into perceptions of the state more generally. While there is little doubt that officer demographics affect citizen–*police* relations in divided societies (Weitzer and Hasisi 2008; Kennedy et al. 2017), empirical evidence linking perceptions of the police with citizen–*state* relations is sparse.

This chapter provides a foundation for the analyses in subsequent chapters by illuminating the process through which police integration translates into citizens' attitudes toward the state. I begin by describing Iraqi and Israeli citizens' perceptions about the integration of their respective police forces. I find some surprising patterns. Not only do citizens in different parts of each country express different perceptions of police demographics in their town or neighborhood, they also perceive national-level integration quite differently, and their perceptions of police integration locally and nationally correlate only weakly with one another.

To analyze this pattern and explain the process through which citizens form perceptions of the police, I ask three sets of questions. First, where do citizens' perceptions of police integration come from? What information do they have at their disposal, and to what extent do their perceptions match reality? The accuracy of perceptions is important because if perceptions diverge too much from actual levels of integration, the government could shift perceptions more efficiently through informational campaigns than through institutional reforms. Interviews with citizens suggest that personal observations of police officers constitute the most influential source of information, and citizens are confident in their abilities to determine an officer's identity. By linking a survey of Israeli citizens with administrative data on the religious identity of Israeli police officers, I find a significant positive correlation between the diversity of officers in a city and the extent to which civilians living in that city believe the local police are integrated. However, the correlation between a city's officer demographics and the extent to which citizens believe the police are *nationally* integrated is much weaker.

Second, who perceives the police as integrated, and what can their characteristics tell us about the divergence between perceptions of police integration at the local and national levels? I find that politically marginalized citizens, meaning religious minorities as well as citizens who report not voting in the most recent election, perceive the police as less integrated nationwide. One possible explanation is that citizens filter their observations through broader political attitudes and experiences. Chapter 4 describes the way that political conflict between the Jewish-dominated Israeli state and Arab citizens shapes Arabs' relationships with the government and makes them skeptical of efforts to integrate the police. In this context, it is perhaps not surprising that non-Jews perceive the Israel Police as dominated by the Jewish majority even though they accurately recognize that many officers in their city are non-Jews.

Finally, how closely are attitudes about the police and attitudes about the government linked? I draw on data from the Arab Barometer, a representative survey of twelve Arab-majority countries, to show that across the Middle East, citizens' attitudes toward their respective national police forces are closely correlated with their attitudes toward the government. However, this link is conditional on the level of government that controls the police. In Iraq's Kurdish region, where the regional government is responsible for policing, the attitudinal link between the police and the federal government is significantly weaker compared to the rest of the country. This finding highlights an important scope condition, that police reform only affects citizen–state relations when citizens can logically interpret that reform as a signal of the way the government intends to treat them.

OBSERVATIONS AND PERCEPTIONS OF THE ISRAEL POLICE

Israeli focus group participants hold dramatically different perceptions of police integration depending on where they live. One Arab-Israeli citizen living in Jaffa, where there are very few Arab police officers, estimates that Arab officers make up only 1–3 percent of the force.[1] Jewish interviewees in neighboring Tel Aviv agreed that there are few non-Jewish officers in their area but believe these groups are represented elsewhere. "In the police today there are Jews, Christians, also Muslims and Druze, and Ethiopians." They disagree on whether these groups are represented fairly, however, and one participant points out that even though there is representation in the lower ranks, there is probably little minority representation at higher ranks.[2] Another participant of the same focus group correctly points out, "In the north [the police have] more Druze. I don't see them in Herzliyah or in Ramat Hasharon."[3] In contrast, a Jewish focus group participant in Haifa recognizes that there are "a lot" of Arabs in the police in his area.[4]

I further explore Israelis' perceptions of police integration using a survey of 804 citizens in nine major population centers, providing a cross-section of both Jews and non-Jews in urban Israel. I detail sampling and interview procedures in the Data Appendix.

The survey asks two questions about perceived integration. First, at the national level,

> In general, how integrated would you say the Israeli police are? By integrated I mean that members of many different ethnic and religious groups serve together side by side. Throughout Israel in general, would you say that the police are very integrated, somewhat integrated, or not at all integrated?

[1] FG2A, Jaffa, March 2019
[2] FG1J, Tel Aviv, March 2019
[3] FG1J, Tel Aviv, March 2019
[4] FG3J, Haifa, March 2019

Then, locally:

> Now please think specifically about your neighborhood. How often do you see or hear about Jewish and non-Jewish officers working together? Often, sometimes, rarely, or never?

Figure 5.1 shows a fairly even distribution of perceptions about integration at both the national and local levels. Among individual respondents, the correlation between the two measures is surprisingly low, at .17. A third measure disaggregates (perceived) non-integration into homogeneous areas in which most officers come from the respondent's group and those in which most officers come from an out-group. About half of all respondents say the police in their area are a mix of Jews and non-Jews. Just over 20 percent say that they are policed primarily by out-group officers.

Where Do These Perceptions Come from?

Israelis have regular contact with the police. One Tel Aviv resident laments that he encounters "police everywhere... every two meters."[5] An Arab from Jaffa agrees, "We see [them] every day."[6] Three out of six focus group participants in Tel Aviv mentioned that they had recently called the police.[7] Unlike many developed countries where employment in the police is skewed toward a particular social or economic class, Israelis of all backgrounds know police officers personally because many young adults serve in the police to fulfill their national service. One focus group participant notes that personal relationships provide information about the institution. "My aunt's husband is a policeman. I am aware of all [their procedures]."[8]

The media provides information about the police, but citizens tend to view this source with suspicion. Focus group participants criticize the traditional media for portraying the police in an unfairly negative light. "Every day you hear about the wrongdoings of the police because it is sexy, it is interesting, it creates a response. If you say that the police did a good job, people would change the channel, so they put more emphasis on the negative aspects of the police... Maybe they could show in part that the police does its work properly most of the time. But you

5 FG1J, Tel Aviv, March 2019
6 FG2A, Jaffa, March 2019
7 FG1J, Tel Aviv, March 2019
8 FG1J, Tel Aviv, March 2019

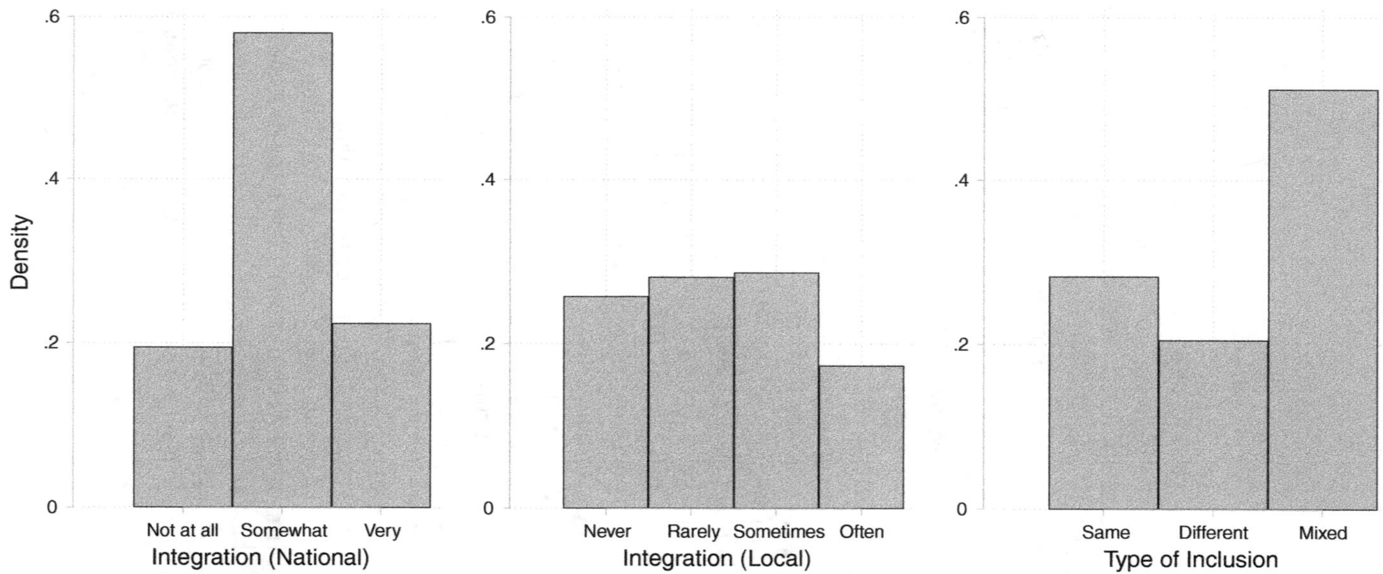

FIGURE 5.1 Israel: Perceived integration at the national and local levels, and whether local officers are perceived to come from the same group as the respondent, a different group, or a mix of each

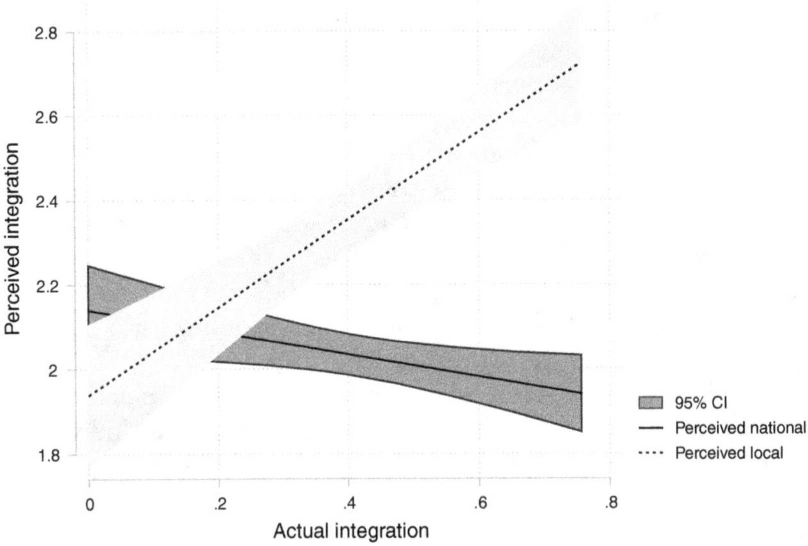

FIGURE 5.2 Police integration in Israel

don't get to hear that. You only hear when they beat up Ethiopians or release a criminal."[9] "In some cases they [media] bring the police spokesperson to respond, and you see that they can barely let her finish before they attack her and accuse her further."[10]

Thus, personal interactions and observations form the basis for Israelis' perceptions because they are frequent and reliable. Israelis distinguish Jews from non-Jews through accents, facial structure, clothing choices, and names. Most are cautiously optimistic about their ability to determine an officer's identity on average, if not in every individual interaction. A resident of Jaffa points out that you can see officers' names on their name tags, usually an unambiguous signal of whether or not they are Jewish.[11] For their part, officers can determine with some certainty whether a driver is Jewish based on where a car is registered, in addition to the cues mentioned earlier.[12]

To evaluate the accuracy of citizens' perceptions of police inclusion, I turn to administrative data on the religious identity of officers assigned to each station. Figure 5.2 shows the relationships between actual local

[9] FG3J, Haifa, March 2019
[10] FG3J, Haifa, March 2019
[11] FG2A, Jaffa, March 2019
[12] FG2A, Jaffa, March 2019

officer demographics and perceived local integration (dashed line), and between actual local officer demographics and perceived national integration (solid line), for each survey respondent based on his or her hometown. While local perceptions are positively and significantly correlated with officer demographics, perceptions of national integration are very weakly negatively associated with officer diversity in the respondent's location. Clearly, citizens' observations of the officers they encounter on a day-to-day basis influence their perceptions of the police in their local area. Yet, there seems to be some intervening variable affecting attitude formation toward the institution at a national level.

In divided societies, citizens' personal experiences accumulate over time to shape their outlook, attitudes, and expectations. Individuals whose minority status has prompted a lifetime of marginalization and poor relations with the police will integrate observations of coethnic officers into their existing perception of the police as an exclusionary institution, while those from the dominant group who have historically been treated well by the police may be more willing to accept at face value that observed officers signal useful information about the makeup of the institution overall. As Warren (2011, 357) points out regarding attitudes toward the police in the United States, "perceptions of the police are not simply a reflection of direct experiences but also a set of cumulative experiences both with police and other social institutions that develop across a person's life course." Members of the marginalized group who observe officers from their group in their neighborhood may still perceive the *institution* as exclusionary, and may surmise that the coethnic officers they observe are not representative of the institution nationwide.

Given the Israel Police's history, it would be reasonable for Arab citizens to be skeptical that Arab officers they observe represent the broader hiring practices of the police. On the other hand, Jewish citizens who live in areas with few Arab officers are exposed to media reports indicating the police's efforts to increase inclusion of religious minorities. While they may not personally observe the results of these efforts, they should reasonably expect that the police will send minority officers to areas with minority civilians. Thus, from a typical Jewish citizen's perspective, the absence of Arab officers in their neighborhood is not necessarily inconsistent with claims that the police include Arab officers elsewhere.

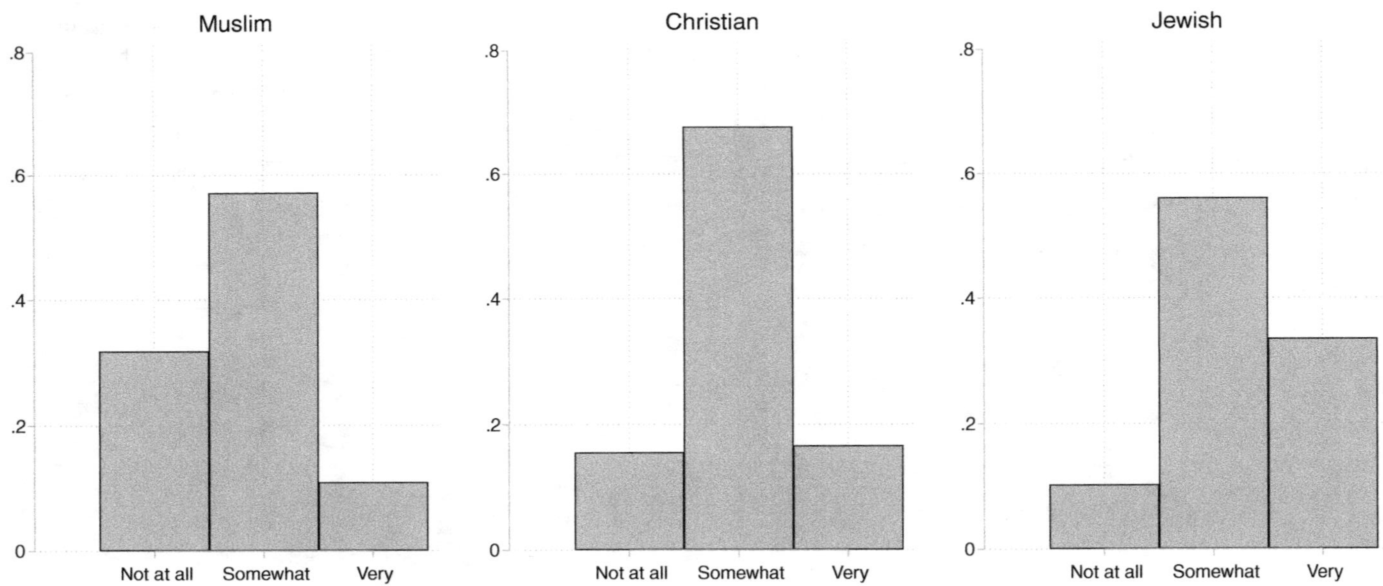

FIGURE 5.3 Throughout Israel in general, would you say that the police are very integrated, somewhat integrated, or not at all integrated?

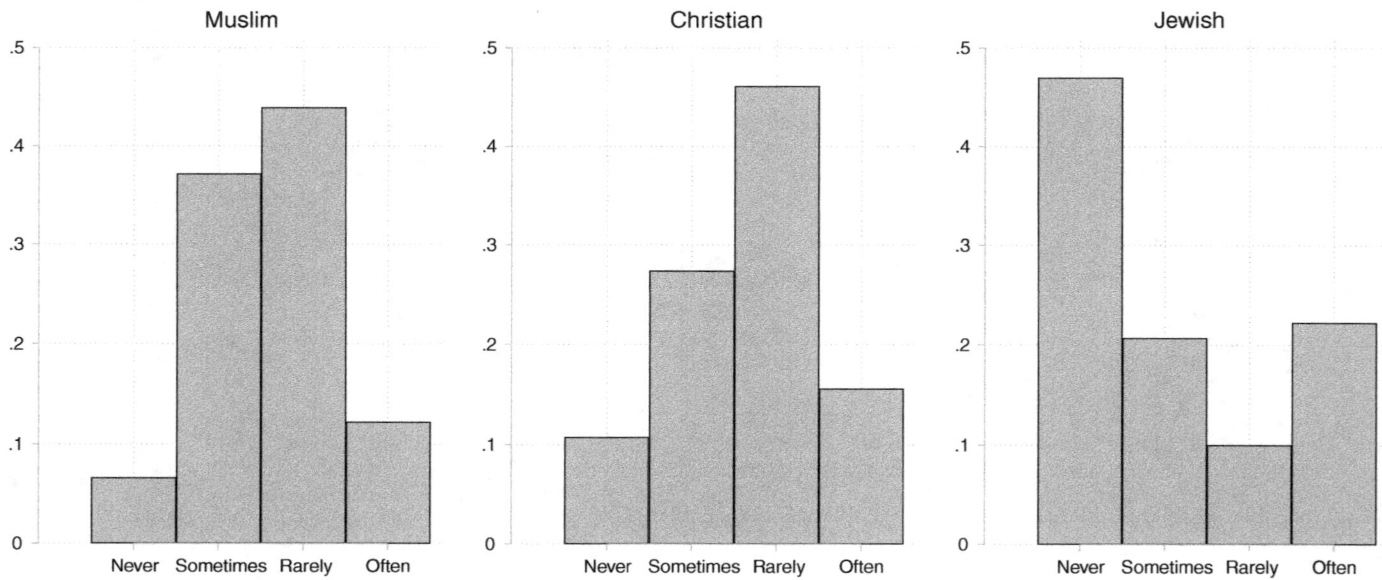

FIGURE 5.4 Now please think specifically about your neighborhood. How often do you see or hear about Jewish and non-Jewish officers working together?

TABLE 5.1 *Israel: Police inclusion by group*

	Jews	Non-Jews	Difference
Actual local heterogeneity	0.37	0.47	0.10***
Perceived local integration	2.08	2.63	0.55***
Perceived national integration	2.23	1.85	−0.38***

$^{***}p < .01$

Locally, Jews rarely report seeing Jewish and non-Jewish officers working together in their neighborhood, while Muslims report seeing mixed policing fairly frequently. At the national level, however, Jews tend to believe the police are quite integrated, Muslims believe the police are not particularly integrated, and Christians fall somewhere in between. It seems that non-Jews who accurately recognize that the police in their area are integrated perceive this local inclusion as an isolated policy that does not extend to the rest of the country. In contrast, although Jewish Israelis do not see many non-Jewish officers where they live, they are aware that there are non-Jewish officers serving in other parts of the country and therefore perceive the police as integrated in spite of their own experiences.

Table 5.1 shows these trends more systematically. The police are relatively *more* diverse in areas with larger non-Jewish populations, and non-Jews correctly perceive the police locally as more integrated. However, non-Jewish citizens are *less* likely to perceive the institution as integrated nationwide.

Figure 5.5 shows the results of several multivariate regression models that predict perceived integration as the dependent variable.[13] Those who have a household member working in the public sector perceive the police as more integrated nationally, but not locally. Consistent with the patterns in Table 5.1, Jews perceive the police as significantly less integrated locally compared to non-Jews, which matches the reality that the police are more diverse in areas where non-Jewish survey respondents reside. The major deviation from that pattern is in East Jerusalem, where respondents (who are almost all Muslims) perceive

[13] Columns 1 and 2 use ordered logistic regression; Column 3 uses OLS. All models cluster standard errors at the primary sampling unit. Figure 5.5 displays 95 percent confidence intervals.

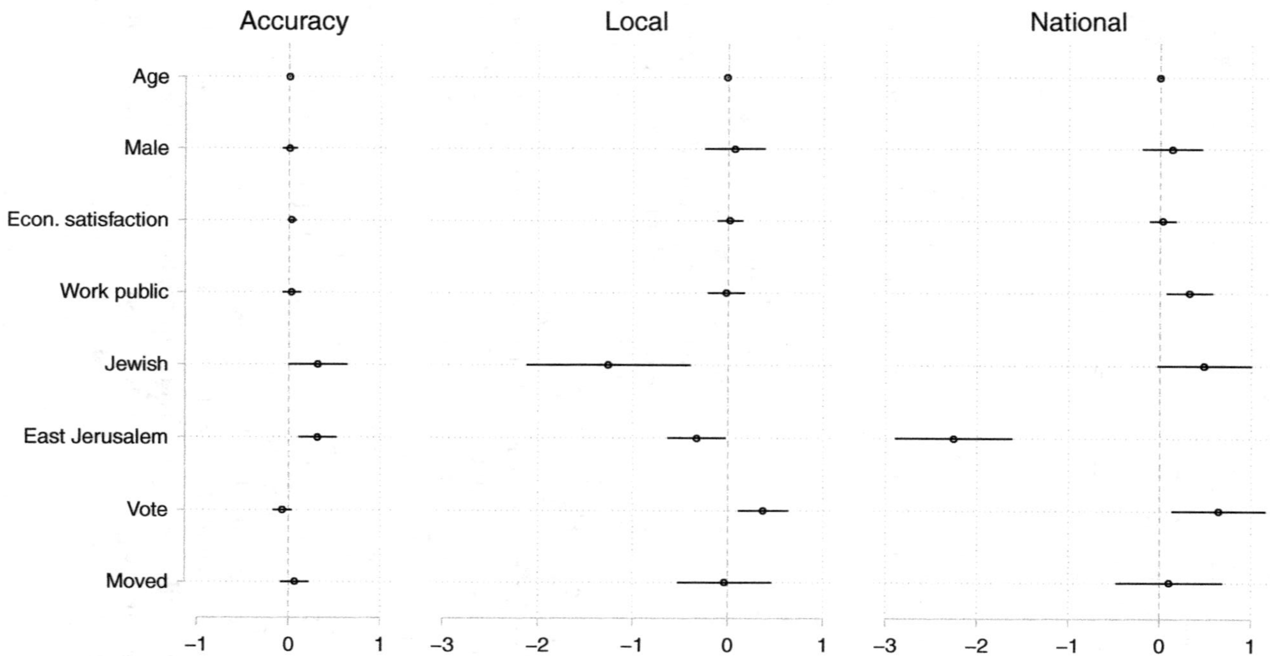

FIGURE 5.5 Who perceives the Israeli police as integrated?

the police as significantly less integrated compared to respondents elsewhere. This correlation is consistent with the political marginalization argument: East Jerusalem residents typically have a worse relationship with the police and the Israeli government, and express less attachment to the State of Israel. This deep marginalization may prevent observations of Arab police officers from influencing their perceptions of the institution overall. Along the same lines, survey respondents who report voting in the last election are significantly more likely to perceive the police as integrated. That this pattern occurs for both local and national integration suggests that it is *not* caused by differential voter turnout rates correlating with local police officer demographics.

Of course, these patterns could be determined by where people with certain characteristics live rather than by the process through which they form perceptions of the police. To analyze the *accuracy* of citizens' perceptions, the first column uses as the dependent variable the difference between police heterogeneity in the respondent's city or neighborhood and the respondent's expressed perception of the extent to which the police in his city or neighborhood are integrated, coded so that higher values indicate greater accuracy (less divergence between the two measures). Older people's perceptions are slightly more accurate, perhaps because they have accumulated more observations over time and therefore have more information. Jewish respondents are accurate in their perception that there are few Jewish officers where they live, as are East Jerusalem residents.

IRAQ

In Chapter 3, I described substantial variation in the extent of police integration across Iraq. As such, citizens living in different parts of the country should perceive different levels of integration. Iraqis interviewed in Mosul and Baghdad varied in their evaluations of the police's level of inclusion, but all agreed that Shias, the demographic majority, hold a majority of officer positions. One Baghdad resident says, "They say [Shias in the police make up] 60%, but when we sit together, we say it's fake news," meaning the actual number is even higher.[14] Ahmed, a Shia resident of Mosul's Jaza'er neighborhood, falls at one extreme: "Minorities are very few, really. Wherever you go you can see that Shia

14 IIACSS interview 01CF, February 2019

are in control, in the police, the army, and Hashd al-Shaabi [state-sponsored militia]. When we go to a police station, we see for example a hundred people, 98% of them are Shia and 2% Sunni."[15] Another interviewee, a Sunni woman in Mosul, thinks the two largest sects are near parity. "Sunni people and Shiite people in the [police] departments are almost 50–50."[16] While most subjects are confident about their ability to identify the sect of officers they encounter, they are not so sure about officers outside of their home city. One Baghdad resident said, "In Baghdad, the majority is Shia. I'm telling you about Baghdad, but I don't know the situation in Mosul."[17] Another Baghdad resident says he has "no idea" how integrated the police are overall, but the majority of the officers he sees are Shias.[18]

To explore perceptions more systematically, I draw on data from my survey of Iraqis living in Baghdad, which I describe in Appendix A. The survey measures perceived inclusion at several levels. First, the survey asks respondents about their perceptions at the national level:

> Throughout Iraq in general, would you say that the police fairly include members of all different ethnic and religious groups? Please answer from 1 to 5, with 1 being not at all fairly and 5 being completely fairly.

Respondents were then asked about the level of inclusion in their neighborhood specifically:

> In your neighborhood, how often do you see ordinary police officers from different ethnic or religious groups working together side by side? Often, sometimes, rarely, or never?

A third question disaggregates non-integration into in-group versus out-group:

> Would you say that security forces in your area are mostly people like you, mostly people from other groups, or a mix between the two?

Figure 5.6 shows the distribution of responses to these questions. Several trends are immediately clear. First, perceptions vary considerably from one respondent to the next. This variation is expected at the

[15] IIACSS interview 02SM, February 2019

[16] IIACSS interview 03NM, February 2019

[17] IIACSS interview 09NM, February 2019

[18] IIACSS interview 11SM, February 2019

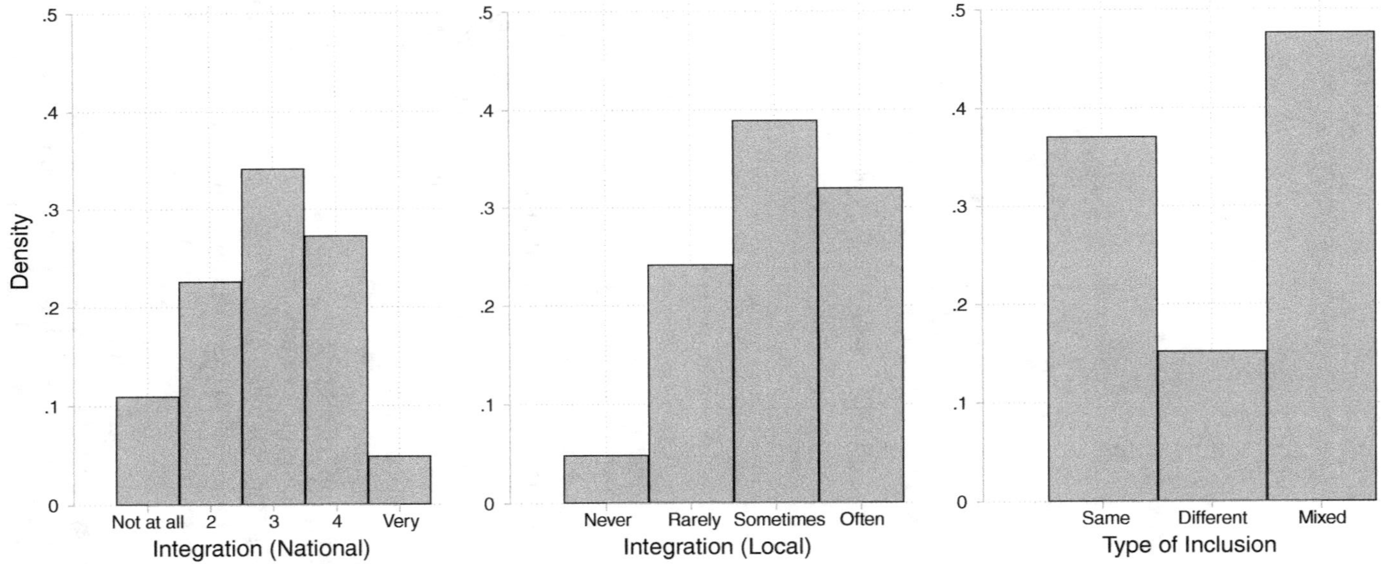

FIGURE 5.6 Iraq: Perceived police integration

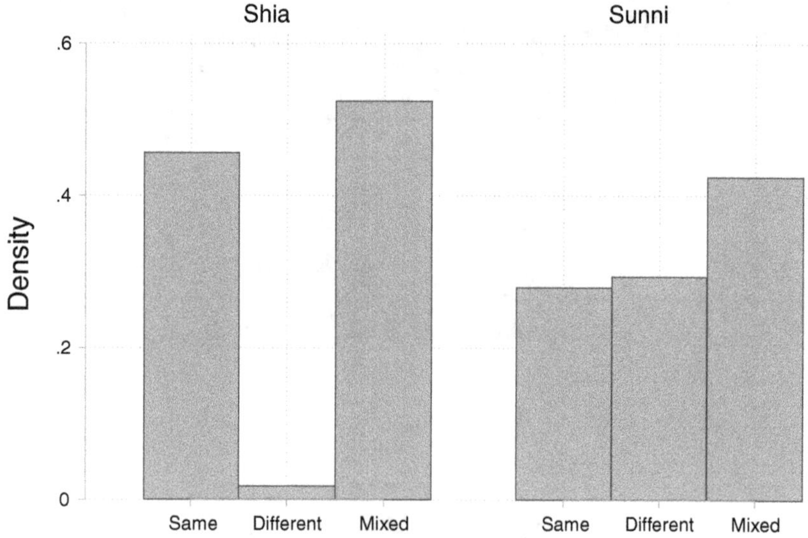

FIGURE 5.7 Perceived type of inclusion, by sect

local level, since actual levels of integration vary across neighborhoods. However, variation in perceptions of how integrated the police are nationwide means that citizens hold differing perceptions at a level at which there is no actual variation. Second, a plurality of Iraqis believe the police are somewhat – but not completely – integrated. This finding is consistent with the description presented in Chapter 3, which indicates isolated instances of inclusive policing throughout the country but no systematic integration at the institutional level.

The third panel of Figure 5.6 shows the distribution of perceived *types* of police inclusiveness. Very few (15.2 percent) subjects believe they are policed exclusively by out-group officers. A plurality (47.4 percent) perceive mixed policing in their neighborhood, while the remaining 37.1 percent believe most officers in their neighborhood are from their own group. At first glance, these figures suggest that the Iraqi police are quite inclusive, at least in the capital city. However, disaggregating responses by sect tells a different story. Figure 5.7 shows that virtually no Shias believe their neighborhood is policed exclusively by Sunni officers. On the other hand, 29.5 percent of Sunni respondents believe that they are policed mainly by Shias, even more than the number of respondents who say they are policed by officers from their own group. Although Shias are a demographic majority in Iraq overall,

Sunnis and Shias hold similar shares of the population in Baghdad. In other words, to the extent that these perceptions are accurate, the Iraqi police in Baghdad are not representative of the population they serve, and even after significant reforms, a large proportion of Sunnis remain policed mainly by the politically dominant out-group.

Citizens' perceptions vary across neighborhoods within Baghdad. Figure 5.8 shows two maps of the capital city. On the left, darker neighborhoods indicate that surveyed respondents perceive the police in their neighborhood as more integrated, while lighter neighborhoods indicate that surveyed respondents perceive the police in their neighborhood as less integrated. Unfilled neighborhoods were not surveyed. The right panel indicates whether a neighborhood is predominantly Sunni (darkest fill), predominantly Shia (lightest fill), or mixed. The maps show no evidence of a relationship between perceived local police integration and neighborhood-level demographics.

Figure 5.9 presents results from two regression models exploring the individual-level determinants of perceived integration.[19] Like in Israel, members of the dominant group (Shias) perceive greater national-level integration compared to members of the marginalized group (Sunnis), suggesting that past experiences interrupt the translation of observed officer demographics into perceptions of the institution. Those who are more satisfied with their economic situation perceive the police as more integrated nationally but less integrated in their neighborhood. Respondents with a household member who works in the public sector perceive the police as more integrated both nationally and locally, perhaps reflecting their privileged status. Educational degree attainment is associated with decreased perceptions of national integration but increased perceptions of location integration. Finally, the number of hours of electricity a respondent receives per day is positively associated with perceived local integration but appears unrelated to perceptions of national integration.[20] Neither age nor gender has any systematic relationship with perceptions of integration.

Forming Perceptions of the Iraqi Police

Iraqis regularly observe police officers. Virtually every Iraqi interviewed for this project in Baghdad and Mosul reported seeing police officers

[19] Results are from ordered logistic regression models, with standard errors clustered by street (primary sampling unit). Figure 5.9 displays 95 percent confidence intervals.

[20] All reported differences are statistically significant using ordered logistic regression with enumerator fixed effects and neighborhood-clustered standard errors.

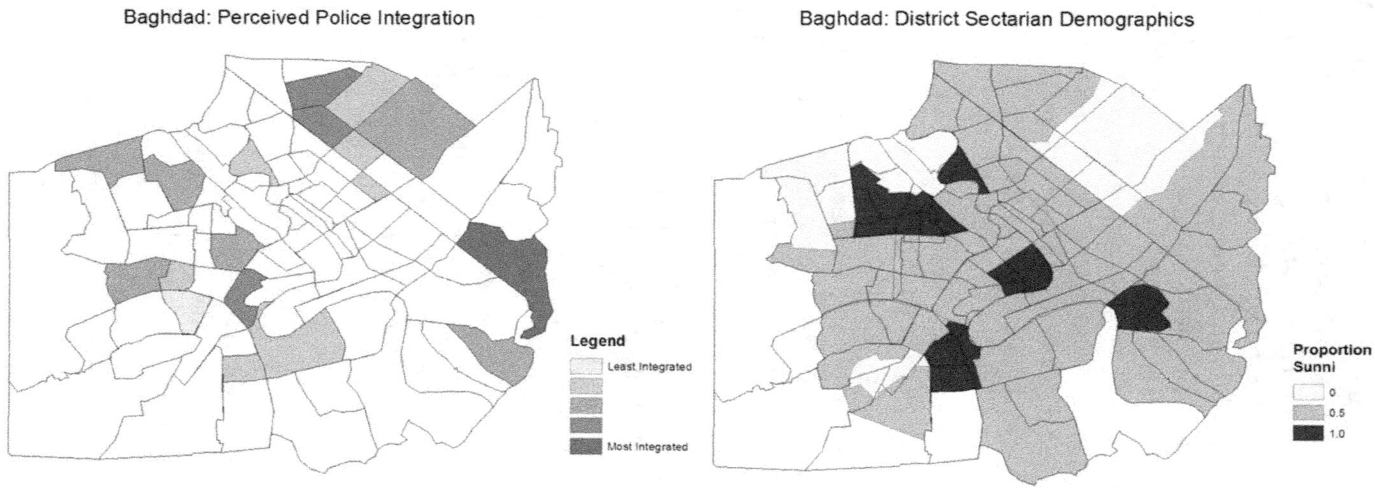

FIGURE 5.8 Local police integration and population demographics

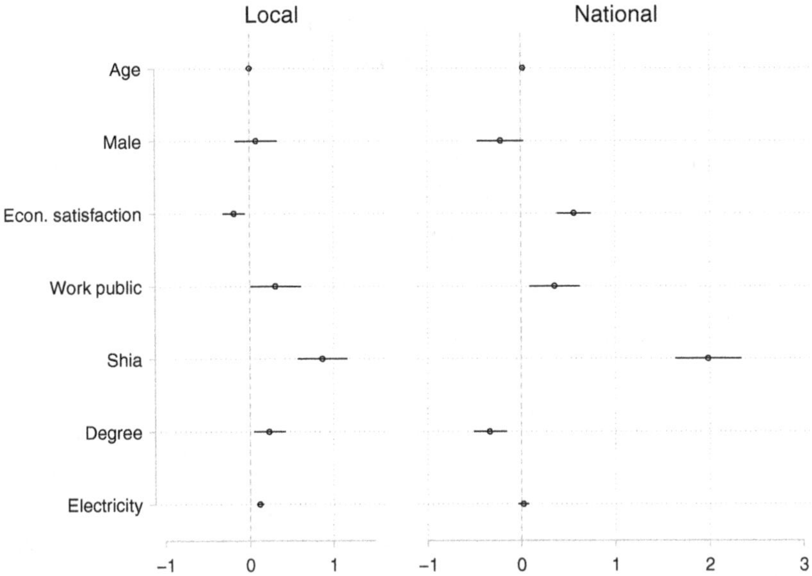

FIGURE 5.9 Who perceives the Iraqi police as integrated?

every time they leave their home. Checkpoints between neighborhoods and on the outskirts of cities are the most common points of contact, but citizens also encounter officers if they need to report a crime, are involved in a car accident, or apply for a permit or residency card. According to a taxi driver in Baghdad, "There's no street or junction without a police officer."[21] Beyond these personal observations, Iraqis also report receiving information about the police from news on the radio and TV, and from talking with friends and family. When asked specifically how he knew whether there were Christian police officers in locations other than Baghdad, the same taxi driver replied, "I've heard about it from a friend or from (a specific acquaintance); for example, if I visit friends or relatives, I would ask them about other families... They would say their son – for example – is working in the ministry of defense or the police and so on." Strikingly, one out of every eight survey respondents lives in the same house as a police officer, providing numerous opportunities for personal interactions.

Given this visibility, can citizens accurately determine the demographic makeup of officers they see? While there are no inherent

[21] IIACSS interview 05CM, February 2019

physical difference between Sunni and Shia Arab Iraqis, cultural and regional differences make group membership observable. Interviewees frequently cited accent as a useful cue. Nasim, a Sunni living in Baghdad, says "The accent of the western [Sunni] people is distinguishable as they talk slowly with a rhythm."[22] A Shia resident of Mosul says, "I notice the accent and the way he talks; if his accent has a lot of 'T' in it then he's Shiite from Tal Afar, if his Arabic isn't good then he's from Bortolla from the Shabak villages, and if his accent indicates that he's from Samaoa, Baghdad and so on, we know that he's Shia, and if his accent indicates that he's from Mosul then of course he's Sunni."[23] Word choice and colloquialisms also reveal sect. Shias address one another as "cousin," or by swearing to specific imams or religious figures. Some interviewees referenced clothing. "Black clothes or the Abaya, the one that goes all the way to the head, and we [Shias] wear black Hijab a lot... It's obvious that only us [Shias] wear it. You can tell from far away that this woman is Shiite from her Abaya."[24] Police officers frequently display flags or posters of religious figures on their vehicles or at checkpoints. Finally, some sectarian cues are context-specific. A Christian woman living in Baghdad says that at checkpoints, the police "know all of the people in GMC [brand vehicles] are Christians, and they let us through."[25]

Names displayed on officers' uniforms and citizens' ID cards also reveal sect in a large number of cases. Recall the anecdote earlier in this book about Ahmed, the Sunni man who was stopped at a checkpoint and solicited for a bribe. The incident occurred because Ahmed's name signals that he is Sunni.[26] Ahmed's experience was not unusual. According to a report by the Finnish Immigration Service on the security situation in Baghdad, "Sunnis have experienced problems at checkpoints because of their names. Back in 2003–2005, during the sectarian conflict, many Iraqis acquired two identification documents, one with a Sunni name and another with a Shia name... In July 2006, the police found 14 young men dead in Baghdad. They were all Sunnis who had been shot in the head. All of them had the same first name,

22 IIACSS interview 12NM, February 2019. As is the case for all citizen interviews in Iraq, the name is changed to protect anonymity.

23 IIACSS interview 02SM, February 2019

24 IIACSS interview 10SF, February 2019

25 IIACSS interview 01CF, February 2019

26 It bears repeating that "Ahmed," like the names used in all references to civilian interviewees, is a pseudonym. The citizen's real name is used almost exclusively by Sunnis in Iraq.

Omar. Meanwhile, Shiites have reportedly experienced problems at the hands of Sunni militant groups such as ISIS due to their names."[27] While the report points out that not every name unambiguously signals sect, many of Iraq's most popular names do so.

Interviewees' confidence in their ability to identify sect varies. One resident of Mosul says he has "total confidence" in his ability to tell if an officer he is interacting with is Sunni or Shia.[28] Others are less certain that they can identify sect in any given scenario, but still receive enough information to form impressions of the institution. "I won't say [people can tell] 100% of the time, but 50%, from their looks, or when he starts talking [with his accent], we're able to tell."[29] Another Baghdad resident says he can identify sect "not 100%, but maybe 70%."[30]

LINKING PERCEPTIONS OF POLICE AND GOVERNMENT

Citizens' perceptions of the police are important in their own right. Yet, for police integration to fully transform citizen–state relations, citizens must associate the police with the government more broadly. Policing is where the rubber meets the road in governance, as officers implement and enforce the laws passed by the state. Police officers wear government-issued uniforms and drive cars with the name of the jurisdiction on the side, symbology that signals the authority on which they act (Ellison 2007). It stands to reason that citizens' perceptions of the police should be closely tied with their perceptions of the government.

I test the link between attitudes toward the police and attitudes toward the state using Round 3 of the Arab Barometer, a nationally representative survey of citizens in 13 Arab countries.[31] The survey asks citizens to evaluate the performance of "the police (security forces)," as well as the "ease of receiving services" from the police and security forces. The surveys also ask respondents to evaluate the performance

[27] Security Situation in Baghdad: The Shia Militias. *Finnish Immigration Service*, April 29, 2015. https://migri.fi/documents/5202425/5914056/61225_Security_Situation_in_Baghdad_-_The_Shia_Militias_29.4.2015.pdf/00c75e2d-9ff7-4894-a851-39228b5a3c5e/61225_Security_Situation_in_Baghdad_-_The_Shia_Militias_29.4.2015.pdf.pdf p. 16–17

[28] IIACSS interview 02SM, February 2019

[29] IIACSS interview 01CF, February 2019

[30] IIACSS interview 07SM, February 2019

[31] Algeria, Egypt, Iraq, Jordan, Kuwait, Lebanon, Libya, Morocco, Palestinian Territories, Saudi Arabia, Sudan, Tunisia, and Yemen

TABLE 5.2 *Arab evaluations of the federal government*

	(1) Eval federal gov	(2) Eval federal gov	(3) Eval federal gov
Eval police	0.560*** (0.00657)	0.484*** (0.0395)	0.455*** (0.0469)
Individual controls	No	No	Yes
Country FE	No	Yes	Yes
Constant	1.700*** (0.0209)	1.901*** (0.104)	1.222 * * (0.478)
Observations	14358	14358	11671

OLS with robust standard errors. *** $p < .01$

of the federal government. Table 5.2 shows that across all countries in the Arab Barometer survey, there is a positive and robust association between evaluations of the police and evaluations of the federal government. As expected, citizens who report that the police and security forces are doing a good job are more likely to say that the federal government is doing a good job as well. Model 3 controls for respondents' gender, education, employment status, religion, and economic well-being. The relationship between police and government approval ratings remains substantively large and statistically significant. Of course, we cannot say whether positive attitudes about the police lead to positive attitudes about the government, or vice versa. Intuition suggests that it is likely a little of both. However, these results support the general claim that under normal circumstances, attitudes toward the police and the national government are associated with one another.

Citizens might *not* associate the police with the national government when a subnational government provides policing services. When policing occurs primarily at the city or county level, as in the United States, we should expect citizens' attitudes toward the police to influence their feelings primarily toward the local government, and less so toward the federal (national) government. While citizens may hold a sense of disillusionment with a system they perceive as unfair, resentment toward a municipal police department is unlikely to lead to rebellion against the national government.

This potential broken link has important implications for Iraq's Kurdish region. The 2005 Iraqi constitution places all authority for domestic security and public safety provision in the region with the Kurdish Regional Government (KRG). The bulk of this responsibility falls on the *Peshmerga*, a paramilitary force formed in the 1970s as a resistance group against the Baathist regime in Baghdad (Lawrence 2009). Today, the Peshmerga is made up of almost 200,000 fighters, the vast majority of whom are ethnic Kurds.[32]

The Peshmerga succeeded in maintaining security and stability in Northern Iraq even during periods of extreme violence in the rest of the country, and were instrumental in stemming the expansion of the Islamic State. At first glance, this effectiveness would seem to favor autonomous in-group policing, with Kurds responsible for their own security. However, the relationship between Kurds and the government in Baghdad is strained by a desire for an independent Kurdish state, a move opposed by Baghdad, the United States, and several neighboring countries. Successful security provision by a Kurdish force might embolden calls for autonomy or independence by decreasing the perceived value among Kurds of a political association with Baghdad and demonstrating Kurdish forces' capabilities in combat. At the very least, unlike individuals elsewhere in the Middle East, Kurdish Iraqis' attitudes toward the police should *not* be associated with their attitudes toward the federal government.

Table 5.3 again uses the Arab Barometer data, but this time restricts the sample to Iraqi respondents and adds interaction terms between a Kurdish indicator variable and three independent variables of interest: evaluation of the police, ease of receiving police services, and evaluation of the local government. The baseline relationship between evaluations of the police and evaluations of the federal government for non-Kurds is indeed positive and significant, indicating that for Arab Iraqis, evaluations of the police are linked to evaluations of the federal government. The coefficients on the interaction terms are negative and significant. The attitudinal link between the police and the national government is substantially smaller for Kurdish Iraqis than for Arab Iraqis, and the difference between the two groups is statistically significant. In other words, Kurdish respondents are less likely to link their evaluations of the police and local government with their evaluations

32 www.bbc.com/news/world-middle-east-28738975

TABLE 5.3 *Iraqi evaluations of the federal government*

	(1) Fed gov	(2) Fed gov	(3) Fed gov	(4) Fed gov	(5) Fed gov	(6) Fed gov
Kurdish	1.209***	0.984***	1.797***	1.014***	2.014***	1.522***
	(0.203)	(0.228)	(0.216)	(0.257)	(0.258)	(0.293)
Eval police	0.638***	0.585***				
	(0.0248)	(0.0306)				
Eval police*Kurd	−0.418***	−0.365***				
	(0.0647)	(0.0685)				
Police service			0.718***	0.583***		
			(0.0434)	(0.0491)		
Police service*Kurd			−0.638***	−0.454***		
			(0.107)	(0.118)		
Eval local gov					0.577***	0.509***
					(0.0292)	(0.0306)
Eval loc gov*Kurd					−0.572***	−0.532***
					(0.0765)	(0.0834)
Individual controls	No	Yes	No	Yes	No	Yes
Constant	1.551***	1.383***	1.421***	1.832***	1.365***	1.654***
	(0.0672)	(0.157)	(0.107)	(0.199)	(0.0962)	(0.160)
Observations	1195	1138	926	881	1189	1127

OLS with robust standard errors.
* $p < .10$, ** $p < .05$, *** $p < .01$

of the federal government compared to Arab Iraqis. Once again, it is impossible to say whether attitudes toward the police affect attitudes toward the government or vice versa, but we can say with confidence that the association between the two variables is weaker for Iraqi Kurds than it is for Iraqi Arabs.

CONCLUSION

Police officers' visibility and frequent interactions with citizens play a powerful role in shaping citizens' perceptions. The positive and significant relationship between local-level police heterogeneity and perceived local police integration shows that integration is more than just a public relations issue. Without real changes in officer demographics, citizens are unlikely to permanently change their perceptions of the police, regardless of any claims the government makes about integration.

At the same time, citizens do not directly translate observations of local inclusion into attitudes about the police as a national-level institution. Rather, they filter personal observations through their accumulated experiences, especially those they attribute to identity-group membership. "Whether it is a stop and search procedure or response to a call, police officers and citizens do not engage each other as neutral bureaucrats and abstract individuals. Rather, it is an encounter loaded, on both sides, with personal and collective histories, negative or positive perceptions, and sets of expectations" (Ben-Porat and Yuval 2019, 195). In both Israel and Iraq, citizens from the politically marginalized group perceive the police as less integrated nationwide compared to citizens from the dominant group despite evidence in both countries that marginalized-group citizens are exposed to *more* marginalized-group police officers.

This disconnect between local-level observations and national-level attitudes poses perhaps the most significant challenge to the use of police integration to improve citizen–state relations. Political leaders from the dominant group who genuinely wish to improve trust must not only recruit minority officers but also convince a skeptical population that the inclusion they observe indicates a genuine attempt at reconciliation by the state. The deeper the historical legacy of marginalization, the more skeptical the population is likely to be. Just as a public information campaign alone is unlikely to sway perceptions of the police, inclusion on its own is also unlikely to shift attitudes toward the institution in a meaningful way. Rather, the government must supplement inclusion with a credible demonstration that the changes citizens observe in their community extend to other communities, and perhaps to other policy domains as well. Even then, changing attitudes in divided societies is likely to be a slow process. Mistrust developed over decades of conflict cannot be forgotten overnight.

6

POLICE INTEGRATION AND ANTI-GOVERNMENT VIOLENCE

On October 24, 2005, an Iraqi civilian parked his SUV in front of the Iraqi Ministry of Agriculture in Baghdad and detonated a large explosive device hidden in the vehicle. As crowds gathered, a second attacker detonated a truck bomb nearby. The combined attacks killed more than twenty people.[1] Less than a month later, on November 18, a coordinated suicide bomb attack on a Ministry of Interior building in Baghdad's Jadiriya district injured at least 40.[2] Between early 2004 and June 2016, civilians and anti-government militias carried out at least 2,173 suicide attacks, causing more than 23,000 deaths and wounding upwards of 53,000. These numbers only include attacks using suicide tactics; the total number of incidents was even higher. While many attacks targeted civilians in crowded markets or mosques, about three in every four took aim at government, police, and military installations, despite these being heavily guarded and harder to reach.[3] Fighters carried out at least four separate attacks against Iraqi police stations in January 2005 alone, illustrating both the frequency and intensity of anti-government violence.[4]

1 Semple, Kirk (2005), "3 bombers strike at Baghdad hotels." *The New York Times*, October 25. www.nytimes.com/2005/10/25/world/middleeast/3-bombers-strike-at-baghdad-hotels.html

2 "Iraq suicide attacks kill dozens (2005), *BBC News*, November 18, http://news.bbc.co.uk/2/hi/middle_east/4448798.stm

3 Chicago Project on Security and Threats Suicide Attack Database. http://cpostdata.uchicago.edu/search_new.php

4 January 10, in southern Baghdad; January 11 in Tikrit; January 26 in Riyadh; January 28 in Dora, Baghdad. *MIPT Terrorism Knowledge Base*. Accessed May 2, 2018, https://web.archive.org/web/20061007163729/http://tkb.org/Incident.jsp?incID=21477

While Iraq's death toll is unusually high among modern conflicts, the nature of the conflict is not unique. Since the beginning of the First Intifada in Israel in 1987, non-state actors have carried out 114 suicide attacks (in addition to hundreds of non-suicide attacks), seventeen of which were aimed at heavily guarded government targets.[5] In 2019, insurgency marked life in portions of Afghanistan, the Philippines, Nigeria, and Egypt.

Police integration affects citizen–state relations on a number of dimensions. In this chapter, I explore its impact on an especially consequential outcome, civilian support for insurgency. Iraq provides a particularly relevant setting for analysis, but the dynamics I identify in this chapter are common to any divided society in which shifts in relative group power foster violence between a marginalized group and the government, including conflicts in Northern Ireland, the former Yugoslavia, and Lebanon.

Civilians play an important role in the state's ability to suppress insurgent violence (Berman and Matanock 2015). Of course, citizens often participate directly in fighting. Existing research identifies a number of possible reasons why citizens might take up arms against the government, including grievances over the quality and distribution of services, low opportunity costs due to a lack of employment opportunities, and as a response to government repression. I show in this chapter that citizens' perceptions of police integration are correlated with all three of these mechanisms. Even if a citizen does not personally participate in violence, his attitudes toward the police and the government impact the realization of violent conflict. Government forces depend heavily on information from civilians to identify and locate insurgents (Department of the Army 2006; Berman et al. 2011b). Noncombatants' decisions to shelter insurgents or provide information about their location to authorities can turn the tide of conflict. This decision rests in part on their attitudes toward the police, which I argue are shaped by integration.

I begin by testing the link between police integration and several motives for conflict that are common in existing research. Using evidence from my survey of Baghdad residents, I find that Sunnis who perceive the police as integrated are more likely to perceive police and government service provision as fair, more likely to expect that they

[5] Chicago Project on Security and Threats Suicide Attack Database. http://cpostdata.uchicago.edu/search_new.php

could get a job in the police if they wanted, and less fearful of repression by the government. Data constraints on police integration and insurgent violence make testing their relationship difficult. Therefore, to identify the causal relationship between exposure to integrated policing and support for anti-state violence, I embed an experiment within my survey which primes citizens with randomly varied information about the Iraqi police's level of integration. I evaluate the relationship between this informational prime and respondents' support for anti-government violence, which I measure using a "list experiment," a technique that ensures the privacy of responses. Overall, recipients of the integration prime were about 60 percentage points less likely to say they would turn to anti-state violence.

WHO REBELS?

Contemporary research on rebellion frames an individual's decision to support or participate in violent anti-state conflict as a function of the costs and benefits of doing so (Olson 1965; Kalyvas 2006; Kalyvas and Kocher 2007; Humphreys and Weinstein 2008; Berman et al. 2011a; Toft and Zhukov 2015). Appropriately for a book about policing, this framework follows from Becker's (1968) classic work on criminal behavior.[6] Just as a person might steal from a shop if the value of the stolen item is greater than the cost and likelihood of punishment, a citizen will take up arms against the state if the expected benefits of winning – gaining access to wealth, improving the quality of service delivery, ensuring one's future security, and so on – outweigh the potential costs of losing or the likelihood of being killed. Empirical research suggests that fighters seek a variety of benefits. For example, they might expect the rebel group to implement policies with which they agree, or the rebels may pay them to fight (Humphreys and Weinstein 2008). Others point out that active participation in a rebellion is often safer than being a noncombatant in a war zone (Kalyvas and Kocher 2007). In divided societies, an individual's costs and benefits likely depend on the group to which they belong (Shesterinina 2016; Tezcür 2016).

Participation in fighting is an extreme outcome, but even tacit support for insurgents affects violence. Government forces typically possess

6 Also see Ehrlich (1973, 1996)

a substantial power advantage over insurgents. In order to benefit from this advantage, they must first identify and locate combatants. Civilian noncombatants are well positioned to provide this information as they tend to be aware of activities in their community. Thus, modern counterinsurgency strategy relies on winning the "hearts and minds" of civilians to convince them to turn in anti-government fighters (Department of the Army 2006; Berman et al. 2011b). Police integration can reduce conflict by signaling to noncombatants that the state intends to treat them well, simultaneously reducing motives for participating in conflict and making noncombatants more likely to provide government forces with information about insurgent activities.

I focus on three common reasons why individuals may side with insurgents rather than with the government: poor or unfair service provision, exclusion from employment, and expectations of physical harm. Anecdotally, Iraqis seem to recognize the importance of these mechanisms. When pressed on why he supports greater integration of Sunnis into the Iraqi security forces, a Sunni man from Baghdad's Saydiya neighborhood explained, "First, you would end unemployment, second, for better security, and third, terrorism would stop."[7] Another resident of Saydiya also believes that more Sunnis in the police would lead to better service provision and physical security: "The Shia are in control [of the police] right now and it's not good … [We] don't expect to get justice, and there isn't much security in the street. Kidnappings are still happening. There is a lot of kidnapping in Saydiya. I don't allow my son to go out alone; I fear for him … If things were balanced, it would be better."[8]

Existing research poses grievances, unemployment, and insecurity as competing mechanisms, but empirical tests find little evidence that these motives are mutually exclusive (Collier and Hoeffler 2004; Humphreys and Weinstein 2008). A more likely explanation is that all of these motives (and others) are relevant some of the time and often occur simultaneously. Rather than pitting them against each other, I ask two questions: First, given what we know about factors which motivate conflict, does police integration mitigate those factors? Second, are individuals who perceive the police as integrated less supportive of anti-state violence?

7 IIACSS interview 09NM, February 2019

8 IIACSS interview 06SF, February 2019

Quality and Distribution of Services

Existing research proposes that relative deprivation, or the belief that one is unfairly worse off relative to others, may motivate grievances and violent behavior (Gurr 1970; Horowitz 1985). In divided societies, the logical comparison for citizens is whether they are worse off than members of the out-group. Grievances may be economic (Russett 1964; Paige 1975; Muller 1985) or political (Cederman et al. 2010). Evidence linking grievances with violence is somewhat mixed. Using data on forty years of civil wars, Collier and Hoeffler (2004) find that while political repression and exclusion are significantly correlated with the likelihood of conflict, other variables have greater explanatory power. Fearon and Laitin (2003) similarly argue that since grievances are ubiquitous, they could not possibly explain variation in conflict occurrence. On the other hand, studies that focus on a group's relative well-being, or "horizontal grievances," find a substantial relationship with conflict (Wood 2003; Østby 2008; Cederman et al. 2011).

Given the political salience of sectarian identity in Iraq, citizens often construe government service provision as a product of sectarianism. A resident of Nassiriya explains how differing levels of electricity provision between Ramadi, a majority Sunni city, and Nassiriya, a predominantly Shia city, were interpreted: "The problem is a sectarian one but at its root it is a class and regional problem. If [the state] provide[s] services to one governorate and not to another it will breed resentment. I mean why was it that in Ramadi [electricity] was cut for only four hours [per day] whereas in Nassiriya it was provided for only two hours? When this kind of a question is posed the easiest and most visible answer is sectarianism: they are Sunnis and we are Shias" (Haddad 2011, 58).

Public safety is arguably the most important good the modern state provides (Olson 1993). It stands to reason that a citizen who believes she receives inferior public safety due to her group identity may develop grievances against the state, especially when most government leaders are from a different group. Inclusive policing reduces opportunities for officers to over-police (harass) or under-police (neglect) out-group citizens by minimizing the frequency of interactions between out-group officers and citizens. Heterogeneous patrols may further reduce the likelihood of biased police behavior by improving officers' attitudes toward out-groups (Allport 1954; Ball and Cantor 1974; Blair et al. 2016). Finally, police integration feeds into a cycle of citizen cooperation which improves the overall quality of service provision. Citizens with a personal connection to the police are more likely to cooperate with and provide information to officers, thereby giving the police better information about the needs of the community (Haim et al. 2019), which the police use to provide services more efficiently (Nanes 2020).

H_I: Individuals who perceive the police as more integrated will be less likely to perceive police or government service provision as biased.

Access to Employment

Conventional wisdom associates unemployment with conflict. Marr (2007) cites the "loss of jobs, income, and status of former army officers, civil servants, and others" as a significant motivator of Sunni Iraqis' participation in the post-2003 insurgency. The Iraqi Ministry of Interior employs more than a quarter of a million citizens, most of them police officers.

Researchers and commentators offer a number of potential mechanisms linking unemployment with participation in conflict. One is psychological; unemployed individuals are said to be disaffected, unhappy, or depressed, leading them to commit acts of violence. According to the White House's National Strategy for Victory in Iraq released in November 2005, one of the primary impediments to peace in Iraq was that "unemployment is high, which fuels popular dissatisfaction and may generate sympathy for the insurgency among some Iraqis."[9]

Another possible link between unemployment and participation in conflict is that unemployment lowers the opportunity costs of participation (Berman et al. 2011a). Fighting against the state requires a significant time commitment and is likely to end in permanent injury or death. Potential fighters may find it difficult to actively participate in an insurgency while simultaneously holding a full-time, wage-earning job. Individuals who are unemployed face a much lower opportunity cost than those holding lawful, stable employment. Empirical evidence on the opportunity costs mechanism is mixed. Research from Africa (Miguel et al. 2004) and Colombia (Dube and Vargas 2013) finds that positive economic shocks, which presumably increase employment, are associated with decreases in civil conflict. Drawing on similar logic, Jablonski and Oliver (2013) find that improvements in the labor markets of countries prone to piracy decrease the frequency of pirate

[9] National Security Council (2005), *National Strategy for Victory in Iraq*. p. 32, November 19, www.washingtonpost.com/wp-srv/nation/documents/Iraqnationalstrategy11-30-05.pdf

attacks. On the other hand, Berman et al. (2011a) find a consistent *negative* relationship between unemployment and insurgent violence in Iraq, Afghanistan, and the Philippines.

Finally, exclusion from gainful employment may generate grievances in much the same way as unfair receipt of policing services (Brainard and Chollet 2007). Particularly in a war-torn country like Iraq in which the police are backed by foreign donors, a job with the police is unusually stable and lucrative. The attractiveness of police employment is even stronger for uneducated, low-skilled individuals who do not qualify for many private-sector jobs. When the state systematically excludes – or is perceived to exclude – members of an identity group from these desirable jobs, citizens from that group may develop grievances which motivate violence against the state.

I remain agnostic about the specific mechanism linking employment with conflict participation, and seek to determine simply whether police inclusion influences citizens' perceptions that they have fair access to employment. Though this hypothesis may seem obvious, the question is not simply how many coethnics an individual believes serve in the police, but whether he would be given fair consideration for the job were he to apply. A citizen may observe police officers from their group but believe that those officers are collaborators who received some sort of special treatment, and therefore still believe that he (or his group) is unfairly excluded from employment in the police.

H_2: Individuals from the vulnerable group who perceive the police and security forces as more integrated will be less likely to perceive their group as unfairly excluded from employment in the police.

Physical Security

A third line of research focuses on the expectations of marginalized group members about their future security. By virtue of being more powerful than the marginalized group, the state struggles to credibly commit not to harm it in the future (Fearon 1995a; Lake and Rothchild 1996). In the shadow of historical conflict, promises alone are rarely sufficient to allay fears. As long as the state retains its power advantage, it can renege on any "commitments" it makes. The resulting security dilemma (Posen 1993) induces the weaker group to invest in building up its defenses, an action which escalates tensions and increases the likelihood that ambiguous behavior by either side will be interpreted by the other as aggression. If either side believes that the balance of power will change in the future, it may decide to strike preemptively. Researchers use variants of the commitment problem to explain group-based civil conflict in the former Yugoslavia (Fearon 1995a), Rwanda (de Figueiredo Jr and Weingast 1997), and Iraq (Dodge 2012; Lake 2016).

Researchers devote a great deal of effort to solving this commitment problem. Most proposals involve institutions which tie the hands of the more powerful party, including third-party peacekeeping (Walter 1997), legislative power sharing (Strøm et al. 2017), federalism and devolution (Horowitz 1985; Roeder and Rothchild 2005), elections and election monitoring (Matanock 2017), and ethnic autonomy (Cederman et al. 2015). I argue that police integration, perhaps as part of a broader power-sharing arrangement, can solve the commitment problem by allowing the powerful state to credibly signal to the weaker group that it does not intend to repress it. As I describe in Chapter 2, police integration raises the costs to the state of future repression by arming and equipping members of the dominant group, providing information about the state's plans and vulnerabilities, and exposing pro-government civilians to out-group police officers. In turn, citizens from the marginalized group who perceive that the police include members of their group should be less likely to expect that the government intends to repress them down the road, reducing their incentives to build up defenses or engage in preemptive strikes and decreasing their tendency to interpret ambiguous actions by the state as aggressive.

Police integration is self-enforcing in that it is costly for the state to purge officers from marginalized groups after providing them with weapons and making service delivery dependent on their participation. The power of police heterogeneity over segregated inclusion becomes especially obvious on this point. Hiring, training, and equipping officers take time. A state which fires a large portion of its police officers *en masse* will inevitably suffer from poor police service provision for a period of time while it rebuilds its force. If all marginalized-group officers serve only in-group civilians, then the state faces lower costs from reneging on inclusion, as presumably it does not care that these civilians receive poor services.

H_3**:** Individuals from the vulnerable group who perceive the police and security forces as more integrated will be less likely to fear future repression by the police/government.

H_3a: The effect of police inclusion on fear of repression will be stronger for integration (local-level heterogeneity) than for autonomy (segregated inclusion).

Alternative Argument: Increased Opportunity for Rebellion

The same tools which make repression costly – arming and organizing minorities, providing them with strategically sensitive information, and making service provision dependent on their participation – increase a group's ability to fight and win against government forces. Thus, police integration might actually *increase* willingness to rebel by raising the likelihood of success. However, participation in violence is risky even for victors (Fearon 1995b; Kalyvas and Kocher 2007), and individuals should prefer to avoid fighting if their concerns can be solved peacefully.

ANALYSIS

High-quality data on violence in Iraq are difficult to come by. Some studies measure insurgent violence using district-level "significant activity" reports (Berman et al. 2011b; Condra and Shapiro 2012). These reports include only events involving coalition forces and cover a time period when police integration (unit-level heterogeneity) was rare, making them ill-suited to my purposes. Iraq Body Count has been aggregating data on fatal violence in Iraq since the 2003 invasion. While not a perfect measure of insurgency, relative numbers of deaths across locations may provide insights into patterns of violence. Figure 6.1 plots the number of deaths that occurred between June 2014, the beginning of the Islamic State's major conflict with the Iraqi government, and February 2017, the last month for which data were available at the time of writing. Most events in Baghdad are identified at the neighborhood level, with about a quarter identified only by district (there are 120 districts in Iraq, including ten in Baghdad). I mapped each event at the center of the neighborhood or district in which it occurred. Larger circles indicate more deaths in a location.

Reports by government agencies active in Baghdad provide another source of information about local levels of violence. A report published by the Finnish Immigration Service in 2015 describes levels of sectarian violence in various neighborhoods of Baghdad, which I use for coding each neighborhood as having low, medium, or high levels of

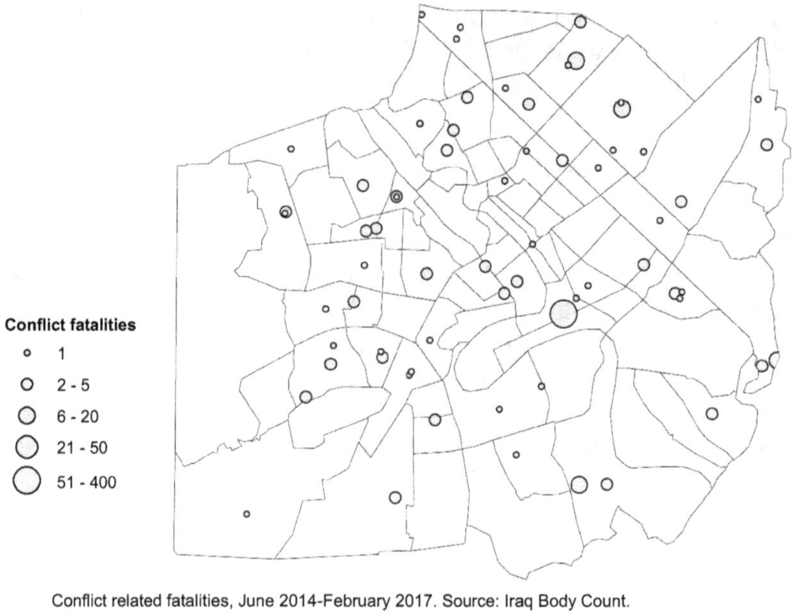

FIGURE 6.1 Conflict fatalities in Baghdad, June 2014–February 2017

violence. The report indicates that it discusses "the districts of Baghdad where considerable Shia militia activity and movement have been reported." However, comparison of the patterns in Figures 6.1 and 6.2 suggests that a neighborhood's omission from the Finnish report does not necessarily indicate the absence of violence.

Ultimately, neither of these sources is appropriate for testing the theorized link between perceptions of police integration and anti-state violence. First, while people form perceptions of police integration based on officers serving in areas where they live (see Chapter 5), they do not necessarily commit insurgent attacks in their home neighborhoods. Second, the location data on violence are noisy and imprecise. Third, I rely on survey data on perceptions of police integration as the independent variable. Obtaining a precise neighborhood-level measure of perceived integration in a large number of neighborhoods would be prohibitively expensive. Given these limitations, I test the effects of police integration on citizens' attitudes and perceptions. First, I look at attitudes surrounding common causes of participation in violence: grievances over service provision, perceptions of fair access to employment, and expectations of security. I then explore integration's effects on a survey-based measure of support for anti-state violence.

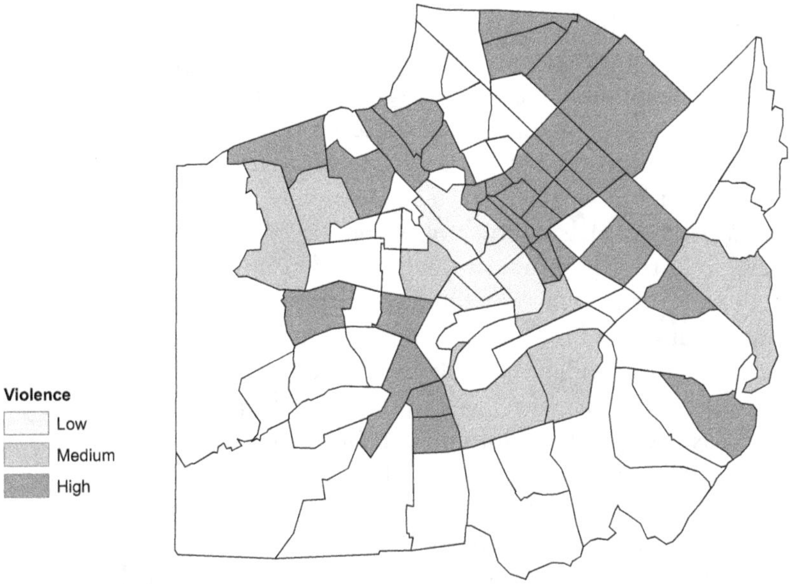

Neighborhood violence, c. January 2014. Source: Finnish Immigration Service, "Security Situation in Baghdad - The Shia Militias." 29 April 2015.

FIGURE 6.2 Sectarian violence in Baghdad, c. December 2014

Measuring Perceptions of Inclusion

I test the link between integration and violence using *perceptions* of police integration measured in my survey of Baghdad residents. While I use this survey-based measure out of necessity, it has the advantage of measuring one slice of the causal chain directly: citizens respond to their *perceptions* of police integration rather than officers' actual demographics. Using the three questions listed in Chapter 5, I measure perceptions of national-level integration, perceptions of integration in the respondent's neighborhood, and whether security forces in the respondent's neighborhood are from the respondent's group, the out-group, or mixed. In this chapter, I analyze only the responses of the Sunni subsample, since integrating the police in Baghdad would mean substantially increasing the proportion of Sunni officers.

RESULTS

To measure citizens' perceptions of how fairly the police provide services, the survey asks, "Do you think the Iraqi Police treat citizens fairly regardless of their religious or ethnic identity? Please answer from 1 to

5, with 1 being the least fair and 5 being the most fair." To measure service provision by the government, the survey asks, "Do you think that the government distributes goods and services fairly to members of your community?" Both questions reference fairness on the basis of group identity to capture the horizontal grievances that existing research links with conflict.[10]

Regression models control for a number of respondent-level characteristics, including gender and age. Education accounts for the possibility that civilians who are better-off or have superior economic prospects might be less likely to support violence. A dummy variable for whether the respondent or a member of his or her household works in the public sector accounts for the respondent's political connections, as well as the quality of information he or she likely has about government institutions. I also control for the number of hours per day of electricity the respondent's household receives as an objective measure of government service provision. A question about economic satisfaction serves as a control for baseline positivity. The model also includes controls for whether the respondent's district is primarily Sunni (versus mixed). Standard errors are clustered by street, the primary sampling unit. All models use OLS and include enumerator fixed effects as a standard safeguard against potential differences in the way enumerators deliver questions. An online appendix presents robustness checks for all tables in this chapter, including nonlinear models and using consistent samples across regressions.

The dependent variable in Models 1 and 2 is perceived fairness of police service provision. In Model 1, an increase of one point on the 5-point scale of perceived national-level police integration is associated with nearly half a standard deviation increase in perceived fairness (significant at $p < .01$). Model 2 considers perceived police integration in the respondent's neighborhood. *Police Same* is a dummy indicating that the respondent believes most officers in her neighborhood are from her own group, while *Police Mix* is a dummy indicating that the respondent believes local officers come from both in- and out-groups. Each coefficient references the difference between that variable and a respondent who believes most officers in her neighborhood are from the out-group. I find a positive and significant relationship between *Police Mix* and perceived fairness; all else equal, a person who believes local officers

10 Portions of this chapter's analyses appear in Nanes (2019).

TABLE 6.1 *Perceived integration and perceptions of service provision*

	(1) Police	(2) Police	(3) Gov.	(4) Gov.
Integration (Nat'l)	0.539***		0.0470*	
	(0.0564)		(0.0267)	
Police Same		0.0450		−0.0265
		(0.165)		(0.0533)
Police Mix		0.610***		−0.0178
		(0.157)		(0.0489)
Male	−0.0327	−0.156	0.0735**	0.0340
	(0.0851)	(0.0958)	(0.0328)	(0.0308)
Age	−4.247	−3.685	0.0600	1.048
	(3.192)	(4.461)	(1.214)	(1.207)
Degree	−0.0363	−0.138***	−0.0332**	−0.0285
	(0.0449)	(0.0451)	(0.0163)	(0.0178)
Econ. satisfaction	0.177***	0.280***	0.0264	0.0324
	(0.0454)	(0.0620)	(0.0265)	(0.0267)
Work public	0.0749	0.152	0.0659*	0.0635*
	(0.0895)	(0.104)	(0.0334)	(0.0321)
Electricity	−3.031	−4.053*	−0.0719	0.233
	(2.049)	(2.338)	(0.645)	(0.642)
District Sunni	0.186*	0.105	0.0120	0.0218
	(0.104)	(0.128)	(0.0431)	(0.0410)
Observations	366	337	352	325
R^2	0.598	0.528	0.220	0.234

OLS regression. Standard errors clustered by street. Enumerator fixed effects.
* $p < .10$, ** $p < .05$, *** $p < .01$

are mixed perceives service provision as 6/10ths of a point higher on the 5-point scale, more than half a standard deviation. On the other hand, consistent with my argument that local heterogeneity provides increased opportunities for monitoring and preventing police misbehavior, there is no observable difference between those who perceive officers as mostly in-groups and those who perceive them as mostly out-groups.

Results on perceptions of government service provision are somewhat weaker. In Model 3, I observe a small and marginally significant relationship between perceived national integration and perceived fairness of government service provision; a 1-point increase in perceived integration (5-point scale) is associatd with a 4.7 percent increase in perceived government service provision, a dichotomous variable. In Model 4, perceptions of the local police's makeup, whether as mostly in-groups or as mixed, are not significantly associated with perceptions of government service provision. It stands to reason that perceived police integration nationally will have a stronger, larger association with perceptions of police service provision compared to other government services.

Respondents who are better educated view service provision as less fair, perhaps because they are more aware of inequalities across groups, while those who see themselves as economically better-off perceive service provision as more fair. Having a household member who works for the government is associated with about a 6.5 percent increase in saying that the government provides services fairly.

Next, exclusion from employment in state institutions may motivate anti-state violence. The survey asks respondents, "Do you think that if someone from your family applied for a job with the Iraqi Police, his or her application would be considered fairly?" I ask about a family member to ensure that the respondent is thinking about someone of his or her sect without explicitly stating that I am interested in sectarian identity. Table 6.2 tests perceptions about police integration against responses to this question. Once again, models use OLS with standard errors clustered by street and include a full set of control variables.

In Model 1, I find a positive relationship between perceived police integration nationally and respondents' expectations that employment in the police is handed out fairly. Sunnis who perceive the police as more integrated (1 point on a 5-point scale) are 14 percent more likely to say a family member's application would be considered fairly. Surprisingly, Model 2 shows no impact of perceiving the local police as mixed (relative to primarily out-groups), while perceiving local officers primarily as in-groups is associated with a 15 percent *decrease* in perceived likelihood that a family member's application would be considered fairly. One possible explanation is that when the government concentrates all Sunni police officers in homogeneous units, Sunnis

TABLE 6.2 *Perceived integration and employment*

	(1) Police jobs	(2) Police jobs
Integration (Nat'l)	0.141***	
	(0.0393)	
Police Same		−0.151***
		(0.0489)
Police Mix		−0.0180
		(0.0511)
Male	0.0471	0.0294
	(0.0388)	(0.0424)
Age	0.0667	−0.232
	(1.130)	(1.461)
Degree	−0.00619	−0.0248
	(0.0204)	(0.0249)
Econ. satisfaction	0.0200	0.0613*
	(0.0238)	(0.0331)
Work public	0.0316	0.0713*
	(0.0434)	(0.0385)
Electricity	0.761	0.471
	(0.856)	(0.825)
District Sunni	0.0835*	0.140**
	(0.0496)	(0.0610)
Observations	330	311
R^2	0.264	0.259

OLS regression. Standard errors clustered by street. Enumerator fixed effects.
$^{*} p < .10$, $^{**} p < .05$, $^{***} p < .01$

perceive it as an attempt to isolate Sunni officers and prevent true integration. Another possibility is that this relationship is an artifact of the small sample and unevenly distributed responses. Only eighty-eight Sunnis say the police in their neighborhood are primarily Sunnis, making the result susceptible to small changes in the way participants respond.

Finally, expectations that one's group might be violently repressed in the future may motivate participation in conflict. I argue that police integration reduces expectations of future repression by making repression more costly for the state, thereby serving as a credible signal of the state's peaceful intentions. Table 6.3 shows the results from several models testing this argument. The survey asks about expected repression by both the police and the government. Specific to the police, "Do you ever feel afraid of the Iraqi Police? Please answer on a scale of 1 to 5, with 1 meaning that you are not afraid at all, and 5 meaning that you are very afraid." Specific to the government, "Do you ever worry that the government might do something to harm you or other members of your religious group?" As in the previous table, all models use OLS, include enumerator fixed effects, and report standard errors clustered by street.

Of the three mechanisms, the evidence linking police integration with expectations of repression is the strongest and most consistent. Model 1 shows that a 1-point increase in perceived national police integration is associated with a .28-point decrease in fear of the police, about one quarter of a standard deviation. Model 2 shows that Sunnis who perceive their local police as mixed are nearly three-tenths of a point less likely to fear the police compared to those who perceive officers as mainly out-groups. On the other hand, there is no relationship between perceiving local officers as mainly in-groups and fear of the police. I find a similar pattern of evidence on expectations of repression by the government, with perceptions that the police are integrated nationally and that they are mixed locally associated with substantial decreases in expected harm among Sunnis. Those who self-report higher economic satisfaction are less expectant of repression, perhaps because they have a more positive outlook in general, or perhaps because they believe their wealth insulates them from mistreatment. No other controls have consistent conditional relationships with expected police or government harm.

The consistent effect of perceived local police heterogeneity (*Police Mix*) and the lack of any significant effect of perceiving local police as in-groups (*Police Same*) is striking. It suggests that minorities do not inherently prefer to be policed by in-groups, and that there is something about local heterogeneity which they believe empowers their group. If this nuance holds for other institutions as well, it would require a substantial change in the way scholars and policy-makers

TABLE 6.3 *Perceived integration and expected repression*

	(1) Police	(2) Police	(3) Gov.	(4) Gov.
Integration (Nat'l)	−0.284***		−0.174***	
	(0.0598)		(0.0462)	
Police Same		0.0347		−0.124
		(0.151)		(0.0802)
Police Mix		−0.297**		−0.204***
		(0.113)		(0.0677)
Male	−0.210**	−0.143	0.0786	0.114**
	(0.0849)	(0.0973)	(0.0529)	(0.0534)
Age	0.435	−1.070	3.779**	3.263
	(2.600)	(2.726)	(1.778)	(2.084)
Degree	0.0299	0.0568	0.00917	0.0273
	(0.0530)	(0.0571)	(0.0240)	(0.0243)
Econ. satisfaction	−0.122**	−0.147**	−0.0638**	−0.0910**
	(0.0468)	(0.0555)	(0.0307)	(0.0341)
Work public	−0.00885	−0.0860	0.0728	0.0626
	(0.112)	(0.109)	(0.0505)	(0.0581)
Electricity	1.946	3.098*	−1.312	−1.292
	(1.367)	(1.611)	(0.912)	(0.954)
District Sunni	−0.103	−0.0890	0.0252	0.0499
	(0.0850)	(0.0861)	(0.0689)	(0.0814)
Observations	374	343	337	312
R^2	0.532	0.534	0.264	0.253

OLS regression. Standard errors clustered by street. Enumerator fixed effects.
$^{*}p < .10$, $^{**}p < .05$, $^{***}p < .01$

think about representation. Conventional wisdom assumes that when it comes to representation, more is better. Such a preference pits groups into conflict with one another, as relative inclusion is necessarily zero-sum. On the other hand, if people prefer heterogeneity, it is possible to build institutions which satisfy all groups. While limited to a single institution in a single case, these results suggest a need for additional research on the distinction between representation and heterogeneity.

Measuring Support for Anti-Government Violence

How do these perceptions affect the realization of violence? Given the limited data on insurgency, I again turn to a survey-based measure of attitudes toward anti-state violence. Asking about support for violence directly would undoubtedly make respondents uncomfortable, leading to high rates of nonresponse and raising concerns about inaccurate responses. It may also place respondents in danger if their anonymity were compromised. Instead, I employ a list experiment to estimate the proportion of respondents who support the use of violence. I randomly assigned subjects either a "short list" or "long list" and asked the following question:

> I am going to read you a list of [4 or 5] strategies that citizens sometimes use when the government does not seem to be listening to them. Please tell me how many of these strategies you would consider using if you felt the government was ignoring your needs. Remember, I don't need to know which ones you would use, only how many of these [4 or 5] you would consider.

Subjects in the "short list" group received a list of four noncontroversial items: voting against the government, writing letters to the government, writing letters to an international organization, and protesting peacefully. The "long list" group received the same four items, as well as an additional item, "using non-peaceful methods."[11] I calculate the proportion of respondents who would use violence as the average response of the long list group minus the average response of the short list group. The mean for the long list group is .300 higher than the mean for the short list group ($p < .01$), indicating that, on average, about 30 percent of Iraqis would consider using non-peaceful methods against the government. Disaggregating by sect, an estimated 24 percent of Shias and 36 percent of Sunnis would consider using violence ($p < .01$). Given that respondents are asked only whether they would *consider* using violence (rather than whether they have used it or definitely would use it), this estimate does not seem unreasonably high. In the Data Appendix, I show that the two groups of respondents

[11] In focus group testing, respondents understood this phrase to imply violence.

TABLE 6.4 *Support for anti-government violence*

Control mean	Treatment mean	Difference	95 percent CI
2.155(.056) $n = 400$	2.455(.067) $n = 400$	.300 * * * (.087)	[.470, .129]

Standard errors in parentheses.
$^{*}p < .10$, $^{**}p < .05$, $^{***}p < .01$

are balanced on all observed characteristics and discuss methodological issues related to the mechanics and interpretation of the list experiment.

To isolate the causal relationship between perceived police integration and support for anti-government violence, I embedded an experiment within the surveys which randomly varies information about the police's level of integration. I first assigned respondents at random to either a treatment or a control group. The enumerator then read what they claimed to be an excerpt from a news report describing the recent crime-fighting success of a police unit in Kirkuk, an ethnically and religiously mixed city in northern Iraq. In the treatment group, the news story attributes the unit's success to the mixed ethnic and religious identities of its officers. A quote from the unit's commanding officer reads,

> When citizens see us patrolling together, they trust us. They see Kurds and Arabs, Sunnis and Shia working side by side and know that we are not a force belonging to one community or another. We are the Iraqi police, and we serve Iraqi citizens.

The news story goes on to say that "According to a high-level official in Baghdad, unit 218 is serving as a new model for policing across the country," emphasizing that this integration is not an isolated occurrence but the result of a broader government policy. Even if respondents have not personally observed such integration, according to this news story, they should expect mixed units like this one to become increasingly common. While the story is fake, it is entirely plausible as there were a number of ethnically and religiously heterogeneous security forces units operating in Iraq during the period.

In the control group, the story attributes the unit's success to new technology that allows police leadership to track crime and allocate resources more efficiently. The structure of the survey and the questions which followed the vignette precluded the use of a pure control with no news story, and the need for a positive frame required that the police's success be attributed to something in order to keep the treatment and control news stories as similar as possible. I elected to attribute the police's success to technology as it was highly plausible in the context, ideologically neutral among civilians, not related to the conflict or to sectarian identity, and not an issue on which respondents should have strong prior expectations. I gave a great deal of consideration to the ethical implications of this measurement strategy. Beyond taking care not to generate potentially dangerous negative reactions toward the police or government, I considered the use of deception in the prime. While the quotes and police unit in question were fabricated, similar integration did occur in certain parts of Iraq. Thus, to the extent that the prime shifted perceptions of the police and the government, it did so in the direction of reality.

In the context of Iraq's tumultuous political landscape, this treatment should substantially shift perceptions on the extent of police integration. The degree to which it does so depends on the strength of subjects' prior beliefs. Those who hold weak perceptions should be more influenced by new information, while those whose beliefs are well entrenched will discount new information which conflicts with their existing beliefs. On average, Iraqis should hold relatively weak priors about the police because of the turmoil the Iraqi police have experienced since 2003. The Iraqi Police Service, and indeed most of Iraq's government institutions, are creations of post-Saddam Iraq. These institutions have evolved considerably since 2003, including several changes to their name, structure, and inclusion of Sunnis. As a result, citizens' perceptions of the police should be malleable.

To test whether increasing information about police integration reduces support for anti-government violence, I cross-randomized the item-count groups with the vignette groups to create four versions of the survey: long-treatment, long-control, short-treatment, and short-control, with equal probability of selection into each. This cross-randomization solves two problems simultaneously. The randomized vignette allows me to measure the causal effect of information about police integration, while the list experiment provides a reliable estimate of a difficult-to-measure outcome.

Testing the relationship between perceived police integration and support for anti-government violence pushes the limits of the scope

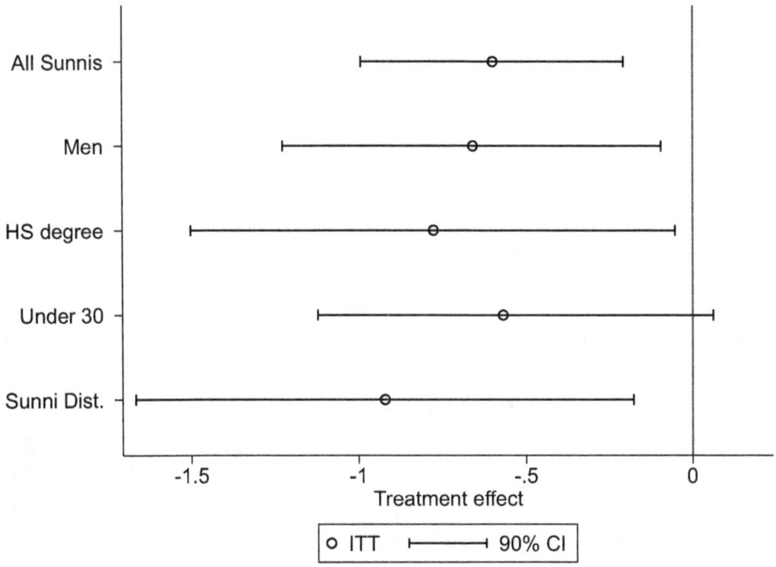

FIGURE 6.3 Effect of information about police integration on support for anti-government violence

condition that integration should matter only if citizens recognize the state's right to govern. However, of the millions of citizens worldwide who likely question their governments' legitimacy, only a tiny proportion turn to violence. Violence is an extreme reaction to an imminent threat of personal or communal harm, coupled with the perception that nonviolent responses are unlikely to mitigate that threat. It is this imminent threat to safety, not merely a lack of government legitimacy, that pushes people to violence. Thus, perceived legitimacy and permissive attitudes toward anti-state violence, while likely correlated, should not fully overlap.

RESULTS: SUPPORT FOR ANTI-STATE VIOLENCE

Figure 6.3 shows the main results. Among Iraqi Sunnis who received the control vignette, 66 percent would consider using violence against the government, compared to only 6 percent in the control group, a difference that is significant at $p < .05$ level using a difference-in-differences estimator. The treatment effect is consistently negative across all tested subgroups of Sunnis, though the sample size is admittedly somewhat small to test for heterogeneous effects.

How can a simple informational cue cause such a large change in support for violence? Several characteristics of the Iraqi case likely increase the magnitude of this effect. First, extreme levels of violence in Baghdad over the past decade and a half should make Iraqis unusually willing to support violence, raising the upper bound and allowing greater room for variation. As discussed earlier, the priming treatment should also have a stronger effect on perceptions of inclusion in Iraq than in countries with well-established institutions. Iraq's institutions are young and relatively unstable; therefore, citizens' attitudes about them should be highly malleable. Next, the survey measures support for violence about ten minutes after the prime. As temporal distance from this cue increases, individuals have more time to weigh the information against their existing perceptions of the police and to integrate new information into their perceptions. Any contradictory information will mitigate the effect of this informational prime on support for violence. Thus, we should expect the effects of a news report about the police being integrated to dissipate over time. Despite these caveats, the clear causal relationship between information about police integration and support for anti-government violence leaves little doubt that perceived police integration affects the likelihood and magnitude of violence.

CONCLUSION

This chapter fills in another piece of the puzzle linking police integration with citizen–state relations. The results are largely consistent with the argument that police integration addresses common motives for supporting or participating in conflict, including grievances over unequal service provision, exclusion from employment, and fears of physical harm. Of these, expected future repression and the associated commitment problem are impacted by police integration in a way that is consistent with my theory. In particular, the finding that local-level heterogeneity, but not same-group policing, addresses expected repression and perceptions of fair service provision suggests that the key mechanism is not just representation but the way in which included officers are distributed within the institution. Citizens do not value representation as an end unto itself, nor is representation in government institutions simply a matter of providing self-determination or allowing coethnics to police one another. Local-level heterogeneity provides previously excluded groups with means of imposing costs on the dominant group or state that are not provided by autonomy and makes it more difficult for the police to renege on inclusion. I speculate that citizens recognize these differences and respond accordingly.

These results support the argument that individual motives to participate in conflict are an important determinant of conflict occurrence. The finding that members of the marginalized group are less, not more, inclined to turn to anti-state violence when their group is empowered by inclusion in the police directly contradicts claims that the likelihood of victory is the most important driver of conflict behavior (Fearon and Laitin 2003; Collier and Hoeffler 2004). The findings in Baghdad suggest that attempts at reconciliation which increase a group's opportunity to rebel are not doomed to fail as long as they sufficiently reduce motives for rebellion. Similarly, this evidence implies that police integration signals future treatment, not just current conditions. If Sunnis expected the state to renege on integration at some point in the future, they should seize the opportunity and rebel while their group is included in the police. Yet, Sunnis who perceive the police as integrated are *less* supportive of violent rebellion, suggesting that they expect integration to persist. Given Iraqis', and especially Sunnis', exceedingly low levels of trust in the government, the most likely explanation for this expectation is that Sunnis believe reneging on integration would be difficult or impossible for the government.

The evidence in this chapter suggests that post-Saddam Iraq might have taken a very different trajectory if the transitional governments and constitution had included provisions for including Sunnis in the police. In the power vacuum that followed the fall of the Baathist regime, minority Sunnis feared not just that they would be excluded from policy-making but that majority Shias would use their newfound power to retaliate for past exclusion and repression. Many decided they could not afford to wait and see how the new Shia-led government would treat their group, as by the time the government showed its true colors it would be too late to do anything about it. Integrating the police would have provided Sunnis with a security guarantee and a credible signal that the government intended to treat all citizens fairly. Failure to integrate the Iraqi police between 2003 and 2014 may have contributed to the country's devastating civil war. The increase in police integration post-2014, while limited to certain parts of the country, may have contributed in some small way to the decrease in domestic support for anti-state violence.

7

CITIZEN COOPERATION AND CRIME

On January 28, 2019, sixty-year-old Hassib Mussa went shopping in Kiryat Tivon, a typical northern-Israeli suburb.[1] As he exited the shopping center, an unidentified assailant shot and killed him. Details of the shooting are hazy, but the police believe the motive was criminal and not related to terrorism. Mussa's murder followed five others in Arab-Israeli towns and villages in the first month of 2019.[2] In each case, the police were unable to gather much information, and they made an arrest in only one of the six incidents. This crime spree in Israel's Arab sector is neither new nor unusual. According to the Knesset Research Center, 64 percent of all murders between 2014 and 2016 took place in Arab communities.[3] The blight of crime in Arab-Israeli towns extends to nonviolent crimes as well, with Arab-Israelis substantially more likely than Jews to experience property crimes like vehicle break-ins.[4]

Arab-Israelis hold a general perception that inadequate police services are responsible for the high crime rate and poor public safety in their neighborhoods. The problem, they say, rests with police who view

[1] Portions of this chapter appear in Nanes (2020).

[2] Shaalan, Hassan, "6 murdered in Arab sector since the beginning of 2019." *Ynet News* January 30, 2019. www.ynetnews.com/articles/0,7340,L-5455297,00.html

[3] Breiner, Josh and Jack Khoury, "Crime is rampant in Israeli Arab communities, but police lack the resources to bring about change." *Haaretz* April 8, 2018, www.haaretz.com/israel-news/.premium-police-struggle-to-fight-crime-in-israeli-arab-communities-1.5978263

[4] Annual Statistical Abstract, Israel Central Bureau of Statistics (2014), "Victims of criminal activities aged 20 and over, by type of offence and selected characteristics." Publication 11.4, www.cbs.gov.il/shnaton66/st11_04.pdf

Arabs as enemies to protect against, not citizens to serve. "They don't help Arabs with anything. The most important thing for them is the security of the state. All of these burglaries and so on, they don't care about that. If Arabs are involved they say 'OK let's settle it and get it over with.' They tell the Arabs, 'you do the work.'"[5] Arab focus group participants want the police "to behave with us as citizens and not as enemies." "They treat the Israelis fine, but with us they are disrespectful." The police, they say, are not interested in serving their community. "They are in the streets as a warning to the Arabs, not to secure the Arabs." One Arab resident of Jaffa, whose population is almost entirely non-Jewish, blames the city's high crime rate on a lack of local knowledge by the police. "What happens in Jaffa, they never solve who does those crimes. So it doesn't give you confidence ... When a Jew commits a crime, they catch him right away. When an Arab did it, they don't know who did it [committed the crime]. There is a difference." Data appear to back up these complaints. Of the 520 reported shootings since 2016 in Umm al-Fahm, a northern town with a population of about 52,000, prosecutors indicted only six suspects.[6]

Frustration over public safety and crime is arguably the single most important feature in the relationship between Arab-Israelis and the government today, even more pressing than the conflict surrounding Palestinian statehood (Ben-Porat and Yuval 2019). "Israeli Arab citizens are interested first and foremost in issues related to their daily lives, and less preoccupied with external issues such as the peace process or matters related to the Palestinian territories" (Rudnitzky and Radai 2017, 12). This chapter focuses on the way that police integration affects crime not just because of its direct importance for public safety but also because of the way perceptions of the police impact citizens' broader relationship with the government.

Arab-Israelis are substantially less willing to contact the police compared to Jewish Israelis. A 2008 study finds that 70.1 percent of Jews said they would call the police if they witnessed a crime, compared to 50.6 percent of non-Jews (Hasisi and Weisburd 2014). Similarly, Figure 7.1 shows that among respondents to my survey, Jews were much more likely than non-Jews to say that they would contact the police if they

[5] All quotes in this paragraph come from Focus Group 2A, conducted in Jaffa, March 2019. To protect participants' privacy and anonymity, the focus group transcripts do not identify individual participants.

[6] Shaalan 2019

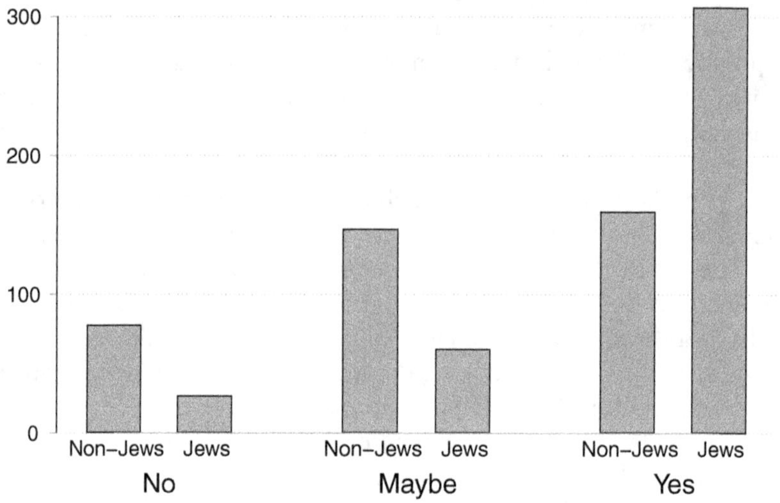

FIGURE 7.1 If you witnessed someone stealing money from a shop, would you contact the police?

witnessed someone stealing from a shop. As I describe later, the resulting dearth of citizen-provided information hinders the police's ability to deter and solve crime, feeding back into further negative perceptions of police service.

For their part, police officers recognize their poor relationship with Arabs but blame lack of cooperation for their inability to identify and apprehend suspects. A commander at a police station in East Jerusalem says that in the event of a shooting, "in the Jewish community, even before the police arrive, there will be a hundred calls to 100 [the emergency number]. [In this Arab neighborhood] I might not get even one call."[7]

Arabs' hesitance to provide information to the police forces officers to operate with incomplete information about the challenges facing Arab communities. In turn, they are unable to allocate resources efficiently toward crime prevention even if they wish to serve these communities. Citizens appear cognizant of this problem. "If someone commits a crime and four or five people saw him, and nobody is willing to complain, how will you arrest him? The court has to have witnesses,

[7] Quoted in Breiner, Josh and Jack Khoury, "Crime is rampant in Israeli Arab communities, but police lack the resources to bring about change." *Haaretz* April 8, 2018, www.haaretz.com/israel-news/.premium-police-struggle-to-fight-crime-in-israeli-arab-communities-1.5978263

but nobody goes. So the police give up."[8] Yet, personal experiences have discouraged these citizens from going to the police for help.

> My neighbor's house got robbed two nights ago. They came back after being in a wedding and saw the house was a mess. They called the police, who told them to come to the station at one or two at night and file a complaint. What is this? [The police] should come right now, check for fingerprints, maybe if they come now they can catch the thief!

Citizens place the onus on the police to change the environment and demonstrate that it is worth their while to go to them for help. According to the same focus group participant whose neighbors were asked to come to the police station in the middle of the night to file a report, "[The police] should give us more tools for security [so that] when something happens, we will not think twice about calling them immediately."[9]

How can the police interrupt this negative feedback loop in which expectations of poor service reduce citizen cooperation, which, in turn, leads to poor service? The Israel Police have improved relations with Arab citizens in recent years by increasing the religious diversity among officers. Inclusion in the police rank and file signals to citizens that the police are more likely to treat them well, thereby increasing their willingness to cooperate with officers and provide them with information (Weitzer and Tuch 2004). Officers then use this information to provide services more efficiently by identifying problem areas with greater accuracy and precision, and devoting appropriate resources to those areas. This information provision mechanism impacts service provision by improving the police's efficiency, and it should lead to net improvements for all citizens in a community, regardless of whether they are Arab or Jewish.

I find that those who perceive the police in their community as inclusive are more willing to report crimes to them. As expected, the effect is strongest for non-Jews, but there is no evidence that inclusion reduces willingness to report crimes among Jews. Thus, as the police become more inclusive, information available to them increases, and the increases are largest in communities with large non-Jewish populations. I then test the effects of integration on crime. Drawing on a large-scale victimization survey to measure crime rates independently of reporting

[8] Focus group 2A, Jaffa, March 2019
[9] Focus group 2A, Jaffa, March 2019

rates, I find that within a given location, increases over time in police integration are associated with decreases in the probability of crime. As expected, the effect is concentrated in locations with large non-Jewish populations, the same locations where increases in information flows should be largest. Within those locations, however, the effect does not differ significantly between Jewish and non-Jewish citizens.

The finding that religious diversity among police officers leads to better, not worse, service provision departs from conventional wisdom that heterogeneity harms public goods provision (Alesina et al. 1999; Miguel and Gugerty 2005; Habyarimana et al. 2007) but is consistent with a growing body of evidence that integration in the police and military improves institutional outcomes (Lasley 1994; Blair et al. 2016; Nanes 2020). I suggest that the rigid structures of security institutions, including a strict chain of command, uniforms, rituals and traditions, and an "us against them" mentality in the struggle against criminals or other opponents, counteract the negative effects of diversity on cooperation.

The central nature of Arab citizens' concerns about poor-quality or unfair service provision makes this success especially important in shaping citizen–state relations. Integration creates a positive feedback loop by credibly signaling to citizens that the police intend to serve them; thus, citizens are more willing to cooperate with the police, allowing them to serve more effectively, which reinforces the signal that the government intends to serve citizens from the marginalized group. This causal pathway reinforces the overarching theme that police integration improves citizen–state relations by allowing the state to credibly signal its positive intentions to a historically marginalized segment of society.

INSTITUTIONAL INCLUSION AND SERVICE PROVISION

Existing research shows that in divided societies, the demographic makeup of service-providing institutions substantially affects the quality and nature of the services those institutions provide, but there is no consensus about the mechanisms driving this relationship. One line of work suggests that civil servants "actively represent" in-group coethnics (Meier 1975; Mosher 1982; Meier and Stewart Jr. 1992; Meier 1993; Andersen 2017)[10] by exerting greater effort at providing services

[10] Also see Taylor-Robinson and Heath (2003) for a similar argument on gender representation.

for members of their own group, potentially at the expense of effort to provide services for out-groups. A related argument suggests that bureaucrats and police officers are better suited to serve coethnic civilians, as they better understand the community (Ben-Porat and Yuval 2012; Abraham Fund Initiatives 2013). Given the fixed resources typically available to the institutions in question, these arguments imply a zero-sum effect in which representation for one group reduces the quality of services provided to members of other groups. This zero-sum outcome raises the possibility of opposition by those privileged by the status quo and calls into question the normative desirability of representation.

Other possible mechanisms acknowledge the potential for institutional inclusion to change officers' attitudes about out-groups or the relative salience of identity. Studies argue that serving side-by-side with bureaucrats, officers, or soldiers from another group humanizes its members and generates shared interpersonal experiences. Samii (2013) finds that soldiers in Burundi who serve in mixed units exhibit less prejudice against out-groups, and Ostwald (2013) shows that soldiers assigned to live-in units in Singapore hold an increased sense of civic identity. Integration may impact the attitudes of marginalized-group officers as well. Newly integrated officers could learn to identify more with the police than with their identity group, raising the possibility that integration may lead to worse treatment of minorities by their coethnics. Yet, the same mechanism could also lead members of the dominant group to "learn" to identify more with their profession than with their ascriptive identity, reducing their mistreatment of out-group citizens.

Finally, diversity among police officers might impact the quality of service provision even without changing officers' attitudes or intentions. Shared identity helps solve collective action problems by improving community members' abilities to monitor and sanction noncompliance (Besley et al. 1993; Fearon and Laitin 1996; Berman 2000; Miguel and Gugerty 2005) or by providing a common language to aid communication (Hardin 1997). Furthermore, if members of different groups have divergent preferences about the distribution of government services (Alesina et al. 1999), integrating the police could create disagreements between officers on how to engage in policing. On the other hand, the rigid institutional structures of policing like a strict chain of command, common uniforms and norms of appearance, and a threat to personal safety may counteract the inefficiencies of heterogeneity by providing a set of heuristics which aid cooperation (Gibson and Hoffman 2013). Studies of the police in Los Angeles (Lasley 1994) and Liberia (Blair et al. 2016) find no evidence that heterogeneity among officers impedes service provision. The highly structured nature of security institutions suggests that the inefficiencies of heterogeneity should be less of a concern among police officers than in most other settings.

Inclusion, Information, and Efficiency

The police rely on citizen-provided information to combat threats to public safety. Just as counterinsurgent forces use tips to combat insurgent activity (Kalyvas 2006; Berman et al. 2011b; Lyall et al. 2015), police officers use information from citizens about suspicious behavior and past crimes in their locality to allocate their limited personnel and equipment as efficiently as possible (Skolnick and Bayley 1988; Akerlof and Yellen 1994; Tyler 2004; Weitzer and Tuch 2006; Ungar 2011). For example, if citizens report a series of vehicle break-ins on a specific street, the police can assign additional patrols to that street, deterring future break-ins and increasing the chances of catching the perpetrator. Without citizens' reports, the police would be unaware that the street warranted extra attention, and they may be allocating patrols to areas where they are less useful. González (2016) clarifies that institutions which are more inclusive of broad swaths of society are better able to harness citizen participation into effective public safety provision.

Where identity is salient, a group's inclusion in the police affects citizens' relationships with the institution. "Minority representation may convey a message of ownership to the minority and undermine the notion that the police are an alien, 'occupying army'" (Weitzer and Hasisi 2008). Shared identity provides citizens with a cognitive shortcut for how they should expect to be treated. Lyall et al. (2015) refer to this shortcutting as "coethnic bias." Citizens need not view integration as normatively desirable or fair. Rather, the accumulation of lived experiences and experiences communicated by family and friends leads reasonable people to develop expectations that individuals from their own group will treat them better than individuals from other groups. Thus, a police force that includes officers from a citizen's group reduces that citizen's expected costs of coming in contact with the police by signaling that the institution is trustworthy (Lyall 2010) and committed to just treatment.

Coethnic bias also raises the expected benefits to citizens of reporting information when the police are inclusive. Citizens contact the police because they expect to benefit from reduced local crime or improved personal safety, or perhaps out of a sense of normative justice. The realization of these benefits depends on the effort the police exert in following up on their information (Blair et al. 2019). Citizens may worry that out-group police officers may not take their concerns seriously. Thus, even if citizens do not fear overt mistreatment, they may be unwilling to incur mundane costs like waiting on hold for an emergency operator or walking to a police station to report a crime if they do not believe the police will reciprocate their effort.

These arguments lead to several expectations about the effects of police inclusion on citizens' attitudes and behaviors:

H_1: Citizens from marginalized groups will be more willing to report crimes to the police when they perceive the police as inclusive.

If increased crime reporting makes the police more effective at preventing crime, then,

H_{2a}: Citizens will be less likely to experience crime when the police in their location are inclusive.

Given that police inclusiveness should increase reporting rates primarily among citizens from marginalized groups,

H_{2b}: The effect of inclusion on crime will be strongest in locations with large populations of historically marginalized groups.

Finally, because public safety tends to be provided non-excludably at the local level, if the gains in crime prevention come from increases in efficiency rather than from coethnic favoritism, those gains should apply to the entire community, not just to those who provide information. All citizens within a community benefit when the police identify crime hotspots and assign more officers to those areas. Similarly, higher conviction rates due to better citizen tips deter would-be criminals throughout the jurisdiction, not just those who would have targeted marginalized groups. Thus, within a location, increased information will improve service provision for all citizens, regardless of whether they personally become more likely to report crimes.

H_{2c}: Within a location, the effect of inclusion on crime should be constant across citizens of all groups.

Several assumptions govern these arguments. First, officers must *want* to provide effective public safety. If the police fail to act on information citizens provide, then improved police–community relations should not influence crime. Similarly, the institution and its officers must be capable enough not to squander information that they receive. As I describe in Chapter 4, the Israel Police is a highly capable institution, with the manpower and equipment necessary to serve citizens and prevent crime.

Second, these hypotheses assume that officers do not intentionally and systematically mistreat civilians from a particular group. For hypothesis 2c to hold, at worst the police must treat each segment of society neutrally. In Israel, there is no question that officers periodically mistreat citizens, and that the highest-profile incidents tend to involve citizens who are religious or ethnic minorities. Thankfully, though, these incidents make up only a tiny minority of citizen–officer interactions.

PUBLIC SAFETY, CITIZEN TRUST, AND CRIME IN ISRAEL

Overall, crime rates in Israel are on par with most Western European countries.[11] As in most places, crime is more common in less affluent cities and neighborhoods.[12] Official figures at the subnational level are difficult to come by. According to the Israel Police, crime in Jerusalem has declined over the past several years,[13] while it has increased in Ashkelon, Modi'in, and Beer Sheva. Tel Aviv has the highest number of crimes per capita.[14] Victimization surveys carried out by Israel's Central Bureau of Statistics provide further insights into the frequency of each type of crime. In 2013, 5.4 percent of Israelis experienced a home break-in and 4.7 percent experienced a nonviolent theft. Two

11 Saunders et al. (2013)

12 US Department of State (2014), "Israel 2014 Crime and Safety Report: Tel Aviv." www.osac.gov/pages/ContentReportDetails.aspx?cid=15230

13 Eisenbud, Daniel K. "Non-terror-related Jerusalem crime rate drops amid heightened police presence." 23 November 2015, www.jpost.com/Israel-News/Jerusalem-crime-rate-drops-434997

14 Levi, Yaakov. "Secret crime stats: Tel Aviv 'most dangerous' town." October 19, 2014, www.israelnationalnews.com/News/News.aspx/186302#.Vvm2nuIrKM8

percent of Israelis had their vehicles stolen and 1 percent were victims of violent crimes. Jews were more likely to be the victim of some crimes, including home break-ins and nonviolent crimes, while Arabs were more likely to experience vehicle break-ins and assaults.[15]

Do Arab-Israelis really prefer to be policed by Arab officers? Some Arab focus group participants initially replied that they do prefer to interact with officers who are Arabs.[16] Some offered pragmatic explanations. "The Arab (citizen) doesn't know Hebrew, so he speaks with the officer in Arabic." However, the discussion soon revealed that the preference for in-group officers is based mainly on the expectation that they are more likely to treat them fairly. On balance, citizens desire fair treatment but care less about an officer's identity. After one participant expressed a preference to be policed by "a regular Jew who is obliged to the law," others agreed that they do not care about identity, only that the officer upholds the law. Yet, their collective experiences lead them to expect that an officer from their own group is more likely to put in the effort to take their reports seriously and generally better equipped to serve them.

TESTING THE MECHANISM: CITIZEN–POLICE INFORMATION FLOWS

To test the relationship between perceived police integration and citizen–police information flows, I draw on my survey of Israeli citizens, which I describe in detail in Appendix A. The key independent variable is the extent to which citizens perceive the police to be integrated. To measure willingness to provide information, the survey asks respondents whether they would report a hypothetical crime: "If you witnessed someone stealing money from a shop, would you contact the police?" This type of crime is unlikely to come to the police's attention unless reported by a witness or victim, reflecting the specific mechanism through which I argue noninclusive policing harms crime prevention. Its relatively trivial nature increases respondents' willingness to admit that they would not contact the police. I further combat any hesitance to admit to not contacting the police by asking an open-ended rather than multiple-choice question. Enumerators grouped responses into

15 Annual Statistical Abstract, Israel Central Bureau of Statistics (2014), "Victims of criminal activities aged 20 and over, by type of offence and selected characteristics." Publication 11.4, www.cbs.gov.il/shnaton66/st11_04.pdf

16 Focus Group 2A, Jaffa, March 2019

three categories: "yes" with no caveat, "maybe," including "probably" or similar responses, and "no." Whereas respondents may have felt pressure to select "yes" when presented with the option, the expectation was that they should feel fewer qualms about answering "probably" when this option was not juxtaposed against an even more positive response.

Regression models control for respondents' religion, age, gender, whether they voted in the last election, economic satisfaction, whether they work in the public sector, and the method of enumeration. All models include dummies for respondents' city and ethnic group, and standard errors are clustered at the primary sampling unit. Models use ordered logistic regression and remain consistent when using OLS instead of logistic regression (not shown).

Table 7.1 shows that respondents who perceive the police as more integrated at the national level (Column 1) are significantly more likely to say that they would report the hypothetical crime. However, citizens' expectations of how the police will treat them should be shaped primarily by the inclusiveness of the officers they actually come into contact with, that is, those in their neighborhood. Column 2 shows that when it comes to perceived police inclusiveness at the local level, there is a significant difference in the effect of perceived inclusion on reporting between Jews and non-Jews. Non-Jews, the historically marginalized group, are significantly more likely to report the shop theft to the police when they perceive the police as integrated (Column 3), while Jewish respondents are neither more nor less likely to report the crime (Column 4).

Controls generally have the expected effects. Non-Jews are less likely to report crimes than Jews. Those who work in the public sector or have a family member who works in the public sector are more likely to report a crime. Finally, respondents living in East Jerusalem, who were surveyed in person rather than by phone out of necessity, are less likely to say they would report the crime to the police, perhaps reflecting the poor relationship East Jerusalem residents have with the police.

The strong, positive association between perceived inclusiveness and willingness to report crimes suggests that inclusion substantially affects the quality of information available to the police, and that it does so primarily in locations with many Arab residents. The next section tests whether local inclusion is indeed associated with improvements in public safety provision.

TABLE 7.1 *If you witnessed someone stealing money from a shop, would you contact the police?*

	(1) All	(2) All	(3) Non-Jews	(4) Jews
Integration (National)	0.319 **			
	(0.126)			
Integration (Local)		0.270***	0.259 **	0.00561
		(0.0933)	(0.109)	(0.128)
Jewish	1.530***	1.659***		
	(0.541)	(0.620)		
Int. (Local)*Jewish		−0.253*		
		(0.147)		
Age	0.00471	0.00669	0.0151*	−0.00115
	(0.00681)	(0.00871)	(0.00809)	(0.0159)
Male	−0.00262	−0.0964	0.171	−0.700***
	(0.187)	(0.213)	(0.256)	(0.241)
Vote	0.376	0.285	0.258	−0.124
	(0.244)	(0.199)	(0.227)	(0.363)
Econ. satisfaction	0.0699	0.0708	0.0913	0.115
	(0.0829)	(0.0932)	(0.0988)	(0.125)
Work public	0.479*	0.462*	0.812***	−0.0183
	(0.263)	(0.274)	(0.240)	(0.489)
In person	−0.840 **		−1.463***	
	(0.343)		(0.352)	
Observations	659	688	374	314

Ordered logistic regression. Standard errors clustered by PSU.
Models include city and ethnic group dummies.
$^{*}\ p < .10$, $^{**}\ p < .05$, $^{***}\ p < .01$

INCLUSION'S EFFECTS ON CRIME

The dependent variable is the probability of crime, which, all else equal, should be lower when the police provide services more efficiently. Data come from Israel's Social Survey, a nationally representative survey of approximately 7,000 respondents carried out by the Central Bureau of Statistics each year. All individuals aged twenty and more living in Israel are eligible to be included in the survey. The Social Survey covers a wide range of topics like economic and employment status, language and technological skills, education, and basic household information. Most relevant to this analysis, it asks a set of questions about crime victimization, including whether the respondent experienced a vehicle break-in, home break-in, or nonviolent theft in the past year. Unlike serious crimes like murder or vehicle theft, these crimes are unlikely to come to the police's attention unless reported by citizens. In the analysis that follows, I code crime victimization as 1 if the respondent experienced *any* of these crimes in the past year, or 0 if they did not.

Survey measures of crime victimization provide advantages for analysis over official crime statistics (Banerjee et al. 2012). The problem with using official statistics for analysis is that they include only the subset of crimes that were brought to the attention of the police. Many of the same factors which make the police more effective at crime-fighting, for example, increased citizen cooperation, also increase the proportion of crimes that are reported to the police. Thus, when trust in the police goes up, actual crime may decrease although increased reporting gives the appearance of increased crime. Survey measures of victimization achieve a more accurate measure of criminal activity by separating crime occurrence from crime reporting.

I test crime victimization against the key independent variable, police inclusion, using the data on police officer demographics described in Chapter 4. I aggregate station-level officer data to the subdistrict level to match the smallest geographical unit in the Social Survey and calculate police inclusion using ethno-linguistic fractionalization (ELF). As I describe in Chapter 4, a measure of 1.00 on *Police Integration* indicates that all officers are from different religious groups, while a measure of 0.00 means that all officers are from the same group. Subdistrict-level *Police Integration* ranges from .014 to .611, with a mean of .211. Since there are no police stations with a majority of non-Jewish officers, an increase in *Police Integration* also indicates an increase in inclusion for non-Jews.

Models include several controls that may influence the likelihood of crime victimization, including gender, home ownership, whether or not the respondent is Jewish, and military service. A dummy variable for urban–rural status of the respondent's neighborhood also comes from the Social Survey. I use district–year unemployment estimates from Israel's Central Bureau of Statistics. Some models include subdistrict indicator variables, while others control for time using a count variable of the number of years since the start of the panel. Standard errors are clustered by subdistrict–year, the level of measurement for police integration, providing seventy-six clusters.

Regression results corroborate the hypothesis that local-level police integration is negatively associated with crime victimization. I include the full regression table, which was originally printed in Nanes (2020) in the online appendix. The results are best interpreted through the visualization in Figure 7.2, which displays the marginal effect of police inclusion on the probability of an individual experiencing at least one crime in the prior year, holding constant the covariates listed earlier.

In Figure 7.2, the left-hand panels show the effect in predominantly Arab subdistricts, while the right-hand panels show the effect in predominantly Jewish subdistricts. Police inclusion is negatively and significantly associated with crime only in Arab subdistricts. This finding is consistent with the argument that police inclusion induces civilians from previously excluded groups to provide the police with information, allowing the police to prevent crime more efficiently. It is also consistent with the finding that non-Jews, but not Jews, who perceive the police in their location as more inclusive are more willing to report crimes. The top panels show the effect for non-Jewish (predominantly Arab) citizens, while the bottom panels show the effect for Jewish citizens. Within a community type (i.e. large Arab population versus small Arab population), there is no perceptible difference in inclusion's effects on crime between Jewish and non-Jewish citizens. This finding is consistent with the argument that the police use information from citizens to provide crime prevention as efficiently as possible, and contradicts the alternative argument that police integration privileges only members of the previously excluded groups because officers provide preferential treatment for their coethnics.

It is possible that shared identity between a criminal and a victim might affect the victim's willingness to contact the police. Unfortunately, there is no systematic data on the religious identities of criminals compared to their victims in Israel. Generally speaking, however, criminals tend to commit crimes very close to home (Phillips 1980; Rengert 2004). Aside from a few exceptional neighborhoods in Akko, Jaffa, and Haifa, Israeli cities and towns are segregated, meaning that most crime

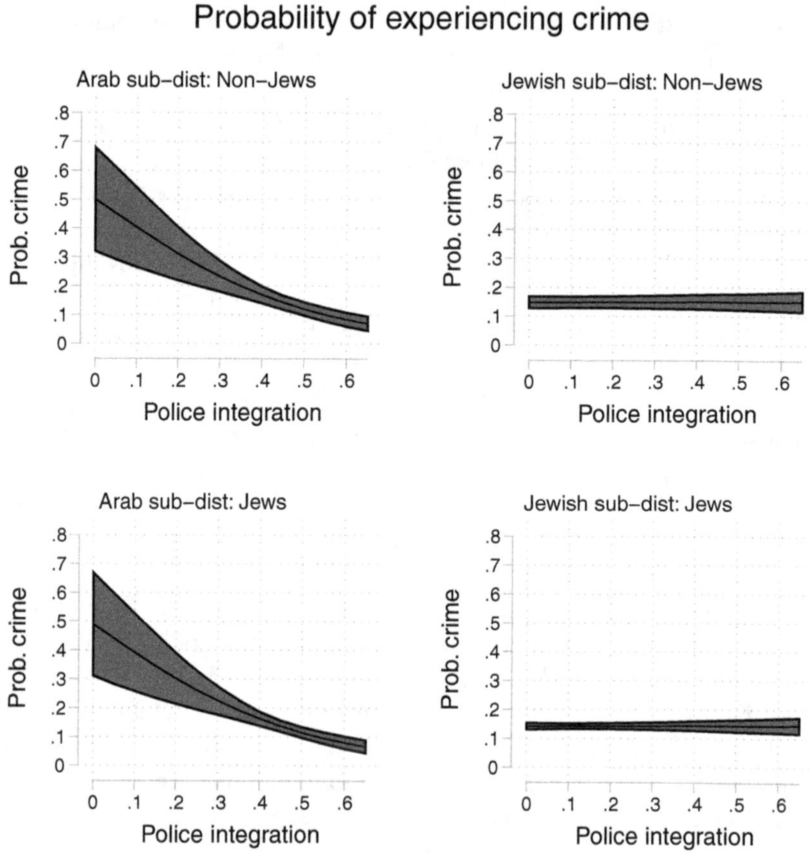

FIGURE 7.2 Effect by community and individual characteristics

in Israel is probably perpetrated by coethnics, and there is little variation in criminal–victim shared identity. Furthermore, victims do not always know the identity, much less the religious affiliation, of the perpetrator. Thus, while shared identity between criminals and victims is an important variable, it is unlikely to explain a substantial portion of the variation in citizens' willingness to report crimes in Israel.

Selection Bias in Officer Assignments

The aforementioned analysis suffers from a potential flaw: If the police assign minority officers to areas with less crime as a matter of policy, the correlation between inclusiveness and crime may be spurious. While the subdistrict dummy variables account for inherent differences

TABLE 7.2 *Predictors of police inclusiveness*

	(1)	(2)	(3)
Unemployment	8.017*** (1.009)		
Pct. male		1.846** (0.765)	
Pct. Jewish			−0.721*** (0.0970)
Constant	−0.285*** (0.0634)	−0.668* (0.377)	0.809*** (0.0811)
Observations	76	82	82

OLS regression with robust standard errors in parentheses
* $p < .10$, ** $p < .05$, *** $p < .01$

between locations, I further explore this possibility by testing whether communities that are crime-prone are less likely to have inclusive police. According to existing research, crime is highest where unemployment and the proportion of male civilians are high (Raphael and Winter-Ebmer 2001), while conventional wisdom in Israel suggests that Jewish cities are less crime-prone than Arab ones due to socioeconomic factors. However, I find a strong *positive* relationship between unemployment and police inclusiveness, as well as between percent male and inclusiveness, and a strong *negative* relationship between percent Jewish and police inclusiveness. In other words, the police are most integrated in areas with *high* baseline probabilities of crime, biasing against the finding that integration is associated with less crime.

The discussion of officer assignments in Chapter 4 further speaks to possible selection bias. According to the Brigadier General I interviewed, while officer assignment is not random, the police do not systematically assign minority officers based on a location's propensity for criminal activity.[17] A closely related concern is that Arab communities which have a good relationship with the police are more likely both to cooperate with the police, improving crime prevention, and to send

[17] Author interview, July 24, 2014

recruits to the police, causing integration. There is little doubt that positive relations between Arabs and the police aid recruitment of Arab officers. However, the police's policy of not assigning officers (especially Arab officers) to their hometowns for fear of corruption means that the areas where positive citizen–police relations cause a greater number of Arabs to join the police will not necessarily receive more Arab officers. Overall, while I cannot eliminate this source of endogeneity entirely, police procedures for officer assignment suggest that its impacts should be limited.

Alternative Arguments: Officer Quality and Institutional Heterogeneity

Hiring practices discussed in Chapter 4 also guard against the possibility that increasing the proportion of non-Jewish officers would negatively impact the overall qualifications of the police. The police use recruitment strategies that counteract societal inequalities, for example, giving hiring preference for university completion, which they view as a signal of maturity, independence, and the ability to follow through on tasks.[18] The use of this and other high-skill indicators as hiring qualifications narrows the educational gap between recruits of different religious groups. Additionally, it is worth noting that the inequalities in Israeli society imply that, on average, the pool of non-Jewish applicants might be less qualified, which biases *against* the finding that including more non-Jewish police officers improves service provision.

Another possibility is that officers may interact less efficiently with other officers from different identity groups than they would have with members of their own group. Ethnic and religious heterogeneity are sometimes argued to adversely impact collective action (Alesina et al. 1999; Banerjee et al. 2005; Miguel and Gugerty 2005; Habyarimana et al. 2007; Laitin 2007). Yet, rather than impeding police service provision, communities in Israel with more diverse police forces benefit from lower crime. I suggest that concerns about inefficient cooperation between out-group officers, while valid, are mitigated by the rigid structures of security institutions. Police officers operate under a strict chain of command and are expected to follow their superiors' orders. Officers

[18] Author interview with a high-ranking officer in the Israel Police whose jobs include managing the recruitment of new officers. July 24, 2014

may also develop a sense of "linked fate" as they work together to combat crime and other security threats, often risking their lives to do so. Police officers develop shared rituals, especially surrounding their own mortality.[19] They foster a similar appearance by wearing uniforms and maintaining similar hairstyles, and officers must meet the same training, educational, and physical fitness standards, leading to a "subculture" which emphasizes fraternity and cohesion (Crank 2014). These shared experiences and rigid formal institutional structures may replace shared group heuristics as a basis for cooperation, even while ascriptive group identity remains salient (Gibson and Hoffman 2013).

CONCLUSION

I find that inclusiveness in the police is associated with an improvement in the quality of public safety provision, and the evidence is consistent with the argument that it does so because marginalized groups are more willing to provide information to security institutions they perceive to be inclusive. Given Arab-Israelis' frustration with crime in their communities and the police's difficulty in preventing it, police integration could substantially improve citizen–state relations by helping the police deliver services that citizens so desperately want.

These results contradict many of the most prevalent arguments against police integration. For example, as I detail in Chapters 1 and 2, some worry that marginalized-group officers will learn to identify more as police than as members of their own group, leading them to treat citizens from their group even more harshly. The evidence in this chapter is consistent with a slightly different version of the same argument: when officers identify more as professionals than with their ascriptive identity, it improves the overall quality of policing while reducing differentiation based on group identity. Furthermore, research on "active representation" implies a zero-sum distributive effect, with well-represented groups receiving government services at the expense of poorly represented groups. In contrast, I find that police inclusiveness improves public safety for all citizens living in communities where information flows increase, regardless of their personal group affiliation. This net-positive effect of integration on service provision makes domestic security institutions an appealing setting for power sharing

[19] Harvey, William L. "Teach our traditions." August 24, 2010, www.officer.com/on-the-street/article/10232484/teach-our-traditions

as a solution to conflict. Even if police integration disproportionately benefits communities where previously excluded groups live, it does not make the dominant group worse off. The results in this chapter give Jewish Israelis no reason to oppose the integration of non-Jews into the police, and indeed I show in the next chapter that they do not express any such opposition. Thus, police integration represents a plausible first step toward resolving hostilities where mistrust between groups challenges cooperation.

8

BARRIERS TO INTEGRATION

If police integration yields such impressive benefits to public safety, why do we observe such inconsistent implementation in Iraq and Israel? After all, reduced support for violent insurgency and net improvements in crime should be universally welcomed. One possibility is that citizens from the dominant group who are privileged by the status quo might oppose change. Depending on the context, dominant-group civilians may fear losing job opportunities that previously "belonged" to their group or might worry that the previously marginalized group will use its newfound power to reinitiate hostilities. While logical, I show that only a small minority of Israeli Jews and Iraqi Shias express such concerns.

Rather, I argue that political elites from both the dominant and marginalized groups often face incentives to resist police integration. In Iraq, Shia politicians seeking to consolidate personal power traded positions in the police as patronage. Faced with international pressure to include Sunnis in the security forces between 2006 and 2014, Prime Minister Nouri al-Maliki, a Shia, avoided integration by consigning Sunnis to homogeneous units in Sunni neighborhoods and regions, and then refusing to properly equip or pay those units. In Israel, police leadership, which is almost uniformly Jewish, is evaluated on how effectively police deliver public safety. Thus, the police actively recruit officers from Arab communities since they view Arab participation in the police as necessary for effective service provision. However, tepid support for police integration by Arab-Israeli elites hampers the police's efforts to recruit Arab officers. These elites fear that participating in the security forces will legitimize the government and undermine calls for Palestinian statehood. Visibly participating in such a critical state institution normalizes the status quo and undermines claims of marginalization that elites use to justify resistance to domestic supporters and the international community.

On the one hand, the lack of opposition from dominant-group civilians points to the police as a promising setting for integration. By demonstrating that cooperation is feasible, police integration may build sufficient trust between groups to allow for further power-sharing measures down the road. On the other hand, police integration's susceptibility to sabotage by political elites from both sides speaks to its fragility and explains why we do not observe its more widespread use. Furthermore, the role of elites in blocking beneficial integration raises questions about the relationship between democracy and police integration. Leaders beholden to the public may be less likely to oppose integration, since they should worry about removal from office if they prevent policies the public wants. Yet, they also have a greater incentive to manipulate institutions and utilize rhetoric which consolidates their personal political influence. Thus, democracy may sometimes push elites to integrate security institutions, but at other times may create incentives to resist integration.

MASS OPPOSITION

Police integration has clear appeal for previously marginalized groups. However, it is less clear whether citizens from the dominant group should be pleased about a change to the status quo. Dominant-group citizens' perspectives matter because their opposition can harm police effectiveness. If dominant-group civilians are so put off by integration that they refuse to cooperate with officers, the police may lack sufficient information about their jurisdiction to provide effective public safety. Dominant-group citizens' opposition can also prevent change in the first place, with citizens threatening to vote incumbent leaders out of office. In an extreme scenario, unwanted police integration could thrust dominant-group civilians into the role of spoilers (Stedman 1997). Opposition to Israeli Prime Minister Yitzhak Rabin's negotiations with the PLO motivated a Jewish Israeli to assassinate Rabin in 1995, derailing the peace talks. Dominant-group civilians vehemently opposed to change could similarly derail police integration.

Civilians from the dominant group might oppose police integration for several reasons. First, if the size of the police force does not increase along with integration, then integration reduces the number of jobs available to their group. We might safely assume that the individual police officers who lose their jobs will be upset. A more widespread concern is whether the loss of hypothetical employment opportunities, or of jobs that previously "belonged" to their group, upsets dominant-group civilians who do not personally work for the police. Byrne and Monaghan (2008) note that job loss was a major concern for working-class Protestants in Northern Ireland due to increased Catholic recruitment. They quote one loyalist as pointing out, "How many people from Loyalist working class areas are in the police? The 50:50 (target ratio of Catholic to Protestant recruits) means it is near impossible for them to join the service" (60). Another interviewee notes that the new recruitment standards blocked applicants who view a career in law enforcement as a family legacy: "I was in the [Royal Ulster Constabulary]... my daughter has applied four times and hasn't got in. Apparently she is from the wrong ethnic group" (60). To what extent do such concerns spark opposition to integration? Does the loss of jobs for "us" become a rallying cry against "them?"

Dominant-group civilians might also oppose police integration if they fear that it makes their group vulnerable to attack by the newly integrated group. Many of the mechanisms which reduce minorities' fears of harm – providing weapons and information, organizing fighting-age individuals, and making service provision dependent upon their participation – simultaneously increase their capacity to violently rebel. There is considerable cross-national evidence that conflict is at least in part a function of how likely a rebel group is to win (Fearon and Laitin 2003; Collier and Hoeffler 2004; Collier et al. 2009). Police integration improves the odds that the marginalized group would win in a fight against state forces by increasing its power relative to those forces. Even if they do not fear large-scale rebellion, dominant-group citizens are vulnerable to harassment by out-group police officers.

Attitudes of Iraqi Shias and Israeli Jews toward Integration

How do Iraqi Shias and Israeli Jews expect police integration to affect their lives? In Iraq, some Shias interviewed for this research said that they prefer to deal with officers from their own group. Ahmed, a Shia living in Mosul, says, "I always prefer that [an officer I'm interacting with] belongs to the same sect as mine. [If] I know that he's Shia I deal with him with pleasure and ease, and I'm sure that he's well educated and knows everything and offered big sacrifices."[1] Ali, a Shia living in Baghdad, concurs: "It benefits me because it is within my sect where the treatment is different… He will treat me better."[2] However, others disagree. Sara, a Shia woman who lives in Mosul, says, "I would call this racism, if I preferred to talk to someone who belongs to the same sect then I would be racist. We want to end it."[3] Ibrahim, a Shia from Baghdad, says he doesn't care about the sect of an officer. If anything, he prefers to deal with Sunnis, because he says those officers are less corrupt.[4] Sara and Ibrahim also believe that police service by Sunnis could improve attitudes toward the Sunni community more generally. Sara says, "They will protect us… If my home got robbed or my purse was stolen, they would help me, and our bond would get stronger."[5] According to Ibrahim, "There should be balance… There must be both Sunnis and Shias included in the Iraqi Police Service because both of them belong to this country. Maybe [including more Sunnis in the police] would change the way I feel about the Sunni community in Iraq for the better." Sunnis joining the police "will lead to a strong [bond] between the Sunni and Shia sects in terms of supporting each other and achieving their duties. This will change the way each sect thinks of the other."[6] Notably, those who say they prefer to be policed by members of their own group cite only minor annoyances in which a police officer they dealt with behaved unprofessionally. Despite the importance of public sector employment in Iraq, nobody mentioned job loss as a concern. Only one interviewee, Ahmed from Mosul, expressed concerns about rebellion, saying a Sunni joining the Ministries of Defense or Interior would have to be checked "to make sure that he doesn't belong to any [terrorist] organization, because… the Sunnis either belong to Al-Qaida or are terrorists. Not all of them of course."[7] However, this opinion stands out as a distinct minority.

Jewish-Israeli focus group participants are also cautiously optimistic about police integration. One woman said she worries about Arabs' loyalties in the event of a conflict. "There is a fear… that their loyalty

[1] IIACSS interview 02SM, February 2019
[2] IIACSS interview 07SM, February 2019
[3] IIACSS interview 10SF, February 2019
[4] IIACSS interview 11SM, February 2019
[5] IIACSS interview 10SF, February 2019
[6] IIACSS interview 11SM, February 2019
[7] IIACSS interview 02SM, February 2019

will not last long, and that if we give them a weapon it might be turned against us some day."[8] However, she says that these concerns extend only to some hypothetical "day of judgement," and she has no objections to Arab participation in the police on a day-to-day basis. "I think that having the Arab minority taking part in society at large is a good thing."[9] The consensus of cautious support was summed up by an interviewee in Haifa: "Recruit them. It is good. But do a careful screening."[10]

In Israel, periodic highly publicized instances of non-Jewish participation in the police contribute to positive relations across communities. On November 14, 2014, two gunmen attacked a synagogue in the Har Nof neighborhood of Jerusalem. Master Sergeant Zidan Saif, a Druze Arab, was one of the first officers to respond. The attackers shot and killed Saif in an exchange of gunfire. In an outpouring of gratitude for his service, the ultra-orthodox Jewish community to whom the synagogue belonged used social media to call on its members to attend Saif's funeral and even provided transportation to them. Israel's President, Minister of Public Security, and Police Commissioner also attended the funeral, hailing Saif as a hero. President Reuven Rivlin's speech at the funeral highlighted Saif's non-Jewish identity. "Terror has struck Jerusalem once more. Terror that does not distinguish between people. Terrorists turned a house of prayer into a house of slaughter. Your son did not hesitate or waver… He stood fearlessly against the terrorists and risked his life to protect the people of Jerusalem."

The terrorist attack, and the role played by a non-Jew in helping to stop the attackers, galvanized parts of the Jewish community in the immediate aftermath. An ultra-orthodox Jewish activist from Har Nof told reporters, "We are calling for widespread solidarity throughout Israel, with an emphasis on gratitude. We will not be ungrateful and will show our thanks for those who sacrificed their lives for us."[11] A few days later, religious leaders from the Jewish, Muslim, Greek Orthodox, and Druze communities gathered outside the site of the attack to denounce terrorism, a highly infrequent show of solidarity across religious groups

[8] FGJ3, Haifa, March 2019

[9] FGJ3, Haifa, March 2019

[10] FGJ3, Haifa, March 2019

[11] Nachshoni, Kobi. "Thousands of Israeli Druze and Jews grieve at funeral for policeman slain in terror attack" *Ynet News*, November 19, 2014. www.ynetnews.com/articles/0,7340,L-4593823,00.html

in a country that has suffered hundreds of deadly attacks in recent decades. It seems that the sacrifice of a non-Jew protecting Jews made a significant impression on the community. The effect is long-lasting. More than a year after the attack, dozens of members of the neighborhood's Jewish community invited Druze from Saif's hometown to share a Shabbat dinner with them.

> Three buses brought some 160 people from four Druze villages in the Galilee to the Shai Agnon synagogue in Arnona on Saturday afternoon. Sheikhs with elegant mustaches and tarbooshes, elderly women whose heads are covered by thin white shawls, young people, teenage girls, and children, all get off the bus one after the other, shaking the hands of their hosts with embarrassed hesitation. Their hosts were waiting for them outside the synagogue with flags combining the Israeli and Druze flags, made by the meeting's organizer, Rabbi Yaakov Kermaier.[12]

Saif's actions appear to have forged a bond between two communities separated by geography and religion.

I further explore dominant-group citizens' reactions to integration using my surveys. The survey in Iraq asks, "Do you think that greater sectarian integration of the Iraqi Police Services would make citizens like you better off, worse off, or about the same?" Recall from Chapter 3 that among members of the Sunni minority, 11.6 percent said integration would make them worse off, 63.8 percent said it would make them better off, and 24.6 percent expected no change. Somewhat surprisingly, Shia Iraqis were slightly *more* positively disposed to integration, with only 6.5 percent expecting it would make them worse off, 67.5 percent expecting to be better off, and 25.9 percent expecting no change. Despite the near certainty that increased integration of the Iraqi police would mean less representation for their own group, a large majority of Shias believe integration will improve their lives.

To further explore the attitudes of dominant-group civilians toward police integration, the survey asks Shia Iraqis and Jewish Israelis about their attitudes on two potential sources of opposition: concerns over subversion by the newly integrated group, and concerns over loss of jobs. Two survey questions explore these possible impediments to peace.

[12] Erlich, Yifat. "Druze and Jews forge special bond in memory of brave policeman. *Ynet News*, Feburary 6, 2016, www.ynetnews.com/articles/0,7340,L-4762603,00.html.

First, on the issue of taking jobs away from dominant-group members, Shias Iraqis and Jewish Israelis were asked,

> Some people worry that a policy of integrating minorities into the police would take jobs away from citizens like you. Do you believe that this is an important concern?

On the issue of dominant-group concern over changing the balance of power, the survey asked:

> Some people worry that including all ethnic and religious groups into public sector jobs like the police, education, and public services might allow them to disrupt the government. Other people say that including minorities in these jobs allows them to do their part in contributing to society. Which view do you think is more accurate?

Figure 8.1 shows that Iraqi Shias are generally not concerned by either of these possibilities. Among respondents who answered the question, less than 16 percent said they would oppose integration due to possible job loss. Approximately 88.5 percent said that integration allows for minority contribution, while 11.5 percent believe that inclusion is dangerous.

Among Israeli Jews, only 20.8 percent of respondents said they might oppose integration because of the potential loss of employment opportunities. Meanwhile, 75.8 percent responded that it is more accurate that integration allows minorities to contribute to society, while less than a quarter say that it could be dangerous. Based on responses to these questions, there should be little concern of a backlash effect in either Iraq or Israel.

Why is there strong support for police integration? Some explanations may be context-specific. In Iraq, Shia Arabs' status as the politically dominant group is relatively new, and there is no guarantee that the status is permanent. Despite holding a demographic majority, Shias were largely excluded from power and governing institutions dating back at least to 1533, first under the Ottoman rule, then under the British mandate, and most recently under Baath Party rule (Dawisha 2009). Each of these regimes concentrated control over security institutions in the hands of a small number of tribes whose members were Sunnis. Only after large-scale international intervention in 2003 and the foreign-imposed implementation of a very shaky democracy in 2004 did the Shia majority take their current position as the politically

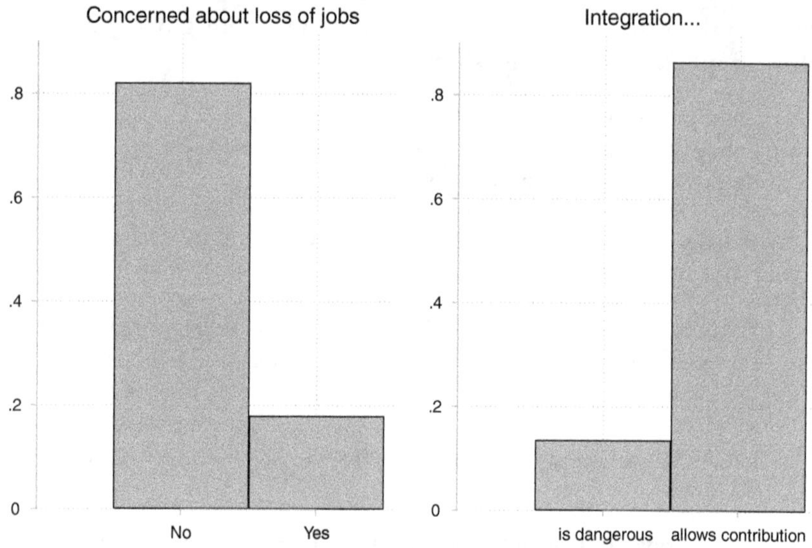

FIGURE 8.1 Iraqi Shias' concerns about integration

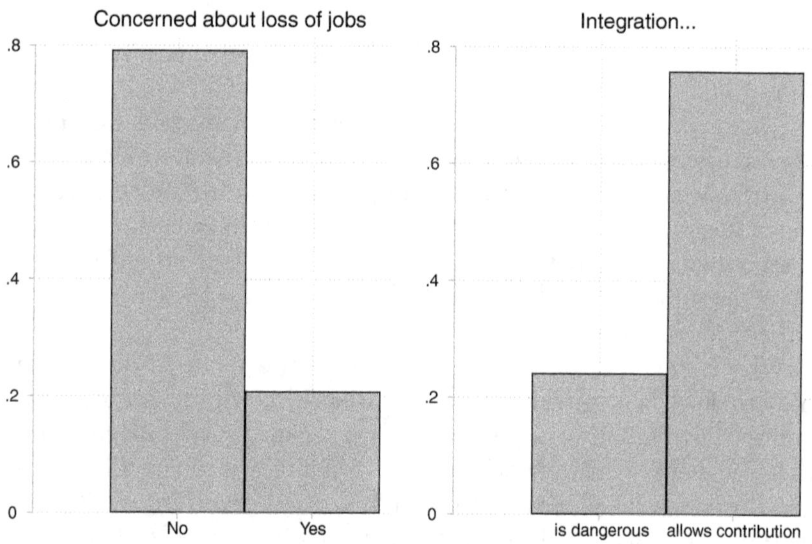

FIGURE 8.2 Israeli Jews' concerns about integration

dominant group. Given the novelty of this power configuration and the significant external involvement that led to its realization, Shias may worry that their group's current status is not assured indefinitely and believe they are better off in a system that balances power across groups.

A second reason for strong Shia support for police integration is that sectarian conflict harms all members of society, regardless of religious affiliation. Militias associated with both Sunnis and Shias have attacked citizens of all sects, leading to tens of thousands of civilian casualties. For example, in February 2016, two attackers detonated suicide vests outside a Shia mosque in northern Baghdad, killing at least twelve civilians.[13] The incident was one of many violent attacks by members of Sunni groups like the Islamic State (IS) against Shias in Iraq. Many Shias therefore oppose sectarian politics, even applications which increase the representation of Shias in government. This rejection of sectarianism was clearly on display in April 2016 when thousands of Shias staged a sit-in at the Iraqi parliament to protest against appointments to ministerial positions on the basis of sectarian loyalties, and to call for the replacement of partisan government ministers with technocrats.[14] More generally, conflict is negative-sum, making it possible for all parties to a conflict to be worse off from fighting (Fearon 1995b). Even with their dominant societal position, there is no doubt that Iraqi Shias would benefit from eliminating suicide bombings from their neighborhoods and bureaucratic corruption from their government.

Next, in some ways, police integration actually raises the costs of rebellion by the newly integrated group. Rebellions require support from several sources, especially foreign actors like governments and international organizations (Salehyan et al. 2011; Sawyer et al. 2017), citizens whom rebel leaders convince to fight, and noncombatants whose shelter the rebellion requires (Berman et al. 2011b; Toft and Zhukov 2015; Tezcür 2016). Rebellions can succeed only if they convince a wide range of domestic and international actors that their cause is worthwhile and their tactics warranted.

To justify violent rebellion and win support from these actors, a rebel movement must claim that violence is its only realistic option for affecting change, that it faces grave threats to its members' safety, and

[13] "Several dead in Baghdad Shia mosque double bombing." *al-Jazeera*, February 25, 2016. www.aljazeera.com/news/2016/02/dead-baghdad-shia-mosque-double-bombing-160225183322410.html

[14] "Iraqi Shia protesters storm Baghdad parliament." *New York Times* April 30, 2016. www.bbc.com/news/world-middle-east-36176910

that its members are illegitimately excluded from the state and society. Participation in the police undermines these narratives because of the police's capacity for violence. After all, how can a group's situation relative to the government be so dire if its members are widely included in this important armed institution? Thus, participation in the police should reduce external actors' tolerance for continued violent rebellion, making it more difficult for insurgents to solicit donations, receive statements of legitimacy, recruit fighters, or foster assistance from noncombatants. A group incurs these costs *only if they use unprovoked, offensive violence*. Participation in the police still provides the capacity to defend one's group through the mechanisms described in the previous chapters. However, the use of unprovoked violence should lead to a loss of support from important foreign and domestic actors. Thus, members of the dominant group may interpret out-group participation in the police as a signal that the group does not intend to initiate hostilities unless provoked.

The distinction between offensive and defensive uses of violence suggests another reason why dominant-group members may not worry about police integration leading to further hostilities: the weapons police typically carry are better suited for self-defense than for insurgency. Facing an army equipped with machine guns, armor, artillery, and aircraft, providing an out-group with a few thousand handguns is unlikely to tip the scales. Of course, this explanation applies more to countries like Israel in which the police and military are clearly differentiated, and less to war zones like Iraq in which the police take on a more militarized role.

Regarding employment, the integration of Catholics into the Protestant-dominated Police Services of Northern Ireland (PSNI) in the early 2000s illustrates several strategies for mitigating costs to the dominant group. Following the 1998 Good Friday Agreement, the PSNI faced the gargantuan task of increasing its share of Catholic officers from about 8 percent to a target of 33 percent while simultaneously reducing the overall size of the police force (Bayley 2008). Finding willing Catholic recruits was not a problem. Shortly after the reforms began, Catholics constituted 35 percent of applicants to the police. However, the police had to create space for these new officers, necessitating a considerable reduction in the number of Protestant police officers. Police leadership feared that the rapid termination of large numbers of Protestant officers might stoke tensions and reignite hostilities. Rather than freezing hiring of Protestants and increasing the number of Catholic officers as quickly as possible, the PSNI mandated that recruitment should be 1:1, or approximately equivalent to the groups' share of the population, and acknowledged that the police force would equalize gradually over time. The police also offered generous severance packages to thin its ranks. From January 2001 to March 2006, the British government spent 179.45 million pounds on retirement incentives for PSNI officers (Ellison 2007). Ultimately, these strategies helped the police downsize the force and increase the ratio of Catholics while avoiding major opposition from Protestants (Ellison 2007; Bayley 2008).

It remains possible that a dominant group's level of support or opposition for integration depends on relative group size. For example, Jewish Israelis' supermajority in both the population and the police allows sufficient room for integration without threatening Jews' political dominance. On the other hand, one can imagine that an attempt to move from 40 percent to 60 percent non-Jewish police officers would elicit opposition from Jewish citizens. There is likely some inflection point at which inclusion of the minority group begins to be perceived as exclusion of the majority group, jeopardizing the cooperation of majority-group citizens. This point is not necessarily at 50 percent of officers from each group, since policing policies are not determined by the majority rule. More likely, the inflection point is determined by the perceptions of dominant-group citizens that their dominant position is being eroded by minority inclusion. Overall, it is encouraging that neither Israel nor Iraq appears to be at this point.

POLITICAL ELITES

If citizens from the dominant group do not stand in the way of police integration, what about elites? In Iraq and Israel, politicians and community leaders often oppose police integration because they fear it will erode their influence. In Iraq, government jobs, especially those in the security sector, offer pay, stability, and authority unmatched by most jobs in the private sector, and politicians believe integration would get in the way of their ability to trade jobs for political support. Prime Minister Nouri al-Maliki also depended on the support of influential Shia elites, many of whom commanded militias. These elites demanded that the state security forces absorb their militias, leaving little room for additional Sunni officers. As a result, the Iraqi police failed to integrate on a meaningful scale under Maliki's leadership. In contrast, during the period of this study, Jewish-Israeli politicians expressed substantial support for integrating Arabs into the police. The Minister of Public Security and the appointed officials serving below him believe including Arabs in the police helps reduce crime, furthering their career interests. However, Arab elites often discourage Arabs from joining the police for fear of legitimizing the Israeli security sector and hampering broader efforts for Palestinian statehood. Thus, in Iraq, dominant-group leaders stymied integration, while in Israel, opposition came mainly from elites of the marginalized group.

Leaders who wish to prevent police integration have many tools with which to do so. Legislators may vote against bills which require police integration, and presidents can veto bills before they become law. Elites may also prevent the recruitment of minorities by appointing ministers and high-level bureaucrats with strong sectarian agendas, or by instituting recruitment criteria which they know most marginalized-group citizens cannot meet. Finally, in the rare circumstances in which incumbent leaders cannot prevent police inclusion from occurring, they can undermine its implementation so as to make it reversible down the road. As I describe later, Iraqi Prime Minister Nouri al-Maliki could not ignore international pressure to include Sunnis in the security forces, but he isolated them in Sunni-only units and ensured that those units received substandard equipment and sporadic pay.

Elite Opposition in Iraq

Upon its arrival in Baghdad in early 2004, the police training team led by Italy, Australia, the Netherlands, and the United States called for recruits to be representative of the country's sectarian makeup. However, over the next decade, Shia Iraqi elites repeatedly stymied attempts to include Sunnis in the police. Opposition came from two levels: politicians in Baghdad responsible for national defense, and regional governors tasked with recruiting cadets to serve in the police. Leaders at different levels opposed Sunni inclusion for different reasons. Oftentimes, opposition was purely pragmatic. Local governors responsible for recruitment refused to provide international training forces with information on the sectarian identity of new recruits, undermining programs meant to ensure balance and inclusion along sectarian lines. Their goal was not specifically to exclude Sunnis but to maintain control over the hiring process, especially their ability to distribute employment in the police as patronage.[15]

In Baghdad, elite opposition to police integration was rooted in sectarian politics. Following the January 2005 parliamentary elections, two groups dominated Iraq's government: the United Iraqi Alliance (al-Itlaaf al-Iraqi al-Muwahad), a coalition of Shia religious parties led by Supreme Council for Islamic Revolution in Iraq (SCIRI), and the Iraqi List (al-Qayima al-Iraqiya), a coalition of Shia secular parties led by Prime Minister Nouri al-Maliki. Shia elites from these powerful political blocs resisted systematic recruitment of Sunnis in the security forces for fear that it would undermine their personal political influence. Maliki relied heavily on SCIRI for political support and distributed ministry positions in return for its leaders' endorsements.[16] He handed the Ministry of Interior portfolio to former SCIRI official Bayan Jabr. Jabr used the position to employ thousands of Shia militiamen from the Badr Brigades, SCIRI's military wing, who then carried out anti-Sunni violence while wearing government uniforms. The government removed Jabr from the post in May 2006 when accusations of police misconduct became too extensive to ignore, but the administration promptly appointed him as the Minister of Finance, where he retained control over funding for the police and other state institutions (Perito 2011).

Maliki did not seek total exclusion of Sunnis from government, and in fact many ministers during his time as head of government were Sunnis. However, where it was convenient, he used sectarian structures to consolidate his political power. For example, he leaned on de-Baathification laws, intended to prevent loyalists of the previous regime from subverting the new democratic government, to remove Sunnis politically opposed to him (al-Ali 2014). When it came to the police, many potential recruits belonged to the tribal militias in Anbar province which helped combat al-Qaeda. Publicly, Maliki opposed their integration into the state security forces on the grounds that their affiliation with tribal militias created potential competing loyalties. In reality, his opposition stemmed from concerns that they might answer to leaders other than his own political allies (Jabar 2014).

15 Author interview with Gerald Burke, January 22, 2016

16 Partlow, Joshua. "Maliki's office is seen behind purge in forces." *Washington Post*, April 30, 2007. www.washingtonpost.com/wp-dyn/content/article/2007/04/29/AR2007042901728.html

Sunni exclusion from the Iraqi security forces reached a turning point in 2007 when the government began hiring former Sunni militiamen to serve in Anbar province. The change occurred not because Maliki's preferences changed but because the United States, and especially General David Petraeus and Ambassador Ryan Crocker, applied considerable pressure to incentivize Maliki. Only after Petraeus personally threatened to withhold funding and logistical support did the prime minister relent on Sunni inclusion in the police, and even then the changes were limited to the specific task of combating the remnants of al-Qaeda in Iraq (AQI). In "Operation Blue Shield," Maliki agreed to expand Anbar's police force to accommodate the integration of 120,000 former Sons of Iraq (SOI) militia members into the official state security forces. The operation coincided with several other programs to include more Sunnis in the police (Robinson 2009, 335).

Yet, none of these programs could be considered integration at an institutional level, as inclusion was isolated to parts of Iraq – primarily Anbar province, but also neighborhoods of Baghdad – with predominantly Sunni populations. The United States' focus on drawing down its forces created space for Maliki to reverse much of the institutional inclusion imposed on him in the previous years. Whereas Maliki had been somewhat receptive to inclusive governance when ruling from a position of strength, his State of Law Coalition's poor performance in the 2010 elections caused him to change strategy. "His sole concern became to capture the state and to divide and conquer opponents, in order to remain in power for as long as possible. He set his sights on the key institutions, starting with the parliament, the armed forces, and the courts" (al-Ali 2014, 130). He used his authority to frustrate efforts to integrate Sunni militia members into the security forces and to disband Sunni units that already existed. The Ministry of Interior failed to pay or properly equip the units of former SOI fighters, and it refused to coordinate security operations with them. "The abandonment of the program allowed al-Qaeda to exploit SOI vulnerabilities, resulting in scores of revenge killings against its members" (Jabar 2014, 1). Maliki went a step further in August 2008, arresting 650 SOI fighters and arguing that the state could not accept the presence of militias operating outside the authority of the government. Yet, SOI fighters who attempted to join the state security forces faced physical fitness and literacy tests that they could not pass (Jabar 2014). To the extent that the security forces included Sunnis, they did so in homogeneous Sunni-only units largely isolated to predominantly Sunni regions of

Iraq. The Iraqi security apparatus easily prevented fighters from acquiring the weapons and equipment that were available to Shia units. At the same time, because security provision in the government's bases of support in Baghdad and the south did not rely on these Sunni units, the government faced few costs from dismantling them and allowing Anbar to return to a state of lawlessness.

Maliki was not the only Shia Iraqi official opposed to police integration. Much of the elite opposition to Sunni integration was led by Bassima al-Jaidri, head of the Implementation and Followup Committee for National Reconciliation (IFCNR). Despite the institution's name, al-Jaidri used her position to minimize the influence of the Sunni militias or their integration into the state security forces following the defeat of al-Qaeda in 2006–2007. al-Jaidri held close ties to Muqtada as-Sadr's Jaysh al-Mahdi (JAM), a Shia militia opposed to US influence in Iraq (Jabar 2014). US military advisors described al-Jaidri on multiple occasions as pursuing a sectarian agenda and noted her ability to influence Maliki in rejecting reconciliation.[17]

Between al-Jaidri and Bayan Jabr, we see a clear image in which the Maliki administration distributed influential government positions to members of Shia sectarian organizations in order to consolidate his personal political power. Those individuals then used their positions to distribute jobs in the security forces as patronage and use the state as cover to settle sectarian scores. Even when this behavior became known, Maliki resisted Sunni inclusion for fear of angering organizations like SCIRI on which he relied for political support. Shia leaders opposed Sunni integration not because of ancient hatreds between groups but for pragmatic political purposes. Had Maliki's political fortunes depended not on Shia organizations but on Sunni ones, all indications are that he would have welcomed Sunnis into the police with open arms. Similarly, governors resisted sect-based quotas for recruitment not because they opposed the creation of an inclusive police force but because they wished to retain total discretion over the distribution of desirable employment opportunities. With the benefit of hindsight, policy-makers could have designed procedures for inclusion which addressed these incentives head-on, for example, by first tackling the pervasive use of police employment as patronage before

[17] Damon, Arwa. "Shadowy Iraq office accused of sectarian agenda." *CNN*, May 1, 2007. www.cnn.com/2007/WORLD/meast/05/01/iraq.office/index.html

attempting sect-based recruitment. Maliki's political incentives to resist police integration also speak to the relationship between police inclusion and the design of other political institutions. Iraq's electoral rules create a party system in which Shia parties are kingmakers. Had Iraq's party system cut across sectarian lines, and had Maliki not found his political survival dependent on parties with strong sectarian affiliations, he may not have been compelled to oppose police integration. In 2014, Iraq changed its seat allocation method in a way that better represents smaller parties and reduces the power of any individual party or faction.[18] Perhaps not coincidentally, the new government of Haider al-Abadi displayed a greater willingness to integrate the security forces.

Elite Support in Israel

During the period of this study, Israel's Jewish political leaders tended to support integrating Arabs into the police, even viewing it as a priority. Consistent with evidence in this book, they believed that citizens in Arab communities respond more positively to officers who are Arab, making them more likely to cooperate and engage with the police and helping the police prevent crime.[19] The desire for integrated policing based on this logic extends to Jewish ethnic minorities as well; the high-ranking officer with whom I spoke specifically mentioned that when the police respond to an incident in an Ethiopian immigrant community, they try to bring at least one police officer of Ethiopian descent "to facilitate. Minority officers have an easier time operating in minority communities. They understand the situation better and respond more appropriately."[20] Police recruitment drives in 2005, 2014, and 2016, which explicitly targeted non-Jewish citizens, stemmed from police leaders' desire to improve citizen–police relations in minority communities.

Public Security Minister Gilad Erdan was a driving force behind the 2016 effort to recruit 1,350 Arab Muslim officers and open twelve new

18 Iraq switched its votes-to-seats formula from largest remainder to Sainte Lague for the 2014 election, and shifted compensatory seats previously allocated at the national level to the governorate level. This followed earlier changes in 2010 which allowed for open list voting. As a result, government formation in Iraq became less dependent on the support of well-organized sectarian organizations.

19 Author interview with a high-ranking police officer, July 24, 2014

20 ibid

police stations in Arab cities and towns.[21] Despite his membership in an administration which took a hard-line stance on Arab–Jewish conflict, Erdan said that the main challenge in enlisting an increased number of Arab police officers is to do it "for them and not against them."[22] In other words, Erdan's public statements imply that police integration should occur not as a means of co-opting the Arab community and recruiting collaborators but as a mechanism for providing superior government services in historically marginalized communities.

Police officers with whom I spoke seemed genuine in their desire to provide better policing services in Arab communities and in their belief that having some number of Arab officers serve those communities would improve public safety. The Israel Police's leaders are evaluated on their abilities to serve citizens and provide public safety effectively. As career police officers, they take personal pride in their institution's effectiveness. It stands to reason that since they believe Arab inclusion enhances service provision, they should enthusiastically pursue this policy.

Other politicians, especially those on the political right, communicated an instrumentalist logic couched in questions of conflict and state legitimacy that nevertheless motivates support for police integration. Speaking in Tel Aviv following a terrorist attack by an Israeli Arab citizen, Prime Minister Benyamin "Bibi" Netanyahu said:

> I view positively the growing integration into the army, the national service and all aspects of national life by the Christian community, the Druze community, the Bedouins in the north and in the Muslim community as well. I call on all Israeli citizens and particularly on Israel's Muslim citizens to choose this path, a path of integration and coexistence and peace and not a path of incitement and hatred and radicalism.[23]

Netanyahu views Arab participation in the police and other state institutions as a *responsibility* for all who enjoy the rights of citizenship. He equates participation in the state institutions with acceptance of the

[21] Hadid, Diaa (2016), "Israel seeking police recruits: Eager, and Arab." *New York Times* September 3. www.nytimes.com/2016/09/04/world/middleeast/israeli-police-recruiting-arabs-to-join-the-force-not-resist-it.html?_r=0

[22] ibid

[23] Staff, Toi. "Netanyahu: We'll root out lawlessness, incitement among Israeli Arabs." *The Times of Israel* January 2, 2016. www.timesofisrael.com/netanyahu-well-root-out-lawlessness-incitement-among-israeli-arabs/

Israeli state and normalization of the status quo. In the same speech, the prime minister also called for a dramatic increase in police presence in Arab towns in response to a terrorist attack. The context of the speech made it clear that this increased presence was to exert state authority in areas the government viewed as hostile, not to provide services to members of those communities. He stated:

> I will not accept two nations within Israel: a lawful nation for all its citizens and a (second) nation within a nation for some of its citizens, in pockets of lawlessness. Those times are over. Whoever wants to be Israeli must be fully Israeli – both in rights and in obligations.

Placed in this context, his calls for police integration sound more like a demand for loyalty than a desire to serve minority communities. Participation in the police by minorities signals acceptance of the status quo. This commitment to the state appears to be the real motive behind at least some Jewish political elites' support for police integration. Regardless of their motives, however, there is little question that the majority of Jewish-Israeli political leaders desire greater Arab participation in the police. Their acceptance of inclusion, if not integration, explains why the proportion of non-Jewish officers in the Israel Police increased during the period of study.

Some Arab-Israeli elites oppose integration for similar reasons as Netanyahu supports it: participating in an institution lends legitimacy to it (Schedler 2002; Magaloni 2008; Ben-Porat and Yuval 2019). They view integration as a means of co-optation by an Israeli state which fails to serve their community fairly or effectively. Government Resolution 922 and its plan to increase Arab recruitment into the police met resistance from some Arab members of Knesset (MKs), nongovernmental organizations (NGOs), and mayors, who argued against collaboration with the right-wing government (Levi and Suchi 2018). Arab MK Ahmed Tibi accused the police of attempting to transfer responsibility for their failures onto the Arab community.[24] According to Tibi, "The problem is with the police, not whether the policeman is Arab or Jewish. When there is a problem with traffic accidents, does the transportation ministry say 'now we need to draft Arab traffic accident

[24] Breiner, Josh. "As number of murders rises, police and Israeli Arabs at odds over solutions." *Haaretz* September 26, 2019, www.haaretz.com/israel-news/as-number-of-murders-rises-police-and-israeli-arabs-at-odds-over-solutions-1.7909272

examiners (who gather evidence for court cases)?'"[25] Former police commissioner Bruno Stein suggests that politicians like Tibi benefit politically by standing in the way of police reforms intended to benefit the Arab community. "Attacking the police and associating with criminals is their way to attack the Israeli regime."[26]

Other Arab leaders were enthusiastic about the early plans to integrate the police but now express frustration at what they see as a lack of results. The police opened a new station in Jisr az-Zarqa amid much fanfare in 2017. Two years later, local council leader Amash Morad Fathi feels that this increased police involvement was a mistake.

> I wouldn't open a police station here today. I wish I hadn't done it... We made absolutely no progress. Twelve people were shot in the legs and drug trading goes on. Last week, a 19-year-old, a regular guy from a regular family, came home from a wedding and left the house. He was shot at close range. He died... The police have no leads... The problem evidently isn't [the police], it's the government. It's convenient for the Arabs to be shooting each other.[27]

Mudar Yunes, head of the Ara-Arara council and chairman of Arab local councils, says,"We don't think police stations inside the villages is the answer [to violent crime]. There needs to be an orderly plan."[28] On the other hand, Fayik Auda, the Arab mayor of Jaljulia, supports Arab recruitment into the police, but only if those officers are deployed to Arab towns. He says that if the police send them to Tel Aviv or Haifa, they will simply be contributing to a "broken system."[29]

Many leaders' skepticism of integration stems from decades of police neglect and abuse of their community. Under such circumstances, integrating the police will not change leaders' (or citizens') attitudes overnight. Although police leadership's recent statements and actions suggest a genuine desire to serve Arab communities, continued opposition by Arab leaders reflects the long-term political context of mistrust.

[25] Lieber, Dov. "To combat rampant crime on their streets, Israeli Arabs heed call to join police." *Times of Israel* November 18, 2016, www.timesofisrael.com/to-combat-rampant-crime-on-their-streets-israeli-arabs-heed-call-to-join-police/

[26] Breiner 2019

[27] Breiner 2019

[28] Breiner 2019

[29] Lieber 2016

CONCLUSION

Far from opposing police integration, civilian members of the politically dominant group support minority participation in law enforcement institutions. Members of the dominant group face real costs from integrating the police, including a reduction in job opportunities. However, carefully designed procedures can mitigate these costs by shifting officer demographics gradually over time and compensating those who lose out due to integration. Survey evidence from Iraq and Israel shows that while members of the dominant groups may lose opportunities for employment, they do not consider it sufficiently costly to oppose integration.

Nor does the threat of rebellion motivate widespread dominant-group opposition to integration. I speculate that participation in the police makes the initiation of hostilities difficult for would-be rebels, as visible inclusion in the police undermines claims of marginalization and vulnerability. These claims are critical to rebels' narratives which they use to solicit support from foreign governments and the domestic population. Thus, members of the dominant group who perceive the police as integrated should be less worried that participating groups intend to renew hostilities without provocation. Indeed, while focus group participants express some concern about arming their potential enemies, on balance this apprehension does not lead to systematic opposition to police integration. On the contrary, an overwhelming majority of dominant-group civilians view participation in the police as an important component of shared responsibility and an opportunity for all segments of society to contribute to the state.

However, political elites from the dominant group sometimes face political incentives to stand in the way of integration. I describe how Iraqi Prime Minister Nouri al-Maliki repeatedly hampered attempts to integrate Iraq's security forces. Motivated by patronage politics and a reliance on Shia sectarian organizations for political survival, Maliki was the single largest roadblock to police integration in Iraq during his premiership. On the other hand, Jewish-Israeli leaders viewed Arab participation in the police as consistent with their own political incentives. For technocratic police leadership, Arab-Jewish integrated policing allows their institution to deliver crime prevention more effectively. For right-wing politicians like Prime Minister Bibi Netanyahu, police participation signals loyalty by Arab-Israeli Jews and legitimizes the Israeli state. Jewish leaders' support for Arab inclusion in the police is consistent with the large increase in Arab police officers since 2008.

On the one hand, the lack of widespread opposition by dominant-group civilians is promising. The expected benefits of integration for historically marginalized groups, and the support for integration these expected benefits promote, do not appear to be matched in magnitude by dominant-group opposition. In deeply divided societies, and especially in those struggling to emerge from violent conflict, police integration provides a rare area of overlapping preferences that make it a plausible first step toward reconciliation. Some skepticism of the other side's motives is to be expected, as we see in some Arab leaders in Israel, but trust can be rebuilt gradually over time. Successful police integration demonstrates that shared institutions are possible, and the increased feeling of security by both sides creates space for further negotiations and compromises.

On the other hand, corruption can undermine police integration. Leaders' opposition may appear as deep-seated intergroup hatred, but the underlying motives stem from a desire to distribute positions in the police and other government institutions as patronage. Leaders who benefit personally from patronage politics may use group identity instrumentally to stoke fears and exclude nonsupporters from access to these valuable positions. Thus, policy-makers seeking to integrate the police must either eliminate patronage politics or find some other way to incentivize leaders to relax their hold on police recruitment and hiring.

9

CONCLUSION: PEACE-BUILDING THROUGH INSTITUTIONAL INCLUSION

In April 2016, Israeli Minister of Public Security Gilad Erdan announced that the Israel Police would begin a massive recruitment drive to increase the number of Muslim officers on the force. All told, the police sought to hire 1,350 additional Muslim officers, which would raise the group's proportion on the force from about 1.5 percent in 2014 to nearly 6 percent just a few years later.[1] The recruitment drive is part of a larger effort to increase policing in the Arab sector at a cost of two billion shekels (about 600 million USD), and coincides with the opening of several new police stations in predominantly Arab towns. The increased emphasis on recruiting Arabs appears to be working – as of September 2016, the police had received 1,420 applications from Arabs in 2016, compared to 543 in 2015 and 687 in 2014.[2]

The goal of the recruitment drive is to provide more effective policing services in Arab communities and to increase trust between Arab citizens and the police.[3] Should we expect increases in the number of Arab officers to have the desired effects on citizen–police relations? What about Muslim relations with the Israeli state more broadly? What effect will the influx of Muslim police officers have on the frequency of ethno-religious violence? The recruitment drive has many of the

1 Hadida, Diaa (2016), "Israel seeking police recruits: Eager, and Arab." *New York Times* September 3. www.nytimes.com/2016/09/04/world/middleeast/israeli-police-recruiting-arabs-to-join-the-force-not-resist-it.html?_r=0

2 Kamisher, Eliyahu (2016), "Help wanted: Police seek Arab recruits for force." *Jerusalem Post*, September 12. www.jpost.com/Israel-News/Politics-And-Diplomacy/Help-wanted-Police-seek-Arab-recruits-for-force-467490

3 ibid

hallmarks of integration: It aims to increase the proportion of Muslim officers severalfold, giving Muslims considerably more influence over the behavior of the police. New recruits are incorporated into the existing policing structure, serving side by side with non-Muslim officers. The evidence presented in this book, not just from Israel but also from Iraq, suggests that this integration should indeed improve citizen–state relations by credibly signaling to Muslim Israelis that the government is committed to treating them better. The changes should enhance the police's ability to tackle crime, contributing to improved relations between Muslim citizens of Israel and the Israeli government more broadly.

SUMMING UP: KEY FINDINGS AND TAKEAWAYS

Throughout this book, I find that minority citizens who perceive the police to be more integrated – which I argue is a function of the officers to whom they are exposed as well as their preexisting political attitudes and experiences – are more likely to expect the police and government to treat them well. These changing expectations spur changes in citizen behavior that contribute to public safety, for example, reporting more information about crime to the police and withdrawing support for violent insurgency. In the process of exploring the causes and consequences of police integration, several noteworthy patterns emerge which contribute to three related scholarly literatures.

The Effects of Police Integration Are Not Zero-Sum

Overall, the effects of police integration are largely similar across ethnic and religious groups. Despite the highly divided nature of politics in Israel and Iraq, in most cases, there is no significant difference in integration's effects between Israeli Jews and Israeli Arabs, or between Iraqi Shias and Iraqi Sunnis. The conventional perspective on integrating the police or other bureaucracies takes an adversarial, zero-sum approach to institutional design, assuming that officers will "actively represent" members of their own group at the expense of other groups (Meier 1975; Mosher 1982; Meier and Stewart Jr. 1992; Meier 1993; Andersen 2017; Kennedy et al. 2017). Extended to conventional power sharing, positions of power in state institutions held by one group detract from the power of other groups (Lijphart 1969). Thus, the allocation of these positions is contentious, and the group that benefits from the status quo should oppose changes to state institutions which give power to other groups.

However, most Israeli Jews and Iraqi Shias support integrating the police, and members of these dominant groups are more apt to perceive service provision as fair when members of the "opposing" group are integrated into the police. I find that most members of the dominant group are not so concerned about a loss of employment that they would oppose integration. At the same time, an overwhelming majority of Israeli Jews and Iraqi Shias believe that minorities' participation in an integrated government institution represents a valuable contribution to society, and only a small number of respondents worry that integrating the police provides more opportunities for rebellion.

I identify a new mechanism linking integration with service provision that avoids the zero-sum approach to institutional integration implicit in existing research. Integration improves crime prevention by increasing cooperation with the authorities, eliciting more information from civilians about problems in the community that the police then use to allocate their resources efficiently. Integration affects public safety not because officers serve members of their own group better, but because they serve *everyone* better when they have a better relationship with the community.

This net-positive outcome to police integration helps move the discussion of the police beyond the direct outcomes of citizen–police relations and frame it as an important component of broader citizen–state relations. Because integration can benefit citizens from both groups, or at least benefit one group without making the other worse off, it makes a promising setting for a first step toward reconciliation where trust is low and each side is skeptical of the other's intentions. Integrating the police can demonstrate to all parties the benefits of cooperation and build the trust necessary to work together in other arenas.

Institutional Inclusion Has Multiple Dimensions

A wealth of research explores the way that institutions affect politics in divided societies (Lijphart 1969; Roeder and Rothchild 2005; Norris 2008; Strøm et al. 2017). Nearly all of it focuses on the extent to which each group is included in the institution. I add a second dimension of integration, the way individuals are distributed within an institution. I theorize a number of mechanisms through which greater heterogeneity within institutional units (police patrols, for example) makes inclusion difficult to reverse, while segregated inclusion allows the institution to limit the power of individuals from certain groups or reverse inclusion altogether.

The empirical tests in Chapter 6 distinguish integration, or the distribution of officers so that officers from all groups work together and serve civilians from all groups, from segregated inclusion (autonomy) in which officers serve primarily members of their own group. Respondents who say their local police are *mixed* between people like them and people from other groups are less likely to exhibit conflict-motivating attitudes compared to those whose local police are mostly out-groups. On the other hand, those whose local police are mostly people *like them* are *not* less likely to exhibit conflict-motivating attitudes. Being policed by members of one's own group fails to elicit many of the positive attitudes and expectations that policing by diverse officers yields.

I theorize that segregated inclusion has a smaller impact because it provides vulnerable groups with fewer mechanisms for defending themselves. Generally speaking, integration prevents the institution in question from becoming dominated by a particular group by fostering heterogeneity within units. Eklund et al. (2005, 131) note that integrating Kurdish troops into the Iraqi army "would prevent the federal army from becoming an Arab army, so there may be a prudential case for partial integration." Integration allows non-coethnic officers to monitor one another's behavior. If an officer mistreats a citizen from another group, there is likely to be an officer from that citizen's group present who can intervene or report the incident the the relevant authority. Additionally, integration makes it more difficult for the government to use officers from the dominant group to repress citizens from the vulnerable group, as vulnerable-group officers would likely get wind of preparations for such actions and tip-off the targeted community. Autonomy, on the other hand, isolates officers from the vulnerable group, keeping them out of the loop. Second, integration makes service provision in dominant-group areas dependent on the participation of vulnerable-group officers. In the event of a conflict, the vulnerable group could withhold valuable policing services from pro-government neighborhoods. Autonomy does not provide this option, as it relegates vulnerable-group officers to communities in which their coethnics live.

For similar reasons, autonomy is easier for the government to reverse than integration, as it allows the government to fire minority officers *en masse* at minimal cost. Unit-level heterogeneity makes it difficult to selectively distribute resources or information on the basis of identity, and marginalized-group officers in pro-government areas would need to be replaced quickly in the event of a conflict.

The distinction between integration and segregated inclusion also reveals a potential problem with using autonomy as a long-term solution to group-based conflict. Even if autonomy reduces immediate threats to security and improves service provision in the short term, it undermines state legitimacy and fails to contribute to durable citizen–state reconciliation. Iraq's 2005 constitution grants the Kurdish Regional Government (KRG) autonomy over several policy areas, including security. All policing in the Kurdish region is carried out by forces controlled by the regional government, the majority of whom are ethnic Kurds (Galbraith 2005). For the approximately five million Kurds living under the authority of the KRG, policing services approximate a system of ethnic autonomy. In Chapter 5, I show that whereas improvements in attitudes toward the police correlate with improvements toward the national government throughout the Middle East, this relationship is substantially weaker or nonexistent in the KRG. Furthermore, this system fails to represent non-Kurds living in the Kurdish region and Kurds living in "Arab" Iraq. This broken link matters because integration reduces conflict by altering attitudes toward the government. If citizens do not associate the police with the government against which they might rebel, then we should not expect changes in police demographics to affect support for anti-government violence.

Differences in configurations of inclusion may also have implications for police-on-citizen violence. Existing research suggests that the police are more likely to "get rough" with citizens who they view as "others," either relative to the officer's identity as a police officer (Westley 1970; Weitzer 2000) or a different ethnic, racial, or religious group (Weitzer 1995). Integration and segregated inclusion may each impact this sense of otherness in divided societies, but in different ways. Integration brings officers from different groups together as equal-status individuals working toward a common goal, potentially reducing the extent to which they view non-coethnic citizens as others and, consequently, raising their threshold for violence. Segregated inclusion may reduce police-on-citizen violence by reducing contact between non-coethnic officers and citizens entirely, though with the caveat notes above. Of course, the evidence in this book pertains primarily to citizen attitudes and behaviors. Future work might explore the impact of integration on officer behaviors more directly.

This book hypothesizes pathways through which individuals' organization within an institution likely matter, and empirically demonstrates the plausibility of these mechanisms. Future research on institutions in divided societies should explore this dimension of inclusion in greater detail. Are integrated institutions actually less likely to be purged than autonomous ones? Do police officers in heterogeneous units treat citizens better, worse, or the same compared to units whose officers match the citizen in question? If so, is the key mechanism monitoring and sanctioning of misbehavior by colleagues, changes in officers' attitudes toward out-groups through contact, or something else entirely?

Reduced Motives for Violence Overshadow Increased Opportunities

Finally, this research contributes to the long-running debate in research on civil wars over the factors that make a society more susceptible to conflict. Broadly speaking, integrating the police addresses people's motives for rebelling against the government, including unfair service provision (Østby 2008; Cederman et al. 2011), exclusion from employment (Marr 2007; Dube and Vargas 2013), and expectation of violent repression (de Figueiredo Jr and Weingast 1997). Addressing these attitudes and expectations would reduce overall levels of conflict if fighting is a function of motives (Gurr 1970; Horowitz 1985). However, "opportunity" explanations for conflict assume that there are always people motivated to fight against the state, and that the costliness of acting on those motivating factors determines whether rebellion occurs (Fearon and Laitin 2003; Collier et al. 2009). Thus, integrating the police and other policy-implementing institutions presents a trade-off by increasing opportunity for rebellion while addressing underlying motives for conflict. On balance, we see a very large reduction in support for violence among Sunni Iraqis who believe the police are integrated. Anecdotally, there is no indication that Israeli Arabs who perceive the police as integrated become more likely to advocate for or participate in riots or terrorism.

Thus, at least in these two cases, it appears that reduced motives trump increased opportunities. This is not to say that the costliness of fighting does not matter, but perhaps motives are a precondition for the influence of opportunity. The lower the motives for fighting, the lower the costs must be in order for conflict to occur. Police integration, it seems, reduces motives more than it increases opportunity, making it a viable solution for group-based conflict. More generally, institutional solutions for conflict which empower potential insurgents are not doomed to fail. As long as they reduce motives for violence, these institutions can withstand some degree of corresponding increase in opportunity for fighting.

POLICE INTEGRATION AS A CURE FOR CONFLICT? POLICY APPLICATIONS, IMPLICATIONS, AND CHALLENGES

The preceding chapters suggest that under the right circumstances, integrating the police effectively mitigates group-based violent conflict. Leaders can signal their commitment to peace, inclusiveness, and the provision of public safety by recruiting police officers from under-represented communities and distributing them widely throughout the force. This section discusses several nuances of implementing police integration as a solution to conflict.

Challenges of Implementation

Even within the scope conditions laid out in Chapter 1, policy-makers wishing to use police integration to prevent anti-government violence must clear several hurdles. The first is to convince members of the previously excluded group to join the police. Particularly in the context of a history of exclusion, divisiveness, and conflict, members of this community may not wish to join the police or other state institutions. The Israeli police struggle in this respect. One problem is the perception among Israeli Arabs that their applications will not be seriously considered, and therefore there is no point in applying. In a 2003 survey of Arab citizens, 31 percent of respondents believed that Arabs are prevented from joining the police because of their ethnic background (Hasisi and Weitzer 2007). However, these perceptions should dissipate as inclusiveness increases and people see officers from their group represented in the police. Another challenge is the possibility that minorities might view the police as a tool of repression and fear that by joining, they would be complicit in harming members of their community (Ben-Porat and Yuval 2012). Once again, however, my findings suggest that these attitudes fade as individuals perceive the police as more integrated. The tallest hurdle for policy-makers, then, comes at the very beginning of the process of integration. The first few recruits may prove to be the most difficult to secure. Once this initial challenge is overcome, subsequent rounds of recruitment will be less difficult. Indeed, despite Arab Israelis' skepticism of the Israel Police, I show in Chapter 4 that the Arab community appears sufficiently willing to participate to make integration possible.

Even if the previously excluded group is willing to participate in integration, integration may fail if the dominant group opposes it. However, as I note throughout this book, police integration provides net benefits for all citizens regardless of identity, including more effective policing services, giving dominant-group members reason to support integration. From a security perspective, Chapter 8 notes that Iraqi Shias and Israeli Jews are not particularly concerned that including Arabs and Sunnis within the police will allow those groups to subvert the state more easily. Rather, dominant-group members view participation in the police by minorities as willingness to contribute to society and willingness to work within the existing political system. In both Israel and Iraq, it is quite clear that opposition from the dominant group is unlikely to pose a serious obstacle.

Finally, policy-makers must communicate to a skeptical audience that the police are actually being integrated. Integration should have little effect on support for violence unless citizens *perceive* that the police are integrated. The evidence provides reason for both optimism and caution on this point. In Iraq, simply presenting Sunnis with a short news story – and a fake one, at that – was sufficient to dramatically alter their attitudes on a number of issues related to the police and the government, and caused a large reduction in willingness to consider using violence against the Iraqi government. While the survey design did not allow for a direct measure of "uptake," or the degree to which these shifts were due to the news story changing perceptions of integration, it is difficult to imagine a more likely explanation for these changes in attitudes.

As I discuss in Chapter 6, Iraq's political institutions, and its political context more generally, are new, underdeveloped, and extremely fluid relative to institutions in most countries. As a result, Iraqis' perceptions of those institutions are poorly entrenched and highly susceptible to new information. The importance of attitude entrenchment is especially important when the new information conflicts with existing beliefs. An Arab Israeli who has interacted with the police for forty years and has rarely seen Arab officers would be justifiably skeptical if he reads in the news that the police are integrated. Empty statements by political leaders not backed up by actual changes in officer demographics are unlikely to change perceptions or attitudes.

In Israel, comparing administrative data on officer demographics with survey data on citizens' perceptions suggests that citizens accurately perceive relative levels of police integration. Chapter 5 shows that officer demographics at the city level are correlated with how often a respondent "see[s] or hear[s] about officers from different ethnic or religious groups working together" with an r^2 of .21. Considering the coarseness of the data on officer demographics[4] and simplistic manner of calculating police integration from those officer demographics,[5] this relationship is not trivial. Clearly more research is needed, but it seems that perceptions of police integration are influenced by actual officer demographics.

What does all of this mean for policy-makers seeking to implement integration in the police? Once again, the most difficult step is likely to be from "not at all integrated" to "a little integrated." During this stage, the police may struggle to find recruits from underrepresented communities. Meaningful political reforms in other areas may help convince previously excluded groups to participate. Once officer recruitment is settled, the police and the government must find a way to credibly communicate the extent of the changes to members of the public. Empty rhetoric, public relations campaigns, and token appointments are unlikely to have lasting impacts. Substantial changes to the makeup and structure of the police are required. Furthermore, this process will be most difficult where the history of exclusion is strongest and where institutions are most developed. Yet, over time, this challenge may be overcome by a clear, consistent message of inclusion backed by observable changes in police demographics and behavior.

Police Integration Is Self-Enforcing

Institutions cause, predict, and explain outcomes only to the extent that they are difficult to change. That is, if the dominant group can alter an institution at will, then no possible design of that institution should have any effect on the attitudes and behaviors of other groups. The

[4] Survey respondents are only geolocated by city, which meant that station-level officer demographic data had to be aggregated to the city level to match with the survey responses.

[5] The formula only includes religious groups, not ethnic ones, and each group is given equal weight regardless of political connotations.

Syrian government could allow for increased representation of opposition parties in the parliament, and opponents of the regime would likely respond positively to this newfound inclusiveness. However, if the regime can revoke this representation just as easily as it allows it, then it will have little effect on the opposition's perception of security. This problem is particularly acute when thinking not about grievances over present conditions but about fears over future conditions. The key, then, is to design institutions that not only affect policy implementation in the present but also make it difficult for the state or dominant group to renege on these arrangements in the future.

Integration achieves this goal because it shifts the balance of power in favor of the newly integrated group. Generally speaking, purges of the police are incredibly rare, and those that occur are possible only when demanded by the masses (Taylor 2014; González 2019). Once officers from a minority group are armed, organized, and provided access to information, removing them from their posts is quite difficult. Even if officers do not actively resist a purge, reversing integration is costly for the state because it removes officers who provide desirable government goods and services. Firing officers *en masse* necessitates rapid replacement by large numbers of individuals who are unlikely to have similar levels of experience and expertise, leading to gaps in service provision that anger citizens. The brief firing in 2003 of nearly all of Iraq's police officers led to looting, riots, and a total breakdown of law and order. To make matters worse, many of the fired officers left their uniforms behind but kept their weapons, flooding the streets with firearms which found their way into the increasingly violent sectarian civil war and insurgency. It took the coalition forces years to rebuild the stability that was lost the moment they purged the police. The costliness of reversing rank-and-file integration explains why it is so effective at mitigating concerns of future mistreatment among vulnerable group members.

Police Integration Is Relevant in Non-Democracies

Most research on institutions in divided societies deals with democratic institutions, particularly electoral rules and representative legislatures. Under autocracy, integration of these types of policy-making institutions is less likely to improve relations between previously marginalized groups and the state. First, while elections and legislative bodies are not meaningless in autocratic settings, they tend to have far less influence over policy outcomes than do similar institutions in democracies.

Perhaps more importantly, they are easily eliminated, reconstituted, and purged by the true seat of power, making their composition a poor signal of the government's *future* behavior. While the relevance of legislatures and other policy-making institutions varies across regime types, the police are critical for all governments. Even the most competent autocrat relies on the police to maintain order. Thus, rank-and-file police officers are relevant to all states, and in divided societies their composition sends a meaningful signal about the way citizens should expect the government to treat them.

Second, in autocracies in which policy-making institutions have real power, autocrats may resist integrating them for fear of appearing weak or eroding their hold on power. Integrating the police is a more palatable option for autocrats because it does not create symbolic "cracks in the wall" regarding the autocrat's hold on policy-making. Autocrats maintain the appearance of iron-fist control over the government while allowing marginalized groups sufficient influence over service provision to placate grievances and fears. Furthermore, whereas top-down power sharing may provide outspoken critics of the regime with a pulpit, creating a coordination point which may lead to rebellion, police integration allows the regime to keep opposition leaders out of the public eye while appeasing the masses.

INTEGRATION IMPOSED BY A THIRD PARTY

The model of integration I lay out in this book assumes that the government, or the dominant group that controls the government, is the first mover. The state implements a policy of police integration, and then members of vulnerable or previously excluded groups respond to that policy. This version of events assumes that the government desires integration, most likely because it sees it as a path toward ending costly conflict. In an alternative scenario, a third party may impose police integration on a state. In this case, the government may not want to integrate the police, but a powerful outside actor, perhaps another state or an international peacekeeping mission, may force the government to integrate its police. Should we still expect police integration to successfully solve sectarian conflict under these circumstances?

I suggest that police integration imposed by a third party will have the same conflict-reducing effects as integration implemented willingly by the host state. The reason is that once rank-and-file integration is implemented, it is costly to undo. Once out-group members are organized, trained, and equipped, and once state service provision in pro-government areas depends on the integrated group' participation, its members are empowered to impose considerable costs on the government regardless of how they achieved their positions. Thus, integration ties the government's hands regardless of its preferences, and integration imposed by a third party on a begrudging government should remain effective even after the third party leaves.

Integration of Iraq's security forces in 2007 illustrates the durability of foreign-imposed police integration. Shias dominated the police and security forces throughout the early years of democratic rule. However, when General David Petraeus took command of the coalition forces in February 2007, and Ryan Crocker became the US ambassador in Baghdad the following month, the two leaders pressured the Iraqi government to integrate Sunnis into the security forces fighting against the al-Qaeda insurgency. Prime Minister Maliki resisted integration because it cut into his ability to distribute positions in the police and military as patronage to reward political supporters (Robinson 2009; Pfaff 2008).[6] Petraeus and Crocker, however, insisted. Their plan, labeled Operation Blue Shield, called for more than 12,000 Sunni recruits to be integrated into the security forces within six months.

Petraeus convinced Maliki to hire thousands of Sunni militia members into the Iraqi police and military in predominantly Sunni Anbar so long as the fighters pledged allegiance to the Iraqi government (Robinson 2009). Convincing Maliki and other politicians to integrate the police in other provinces proved more difficult. "The idea of bringing large numbers of former opponents back into the government, particularly under arms, set off all the alarm bells of the Shia politicians who lay awake at nights fearing the return of a repressive Sunni-dominated regime" (Robinson 2009, 253). To address these fears and leave Maliki without a smoke screen for his patronage-motivated opposition, coalition and Iraqi forces jointly conducted background checks, fitness and literacy tests, and medical exams on all new recruits. To avoid meddling in the process by the Shia-dominated Ministry of Interior, local councils or tribes provided endorsements for candidates (Robinson 2009, 254).

Maliki, however, continued to resist. The Americans made little progress over the course of several meetings in summer 2007. Brigadier

6 Also see Chapter 7

General John Campbell, a key player in Baghdad's security plan, managed to secure the endorsement of Iraqi head of Baghdad Operations Lieutenant General Abboud Qanbar. Yet, even then, Maliki was not swayed. After several unsuccessful meetings between Petraeus, Qanbar, and Maliki in which Petreaus failed to convince Maliki that the Sunni recruits could be trusted, Petraeus switched tactics.

> Petraeus had learned over the past year that he would occasionally have to show the full range of emotion, something other than an even temperament, to prevail in such disagreements. At times he feigned anger to convince Iraqi officials to do what he felt was necessary – particularly when he suspected a sectarian agenda was at work. Other times, the vein in his temple stood out and his emotion was authentic. This was one of the latter moments.
>
> "It's make or break time. These guys used to point their guns at us and you. Now they are pointing their guns at [Al Qaeda in Iraq]," he said, turning up the emotional pitch. "Do you want them to point their guns back at us, to shoot and kill our soldiers and yours?"... It took the commander of all U.S. Forces in Iraq to overcome the prime minister's dogged resistance; no one else could budge him. (Robinson 2009, 260)

Finally, in late summer 2007, Maliki agreed to allow Sunni militia members to join the police in parts of Baghdad. To avoid further opposition from the Interior Ministry and existing security forces, the US forces airlifted hundreds of recruits to the Baghdad Police College so their arrival would not be impeded. Slowly but surely, the former Awakening fighters were integrated into the Iraqi police and security forces. The entire process, from start to finish, required significant pressure from the Americans and would not have occurred had Maliki had his way, making it a clear example of a policy imposed by a third party.

By and large, imposed integration in Iraq was successful in areas where it was implemented. Within central Baghdad, the Iraqi Police integrated most extensively in the A'amiriya neighborhood, an upper-class neighborhood home to both Sunnis and Shias. Before integration, A'ameriya was one of Baghdad's most violent neighborhoods, with most fighting instigated by Sunni militias seeking to push out Shia residents.[7] In the first half of 2007, the Iraqi government claimed that the area

[7] Cave, Damien (2007), "Amiriya: Walls and checkpoints bring hope and frustration." *New York Times* September 6. www.nytimes.com/interactive/2007/09/06/world/middleeast/20070907_BUILDUP_DETAIL_GRAPHIC.html?neighborhood=amiriya

was too dangerous to provide public services like trash removal, and electricity was only available for a few hours per day.[8] In the 2016 survey conducted for this project, five years after US troops withdrew, residents of A'ameriya reported similar levels of trust in the police as did Sunnis elsewhere in Baghdad, were similarly likely to say that the police treat members of different religious groups fairly, and were slightly more likely to indicate willingness to report criminal activity to the police.[9] A'ameriya residents report seeing Sunni and Shia officers working together slightly more often than the citywide average. Electricity is now provided for about 14 hours a day, compared to the 15.7 hour per day average reported across the rest of the city. In what was one of Baghdad's worst neighborhoods only ten years ago, these numbers indicate substantial improvement which persisted long after US troops left the area.

There is little doubt that Maliki's resistance to police integration prevailed in many, if not most, parts of Iraq. The majority of the Anbar militias were never integrated into the state security security forces, and it was not until the administration of Haider al-Abadi took control of the Iraqi government in 2014 that the government began widespread *voluntary* efforts to integrate the Iraqi police. Furthermore, as I discussed in Chapter 8, Maliki easily reversed inclusion in areas where Sunni soldiers and officers were isolated from their Shia colleagues. However, the experience of A'ameriya in which the police were integrated under pressure from the United States is consistent with the underlying logic that once implemented, however grudgingly, police integration is difficult to reverse.

BEYOND POLICING: BUREAUCRATIC INTEGRATION IN DIVIDED SOCIETIES

This book, as well as the data and evidence I report in it, focuses on the police. However, the theory of rank-and-file integration is a general one that should apply to many bureaucratic institutions which implement policies or enforce laws. Four scope conditions govern whether an institution may serve as an effective setting for integration. First, citizens

8 ibid

9 I report only general trends here to avoid leaning too heavily on a very small sample. The survey included only thirty residents of A'ameriya, providing an insufficient number of responses to claim representativeness with any precision.

must have information about the demographic makeup of the institution's rank and file. As we see with the police, this information often comes from direct observation of employees, meaning that employees must operate in the public view. Second, the institution in question must be responsible for distributing a good or service of substantial value. The police, of course, distribute public safety. Other valuable services bureaucrats provide include infrastructure like roads and electricity, education, healthcare, and permits for construction or running a business. The way government institutions distribute these goods and services has a substantial impact on citizens' well-being. Third, the rank-and-file employees of the institution must have significant discretion over the way the good or service is distributed. Police officers have broad leeway in how laws are applied and enforced to different segments of the population, as well as how scarce police resources are distributed throughout communities. I suggest in the following text that educators and healthcare workers have similar discretion. Finally, the rank-and-file employees of the institution must be in a position to use their discretion to impose costs on the state in the event of a conflict. The police can impose costs by turning their weapons against the government. Other institutions, however, are more likely to impose costs simply by withholding their participation, leading to inferior service provision to citizens to whom the government is accountable.

Several policy-implementing institutions meet these conditions and may make suitable candidates for rank-and-file integration as a solution to conflict. Policy-makers seeking to credibly commit to the positive treatment of previously excluded groups may integrate the public education system, for example. Schoolteachers and professors work in the public eye, and their group membership is easily observable by students and their parents. Arab Israelis cite poor education provision as a key grievance against the government. "The education system is failing also. In the Arab sector, I mean. A kid who is 14, 15, 16 cannot read his own name."[10] Teachers are, of course, responsible for distributing a very important service, education, and their level of effort influences the quality of education that students receive. Just as importantly, teachers are in a position to determine the *content* of the education that students receive, including the perspective from which history is taught, giving them significant political power. Teachers can impose costs on the

[10] FG2A

government by manipulating the information they transmit to students in a way that subverts government support. Reneging on schoolteacher integration is also costly, as the supply of teachers looking for work is limited, and hiring large numbers of new teachers at once is highly disruptive.

The healthcare system provides another likely setting for integration. Citizens from all groups depend on doctors, nurses, and hospital employees to provide healthcare. Especially in countries in which the government provides most healthcare services, integrating these positions gives power to previously excluded groups, places their members in a position to prevent biases in healthcare provision, and provides desirable jobs for many people. At the very least, integrating the healthcare system can help prevent the dominant group from abusing its power, as occurred in Iraq shortly after democratization. In May 2006, Iraq's Health Ministry came under the control of partisans of Shia leader Muqtada al-Sadr, leading to the denial of services or worse in Sunni areas of Baghdad. "Some of the most egregious abuses were occurring in Baghdad's hospitals. The Sadrist health minister had packed the ministry and hospitals with militia members. Sunnis were going in and not coming out" (Robinson 2009, 154). The presence of large numbers of Sunni doctors, nurses, and staff might have prevented hospitals from being used in this way.

Less glamorous institutions like public works and sanitation may also be effective settings for integration. Public works employees work in the public eye, maintaining infrastructure and providing services. Citizens value the smooth highways, clean streets, and reliable electricity that these institutions distribute. In Iraq, insurgents seeking to undermine the newly democratic state frequently targeted the employees responsible for building infrastructure. "The state's legitimacy depended on its delivering services to the people; so the less electricity people received, the less legitimate was the state. Thus power lines and engineers came under regular attack" (al-Ali 2014, 107).

Workers may shirk, which includes not working as hard as they should or intentionally doing substandard work out of malice. The nature of public service delivery makes monitoring costly: public works projects are scattered throughout the country, their evaluation requires specialized knowledge and expertise, and it is difficult to say with certainty whether poor-quality work is the result of shirking or environmental factors. In his quest to directly observe corruption on road-building projects, Olken (2007) hired a team of engineers to extract and analyze core samples from newly built roads. Such an extensive procedure is hardly feasible on a regular basis, meaning road builders have leeway in the quality of work they choose to do. If road builders in a divided society are more likely to shirk when they are building roads in out-group neighborhoods, then integration allows workers with different preferences for shirking to monitor one another's behavior and prevent biased behavior.

The saga of Beirut's trash collection in winter 2015–2016 illustrates how politically relevant seemingly mundane services can be. The city's waste removal contractor suspended trash collection after its contract expired in early 2015.[11] Over the next eight months, trash piled up throughout the city's streets and sidewalks. The trash piles became so extensive that they blocked traffic, and residents complained that the unsanitary conditions were causing health problems. The lack of trash removal turned into a major political crisis for the Lebanese government. What began in July as a small protest outside of the parliament building grew into major anti-government demonstrations, along with a social media campaign under the hashtag "You Stink" aimed at politicians responsible for failing to provide basic services. Some protesters explicitly demanded the government's resignation.[12] By August, protests became sufficiently violent for the government to call on the army to maintain order on the streets of the capital.[13] Public works are relevant in other countries as well. During the summers of 2012 and 2013, residents of Basra, Iraq, protested nightly, and often violently, against the lack of government service delivery (al-Ali 2014). Although these crises were not caused by sectarian divisiveness, they demonstrate that rank-and-file bureaucrats can impose significant costs on the government by withholding services.

While integration may be effective in a wide range of policy-implementing institutions, it is likely to have an especially strong effect when applied to the police. Public safety is arguably the most important service that the modern state provides, and the police's capacity for violence amplifies any effects that institutional changes may have

[11] Bulos, Nabih (2015), "Beirut garbage crisis has Lebanese telling government: 'You stink!'" *Los Angeles Times*, July 26. www.latimes.com/world/la-fg-lebanon-trash-20150727-story.html

[12] AlJazeera.com (2015), "Lebanese protest against waste disposal crisis." *Al Jazeera.com*, July 26. www.aljazeera.com/news/2015/07/lebanon-beirut-trash-rubbish-crisis-150725060723178.html

[13] Conlon, Kevin (2015), "Army deployed to Beirut after anti-government anger boils over." *CNN.com*, August 30. www.cnn.com/2015/08/23/asia/beirut-lebanon-garbage-clashes/

on society. If integration of other policy-implementing institutions generally reduces citizens' fears of being mistreated by government, integration of the police should do so to an even greater extent. Nevertheless, the police are hardly unique in providing goods and services that citizens care about, and the discretion of bureaucrats from a wide range of institutions over policy implementation means that in divided societies, citizens should care greatly about the integration of these institutions.

EXPANDING TO MULTIPLE GROUPS

The theory I propose in this book describes interactions between two groups, one powerful and one marginalized. In reality, of course, communities and political units tend to have many groups. An extension of the theory might ask how a third, very small minority will behave when the larger marginalized group becomes integrated into the police. While I did not explicitly set out to examine this complication, a few anecdotes suggest building-blocks for future work on the issue. Selda,[14] a Christian woman living in Baghdad, says the idea of Sunnis joining the police "makes me happy because things will be balanced. If you feared one of the sides you will go to the other. I can take advantage of what's going on between them, so I go to one side and they'll probably bring me justice to spite the other." As outsiders to the Sunni–Shia conflict, Selda feels that Christians are able to play the sides against one another to get what they want. Furthermore, the balance that integration creates prevents hegemony by either side. In the absence of any real power for Christians – a foregone conclusion in Baghdad given their lack of numbers – the next best thing for them is to ensure balance among other groups.

A more complex extension might acknowledge the multidimensional nature and cross-cuttingness of group identity. For example, Israeli Arabs are divided between Muslims, Christians, and Druze, who in some areas are further divided into extended families or *hamulas*. Jews, meanwhile, are divided ethnically between Ashkenazim and Sephardim, and further by specific country of origin. A discussion among Muslim Israeli focus group participants outside of Haifa reveals the complications of cross-cutting cleavages. The participants

[14] IIACSS interview 01CF, January 2019. Subject's name changed to protect anonymity.

expressed substantial distrust in police officers who are Druze – coethnics in that they are both Arabs yet distinct in their religious beliefs and cultural practices.

> If you try to talk with a police officer, even if he is a Druze, in Arabic, he will ignore you. Last Friday, at the Temple Mount, a Druze came in, with shoes, to the temple. The worshipers told him in Arabic to step outside, or take off his shoes, or put a plastic bag on them before he enters. This is a holy place. They talked to him in Arabic, and he replied back in Hebrew. It caused damage to the police, to the government, to the country. He was a police officer, in the police uniform. A police officer with a walkie-talkie and a gun and everything.[15]

Other focus group participants agreed with this frustration toward Druze officers, saying they prefer to be policed by other minorities instead. One said, "I prefer Ethiopians over Druze. I prefer [just about anyone] in the police other than the Druze," while another expressed a preference for Bedouin officers – Arab Muslims, but culturally distinct from these residents of cosmopolitan Haifa.

Finally, this research focuses almost exclusively on group identity in the form of religion, ethnicity, race, and language. Gender constitutes another relevant source of group identity with theoretically distinct characteristics. First, men and women nearly always make up equal shares of the population, creating a different dynamic than the one between majority and minority groups. Second, men and women are far more societally integrated than members of different ethnic or religious groups tend to be, living together in the same homes and family units, perhaps explaining why violence organized around ethnicity or religion tends to look so different than gender-based violence. On the other hand, many of the dynamics I discuss with regard to group identity are also relevant to gender integration in the police, including female officers' abilities to empathize with and elicit information from female civilians (Messner and Sampson 1991; Paoline III et al. 2000; Karim and Beardsley 2017; Karim 2019). All told, while this research takes a substantial step forward in understanding institutions in divided societies, the two-group model only begins to scratch the surface of group politics in divided societies.

[15] FG2A

THE WAY FORWARD

Group politics is here to stay. Political organization around group identity pre-dates the modern state, and so long as power, influence, and treasure are at stake, there is no reason to expect the political relevance of group identity to disappear. Yet, the vast majority of intergroup cleavages are peaceful. Political organization along group lines need not become violence along group lines. This book builds on a large body of research that suggests that institutions which incorporate group cleavages into their design, ensure access to influence for each group, and mitigate fears that today's vulnerabilities will lead to future exclusion allow states to govern diverse populations peacefully and effectively. The peaceful coexistence of diverse identity groups in Canada, Belgium, Switzerland, and countless other states illustrates that borders need not be redrawn to accommodate societal differences.

I close with two overarching conclusions about conflict and representation. First, individuals fight because they have reason to do so, not simply because they can. This assumption implies that institutions should focus not on raising the costs of conflict, for example, by separating members of groups in conflict or ensuring hegemony by a particular group, but by addressing the underlying motives that drive individuals to violence in the first place. I investigated the effects of institutions on a handful of motives, including grievances over service provision, exclusion from employment, and fear of repression. I do not suggest that these are the only things that drive people to fight. Institutional solutions to conflict must focus on the unique conditions of the conflict in question. Thus, while the framework of integration should generalize to a wide range of contexts, the details of integration must address the unique drivers of conflict in each setting. In all cases, however, integration must not only address the underlying motives in the present but also find a way to commit to their resolution indefinitely into the future.

The second conclusion is that inclusion in political institutions is a means to an end, not an end unto itself. Police integration works not by addressing a normative desire for representation but by increasing the *influence* of each group over policy outcomes. The location of policy-implementing institutions at the end of the chain of governance makes these institutions especially important for influencing the outcomes of governance that individuals care most about, and about which they are most likely to fight. Symbolic inclusion in lawmaking institutions may be normatively desirable, but so long as policies affect individuals in a way that generates grievances, or so long as individuals do not feel secure in their future prospects, symbolic inclusion alone is unlikely to prevent or solve group-based conflict. Inclusion in government matters to the extent that it affects people's well-being and quality of life. Integration addresses not just an innate desire for inclusion but a more urgent need to be treated in a certain way. By creating balance within the institution which determines how laws affect citizens on a day-to-day basis, police integration prevents biases, exclusion, and fear that motivate conflict while allowing members of different groups to coexist under the umbrella of a shared state.

APPENDIX A

DATA AND METHODS

This book draws on a number of original qualitative and quantitative sources of evidence. Here, I provide details on how I collected this evidence with an eye toward transparency and replicability. Survey instruments, interview guides, data sets, and analysis code can be retrieved from my website.

While I draw on a number of data sources throughout the book, my evidence leans heavily on survey measures. This dependence has strengths and weaknesses. On the positive side, surveys are the best tool to measure my main independent variable, perceptions of police integration, and my main dependent variables, citizens' attitudes and expectations. While police integration depends on real changes in officer demographics, citizens' attitudes depend on their *perceptions* of integration. The surveys allow direct measurement of that construct. Similarly, measuring attitudes and expectations directly allows a more precise exploration of the mechanisms underlying changes in security. Individual-level surveys allow me to ask not just "whether" integration affects outcomes like crime, but also "why" it does so by exploring the attitudes of individual people.

For different reasons, my measures of security – support for anti-state violence in Iraq and victimization by crime in Israel – also come from surveys. I provide an overview of violence in Iraq in Chapter 6, using data on conflict fatalities, but these data are ill-suited to test against perceived integration due to their coarseness. Instead, I rely on a survey-experimental measure of individuals' support for anti-government violence which provides a more precise measure of attitudes, if not action. In Chapter 7, I measure crime prevention in

Israel using a large-scale victimization survey in which subjects are asked whether they experienced crime in the past year. Such victimization surveys are commonplace in analyses of crime as they avoid many likely sources of bias in official crime data (Banerjee et al. 2012). In particular, official crime statistics only reflect crimes of which the police are aware, and the main method through which the police learn about crimes is citizen reporting. Thus, the more willing citizens become to cooperate with the police, the higher the proportion of crimes the police include in their statistics, potentially creating the appearance that crime has increased when in fact it is only citizens' cooperation that has increased. Measuring crime with a survey avoids this problem to the extent that people are willing to answer truthfully to an unprompted "yes or no" question about victimization.

Of course, surveys alone cannot paint a complete picture of a society or its politics. First, perceptions may be divorced from reality. In my research, the extent of this gap determines whether police integration is consequential. If police officer demographics have no bearing on citizens' perceptions of integration, the pathways through which I propose integration affects security could not possibly occur. The administrative data on Israeli police officer demographics, which I present in Chapters 4 and 5, were therefore critical for testing this particular mechanism, and for painting a complete picture of trends in police integration in Israel. Sadly, as I detail in Chapter 3, similar data on Iraqi police demographics do not exist.

Second, while surveys' analytic strength comes from their systematic nature, the trade-off is that they constrain the information interviewees are able to provide. Thus, I supplemented the surveys with dozens of open-ended, informal interviews, as well as three semi-structured focus groups. These interviews, conducted both before and after I analyzed the survey data, sought to bring to life the stories hinted at by trends in the systematic data and ensure that the overall story I told reflected the nuances of real people's experiences. I describe each of these data collection efforts in detail in the following text.

FIELD RESEARCH STRATEGY AND TIMELINE

Much of the data I use in this book, including surveys, interviews, focus groups, and officer demographics data, are the product of several rounds of field research. The first occurred in summer 2014, when I traveled to Israel with three goals: first, to determine whether data existed on the religious makeup of police officers at each station and to acquire these data if possible; second, to probe the plausibility of my theory by interviewing police officers, citizens, and academics familiar with the Israeli police; and third, to collect ancillary data on other relevant indicators. It was during this trip that I conducted the interview with a high-ranking officer in charge of recruitment cited in Chapters 4 and 7, had the conversation with the police officer quoted in Chapter 2, used a Freedom of Information request to acquire the data on police officer demographics used in Chapters 4, 5, and 7,[1] and retrieved the Social Survey data on crime victimization from the Central Bureau of Statistics. I made a second significant data collection effort in winter 2016. I returned to Israel for several weeks to conduct additional interviews with Israeli citizens about their experiences with the police and to collect additional administrative data from the Central Bureau of Statistics. I made two additional trips to Israel while working on this project which contributed to my perspective on citizen–police relations.

Not surprisingly, fieldwork on Iraq proved to be more challenging. My efforts at data collection occurred during the height of conflict between the Islamic State and government forces. As fighting between these forces raged in the northern parts of the country, insurgents affiliated with other local and foreign groups, including al-Qaeda, carried out bombing and shooting attacks throughout Iraq. Insecurity made unstructured interviews and informal observations unfeasible. Even if traveling to Baghdad had been possible from a safety perspective, it is unlikely to have been productive. The legacy of the United States' occupation and a palpable sense that the United States was to blame for Iraq's suffering made my identity as a US-based researcher a liability. With the wounds of the Coalition Provisional Authority, de-Baathification, and other failed policies still fresh, Iraqi politicians were in no mood to hear from another American about the imperative of sectarian integration. Leaders in the police and the Ministry of Interior rebuffed several of my approaches through an Iraq-based research firm as soon as they discovered the project was run by an American. Given recent history, I do not blame them.

[1] Upon my initial approaches, the police indicated a refreshing willingness to release this information. Their officers guided me through the process of filing the Freedom of Information request, and the police released the requested data promptly thereafter.

Thus, for the sake of security as well as productivity, I elected to study Iraq from neighboring Jordan. While I could have worked safely from Iraq's Kurdish region, which experienced little violence during this period, basing in Jordan provided greater access to relevant voices. The Kurdish Regional Government maintains its own security forces, which are nearly uniformly Kurdish. While interesting and worthy of study, policing in the Kurdish region was tangential to this study. On the other hand, Jordan hosts both a large Iraqi expatriate community and a number of officials who had been involved in training Iraqi police officers. As I describe in Chapter 3, the Iraqi government and international coalition trained tens of thousands of Iraqi officers at the Jordan International Police Training Center on the outskirts of Amman between 2004 and 2007. While no longer used by the Iraqi police, the training center still exists, and many of the staff and trainers still work locally. Several of these individuals agreed to meet with me, some on the record while others preferred not to be quoted directly. Finally, the research firm that conducted the survey in Baghdad I describe later has an office in Amman, allowing me to coordinate closely with their researchers and staff. Thus, I conducted fieldwork in Amman in winter 2016, and returned several times over the next three years to coordinate the survey and interviews described in the following text.

INTERVIEWS AND FOCUS GROUPS

Broadly speaking, I conducted two rounds of interviews, one before conducting systematic analyses, which I used to develop my theory and hypotheses, and a second round after conducting the main analyses, which I used to add nuance to the discussion and verify my results. I quote interviewees from both rounds throughout the text. With a few notable exceptions, mainly current and former police trainers who worked with the Iraqi police, I use pseudonyms to protect interviewees' identities. I maintain the same unique pseudonym and/or numeric identifier for each interviewee throughout the book to allow readers to keep track of their statements. Locations and other details like employment, age, and gender are real. In addition to the interviewees quoted directly in the text, I spoke with a number of other individuals who provided background information on policing in Iraq and Israel but preferred not to be quoted.

I conducted the first round of interviews personally during my fieldwork in 2014 and 2016. All quoted interviews occurred in person, though I conducted a few background interviews by phone. In some cases, I cold-emailed individuals whose names I found by reading journalist accounts, while in other cases, academics, especially Badi Hasisi, David Weisburd, and Simon Perry, were gracious enough to make introductions for me. Interviewees often suggested additional people with whom I should speak.

In February 2019, I commissioned structured focus groups in Tel Aviv, Haifa, Jaffa, Baghdad, and Mosul. In the Israeli cities, three groups of citizens – two made up of Jews and one made up of non-Jews – spent two hours discussing their experiences with the police under the guidance of a professional interviewer from Brandman Market Research. I provided Brandman with a discussion guide and discussed the purpose of the project at length beforehand, but for the most part, participants were encouraged to speak their minds on anything related to policing or identity. The focus groups were conducted in Hebrew. Brandman delivered transcripts in Hebrew and English.

In Iraq, security concerns and the sensitivity of the topic prevented me, an American, from conducting interviews with citizens on their experiences with sectarian violence and the police. Instead, I developed an interview guide which professional interviewers from IIACSS, an Iraqi research firm, used to conduct one-on-one interviews. They interviewed twelve citizens, eight from Baghdad and four from Mosul. The interviewees included five women and seven men; five Sunnis, five Shias, and two Christians; ranging in age from twenty-five to fifty-five, with a variety of educational backgrounds. Interviews took place in Arabic and lasted between about 30 minutes and 1 hour. IIACSS delivered an audio recording of the interview, along with a transcript translated into English.

ADMINISTRATIVE DATA

In Israel, I collected new data on the religious makeup of officers at every station in the country, measured yearly from 2008 to 2014. I use this demographic data to calculate local-level integration, which I show matches closely with Israelis' perceptions of police integration. Early in the project, I noted that the Israel Police listed yearly national-level data on officer religious demographics on its public-facing website, making it highly likely that such data existed at lower levels of aggregation. Inquiries to several administrative offices in the Israel Police confirmed that they had the data, but no individual I spoke with was authorized to release it to me. Instead, they recommended that I file a request under Israel's Freedom of Information law, which I accomplished using a simple web form. The police mailed a disk with the requested data to me several weeks later. The disk contained a file with station-level officer demographics data for each year from 2008 to 2014. The file for 2010 was corrupted; therefore, that year is excluded from all analyses using these data.

After considerable effort, I determined that the Iraqi government does not maintain systematic records of its officers' sectarian identity during the period of this study, nor did the United States collect such data during its involvement. The absence of data in Iraq likely results from a strategic calculation by federal and provincial politicians who sought to distribute positions in the security forces as patronage. The more data existed on the makeup of the force, the more pressure the United States could impose to recruit officers of particular demographic backgrounds, thereby constraining politicians' abilities to staff the police as they wished.

SURVEYS

The analyses draw from original surveys in Iraq and Israel, each conducted in early 2016. I describe them here.

Iraq: Sampling Procedures

Safety concerns precluded surveying in much northern Iraq. The Islamic State controlled large swaths of Anbar and Nineveh provinces in late 2015, including major population centers like Fallujah and Ramadi. Although Iraqi security forces had begun to retake territory by the time the survey began, fighting remained fierce and unpredictable, making research in many locations impossible. Restricting the sample to Baghdad also improved comparability across respondents. While there are substantial social, economic, and cultural differences from one neighborhood to the next, those differences are likely smaller than the differences between residents of cities hundreds of miles apart. Finally, within Baghdad, the federal and local police operate interchangeably, simplifying both citizen perceptions and the questions needed to accurately measure those perceptions. The survey included 800 randomly selected respondents, stratified to achieve a sample of half Sunni Arabs and half Shia Arabs, which roughly matches Baghdad's Sunni–Shia makeup.

Because of the sensitive nature of sectarian identity in Iraq, respondents were not asked directly about their sectarian identity. Instead, enumerators coded whether they believed the respondent to be Sunni or Shia based on factors like name, manner of dress, facial hair, and visible items around the home. Enumerators then listed how confident they were in their coding. In total, enumerators described 85.5% of codings as "completely certain," 14.25% as "fairly certain," 0.25% as "more likely than not," and none as "unsure."

Baghdad Governorate is divided into nine administrative districts, which are further divided into subdistricts and census blocks. A 2010–2011 household census served as the sampling frame. Subdistricts were chosen proportionally based on population, and then blocks were chosen within each subdistrict, again proportionally based on population. Within each subdistrict, streets were selected using a simple random sample from a list maintained by the survey team. Interviews were conducted on sixty-seven different streets. Enumerator teams were provided with the sample at the street level, and then the team leader selected households randomly based on a map of occupied households. Within each household, the interview was conducted with the adult who had the next birthday.

If enumerators failed to reach a resident at a selected location after several attempts, or if the resident declined to participate, another household was selected from the remaining occupied households on the street. Among respondents who completed the survey, item nonresponse rates were no higher than 15 percent. Enumerators were primarily part-time employees of the survey company, and most had worked as enumerators on previous projects for this company. Enumerators worked in teams of five to eight, with each team overseen by a supervisor. An effort was made to assign enumerators to their home neighborhoods. Female enumerators were present in every team so that female respondents could be interviewed by a woman. Each interview was conducted by a single enumerator, sometimes overseen by a field supervisor, to minimize conspicuousness.

Iraq: Sample Characteristics

Fifty-two percent of respondents in the sample are male. The youngest respondents were eighteen (by design), while the oldest was seventy-two, with an average age of 35.5. Respondents' ages are particularly important in the context of Iraq because of the dramatic shifts in political power that occurred with the fall of the Baath regime in 2003. Older respondents have experienced periods of both Sunni and Shia political dominance during their lifetimes. In contrast, respondents in their twenties were very young when Saddam Hussein ruled Iraq, and their political and social attitudes formed primarily during the post-Saddam civil war. About 42 percent of respondents have lived their entire adult lives under a Shia-dominanted government. The other 58 percent were adults during the Baath regime and have experienced both a Sunni-dominated dictatorship and a Shia-dominated democratic government.

In terms of education, just over half had at least eleven years of formal schooling. More than 82 percent of respondents report living in the same neighborhood now as they did ten years ago. This figure is likely inflated by the fact that many Iraqis who were forced to flee their neighborhood due to security may have left Baghdad entirely, removing them from the sampling frame. Most respondents were displeased with their current economic situation, with only 32 percent either "somewhat satisfied" or "very satisfied." As an objective measure of government service provision and a general indicator of neighborhood characteristics, the survey asked respondents how many hours of electricity their household receives each day. Respondents reported receiving between 10 and 22 hours of electricity per day, with a median of 16 hours. Sunnis reported receiving about half an hour *more* per day than Shias, a small but statistically significant difference that contradicts arguments that the Shia-dominated government biases the distribution of services in favor of Shias.

Finally, 44 percent of respondents either work or have worked in the public sector, or have someone else in their household who works or has worked in the public sector. Of those, 100 (out of 800 total respondents) work or have worked for the police. These numbers may seem high, but in the context of Iraqi society, they are quite reasonable. Iraq's public sector is very large. A report published in 2016 estimates that the bureaucracy employs seven million people for a population of about thirty-three million people.[2] Considering that bureaucrats are disproportionately likely to reside in Baghdad, and that

[2] Cockburn, Patrick. "Iraq's Interior Minister on why state corruption is helping the murderous campaign of Isis." *Independent*, March 1, 2016. www.independent.co.uk/news/world/

TABLE A.1 *Survey sample statistics (Iraq)*

Variable	Obs	μ	σ	Min.	Max.
Sunni	800	.50	.50	0	1
Age	800	35.48	12.23	18	72
Male	800	.52	.50	0	1
Electricity (hours/day)	800	15.74	3.03	10	22
Econ. satisfaction	800	2.81	1.18	1	5
Work public	800	.44	.50	0	1

Iraqi households tend to be quite large, it is not surprising that nearly half of respondents have a member of their household who works in the public sector. The high number of households with a current or former police officer – one in eight – speaks directly to the sources of information Iraqis have about the makeup of the police, information which no doubt shapes their perceptions of the institution.

Iraq: Measuring Support for Anti-Government Violence

To obtain a reliable measure of citizens' support for anti-state violence without risking the safety of either respondents or enumerators, I use a list experiment, a measurement device which keeps individual-level responses private while allowing for analysis of aggregated group-level responses.

Table A.2 shows the distribution of responses to the item-count measure on support for anti-government violence. The logic behind the item-count measurement strategy is that subjects do not reveal their individual response. It is possible for the researcher to determine only how many items on the list a respondent would choose, but not which one(s) he or she would choose. Of course, anonymity breaks down if respondents select all of the items on the treatment list. Such a "ceiling effect" makes it obvious that the respondent has selected the controversial item.

Table A.2 shows that twenty-five respondents answered "5." In doing so, they revealed their willingness to consider using violence against the government. One possibility is that these subjects were being honest, and either did not understand that answering this way revealed

middle-east/war-with-isis-iraq-s-interior-minister-on-why-his-country-is-impotent-against-the-militants-a6905941.html

TABLE A.2 *Distribution of list experiment responses*

Number of items	Control	Treatment	Total
0	4	3	7
1	135	128	263
2	134	95	229
3	49	57	106
4	78	92	170
5		25	25
Total	400	400	800

their response or simply did not care. If this is the case, it is also likely to be true that other subjects also would have considered all five but did not say so for fear of revealing their answer on the controversial item. This scenario would cause me to underestimate the proportion of respondents who support the use of non-peaceful methods. A second possibility is that these subjects, or some subset of them, either were not paying careful attention to the survey question or did not understand the question and simply picked an answer. As long as they arrived at the answer of "5" randomly, then we are simply observing noise in the data.

A related concern is that additional respondents may have wanted to truthfully answer "5" but did not do so because they understood that this response would reveal their willingness to use violence. It is not possible to determine how many subjects provided inaccurate answers due to such a "ceiling effect." However, any ceiling effect would bias the overall estimate of willingness to use violence downward. Therefore, the proportion of the sample estimated to support anti-government violence should be considered a conservative estimate. It may undercount the proportion of respondents who would consider using violence but is unlikely to overcount them.

Critically, however, the ceiling effect *does not affect the interpretation of the main result* in Chapter 6. There is no reason to expect that the ceiling effect influenced responses differently depending on which vignette respondents received. Therefore, while the estimated support for violence may be biased downward, the *difference* between support in the treatment and control groups is not affected since these conditions were randomly assigned.

TABLE A.3 *Cumulative responses*

Num. Items	Short	Long
0	4	3
1	139	131
2	273	226
3	322	283
4	400	375
5		400

Related to the ceiling effect is a floor effect in which respondents in the treatment group perceive the "non-controversial" items as so rare that they think answering "1" reveals their preference for using violence. Only 1 percent of respondents in the control group answered "0," providing no evidence of a floor effect.

Another potential design effect occurs when respondents' answers to the nonsensitive items are conditional on the presence of the sensitive item (Blair and Imai 2012). If there is *no* design effect, we should observe two characteristics. First, for each item response from 0 to 4, the probability of observing that response or lower in the short list is greater than or equal to the probability of observing the same response or lower in the long list. In other words, 273 respondents in the short list group responded 0, 1, or 2. If there is no design effect, there should be 273 or fewer respondents in the long list who responded 0, 1, or 2. Second, for each item response from 1 to 5, the probability of observing that response or lower in the long list group is greater than or equal to the probability of observing one minus that response or lower in the short list group. For example, 283 respondents in the long list group selected 0, 1, 2, or 3 items. If there is no design effect, 283 respondents or fewer should have selected 0, 1, or 2 items. A formal representation of these conditions is found in Blair and Imai (2012, 64). Taken together, they imply that the introduction of the sensitive item increases responses, and that it does so by *at most* one item. Table A.3 shows the cumulative number of responses up to and including each line. The table clearly shows that both the aforementioned conditions are met, meaning there is no evidence of this type of design effect.

Finally, I observe a nontrivial increase in the average number of items selected by the four-item (short list) group between those who

TABLE A.4 *Iraq – list experiment*

Variable	Control mean	Treatment mean	$Pr\|T\| > \|t\|$
Male	.55	.50	.157
Age	35.61	35.35	.757
Degree	.82	.84	.665
Economic satisfaction	2.79	2.82	.675
Electricity (hours/day)	15.74	15.73	.963
n	400	400	

received the control vignette and those who received the treatment vignette, from 1.92 items to 2.09. Ideally, this response would have remained stable, indicating that the vignette affected support for violence but not respondents' willingness to use any of the noncontroversial items. While the change may be caused by random noise, it is also possible that informing subjects that the Iraqi Police are integrated emboldened them to engage in nonviolent anti-government activities included in the control list like writing letters to an international organization or participating in peaceful protests. In other words, it is possible that believing that the police are integrated not only decreases incentives to use violent measures but also simultaneously increases willingness to use peaceful measures. Regardless, the increase in the average number of items by the short list group makes the decrease in the number of items within the long list group all the more powerful, as inflation in the short list group biases *against* the observed effect of the treatment on support for violence.

Iraq: Experimental Prime on Police Integration

In the analysis in Chapter 6, I randomly prime respondents with information about the extent to which the Iraqi police are integrated using the following vignettes. The stories are fake, but were designed to read like real news stories. I discuss the reasoning behind the construction of the stories in Chapter 6.

Treatment (Police Are Integrated):

I would like to read you a few paragraphs from a news story that was in a newspaper just the other day. The story is about a police unit in

Kirkuk. The title of the article is, "Police Break Sectarian Barriers to Serve Citizens."

Unit 218 of the Iraqi Police Service has been receiving attention lately thanks to its successes in maintaining order in the Arrapha neighborhood of Kirkuk. The secret to the unit's success, according to one lieutenant, lies in its officers' diversity:

> Of the 140 officers in my unit, we have individuals from all different religious and ethnic groups of Iraq. We are Shias, Kurds, Sunnis, Turkmen, and we all work together to serve the community.
>
> When citizens see us patrolling together, they trust us. They see Kurds and Arabs, Shia and Sunni working side by side and they know that we are not a force belonging to once community or another. We are the Iraqi Police, and we serve Iraqi citizens.

According to a high-level official in Baghdad, unit 218 is serving as a new model for policing across the country. The Ministry of the Interior has announced an initiative to increase the diversity of police recruits from each of Iraq's sects in the coming months in an effort to improve the quality of service.

This is the end of the news story.

Control (No Information about Integration):
I would like to read you a few paragraphs from a news story that was in a newspaper just the other day. The story is about a police unit in Kirkuk. The title of the article is, "Police Use Technology to Serve Citizens."

Unit 218 of the Iraqi Police Service has been receiving attention lately, thanks to its successes in maintaining order in the Arrapha neighborhood of Kirkuk. The secret to the unit's success, according to one lieutenant, lies in its officers' use of technology:

> We have adopted a computerized reporting system. The system allows us to record crimes and incidents in a centralized database. We can use all of the information to find patterns and decide where to send resources.
>
> Instead of waiting for citizens to call us after a problem has already happened, this new technology helps us know where to go to prevent incidents from happening in the first place.

According to a high-level official in Baghdad, unit 218 is serving as a new model for policing across the country. The Ministry of the Interior has announced an initiative to increase the police's use of technology in the coming months in an effort to improve the quality of service.

This is the end of the news story.

Balance Across Treatment Groups

TABLE A.5 *Iraq – vignette experiment*

Variable	Control mean	Treatment mean	$Pr\|T\| > \|t\|$
Male	.50	.51	.322
Age	35.97	34.99	.258
Degree	.87	.79	.167
Economic satisfaction	2.85	2.76	.281
Electricity (hours/day)	15.75	15.72	.907
n	400	400	

Safety and Research Ethics

All procedures involving human subjects were reviewed and approved by the Institutional Review Board at the University of California, San Diego, prior to implementation. All subjects provided informed consent. I am not aware of any harm to subjects or enumerators resulting from the research.

Research in Iraq presented two main categories of threats to safety. First, the topic of the research was sensitive, as supporting or participating in anti-state violence may lead to arrest, prosecution, or violent retaliation. To reduce the physical dangers of asking about these sensitive topics, the survey procedures placed a heavy emphasis on anonymity and data security. The survey did not record any information that could be used to identify the respondent once the research team left his or her home. The design of the list experiment prevented anyone, including the enumerator, myself, or bystanders, from knowing whether any individual respondent personally supported anti-government violence. Beyond physical dangers, the topic may have brought up unpleasant memories or emotions. Before asking selected individuals to consent to participate in the research, the enumerator warned the individual that the topic was sensitive and may bring up bad memories. During the survey, subjects were free to skip any question at any time without losing the opportunity to complete the rest of the survey if they wished. As described in the main text, the wording of the list experiment was intentionally selected to reduce the shock factor of the subject by avoiding direct language about violence.

Second, an individual's mere presence in Baghdad in 2016 posed a significant threat of random violence, including harm from suicide bombings, kidnappings, improvised explosive devices, and gun battles between militias and the authorities (or between multiple militias). Perpetrators of this second category of violence did not target research subjects or enumerators specifically, but these activities nevertheless raised the danger of going house-to-house to collect data in Baghdad. These concerns are mitigated for subjects because they were interviewed in their own homes. Consequently, participation in the research did not affect their exposure to random violence. As much as possible, the research team used enumerators who were local not just to Iraq but also to Baghdad specifically, mitigating the impact on their exposure to random violence as well. Of course, going door-to-door made it impossible to eliminate this impact on enumerators entirely. Thus, efforts were taken to minimize travel time between subjects. Limiting the sample to Baghdad helped tremendously, as did clustering respondents by street. Finally, each team of enumerators had wide latitude to alter procedures or abandon questioning as needed based on security conditions at the moment.

Israel: Sampling Procedures

I surveyed individuals in nine urban centers across Israel. The sample was designed to allow for an efficient comparison of Jewish and non-Jewish citizens across a wide range of social and economic contexts within the constraints of the sampling frame. Cities were selected purposively based on known demographic and political characteristics to include a representative cross-section of both Jewish and non-Jewish Israeli citizens living in urban centers, as well as a diverse cross-section on social, religious, and economic factors. The included cities vary not just on their religious makeup but also on their level of intergroup tension. For example, Haifa and Akko are very diverse and have low levels of tension, Jerusalem/East Jerusalem is very diverse and has high levels of tension, and Tel Aviv is not diverse and has lower levels of tension.

TABLE A.6 *Distribution of respondents*

City	Non-Jews	Jews
Akko	34	36
East Jerusalem	104	0
Haifa	65	65
Jerusalem	0	100
Nazareth	123	2
Nazareth Illit	0	50
Rahat	50	0
Sderot	0	50
Tel Aviv-Jaffa	25	100

Table A.6 shows the distribution of respondents by religious identity from each city.

In all cities except East Jerusalem, interviews were conducted by phone. The sampling frame was a list maintained by a market research company of hundreds of thousands of phone numbers of residents of metropolitan areas. I randomly selected phone numbers using a simple random sample within each city. The interview was conducted with the individual who answered the phone so long as he or she was at least eighteen years of age and willing to take the survey. If there was no answer, the number was dialed up to three additional times at a later date. If, after the third call-back, there was no answer, or if the individual who answered was not willing to take the survey, another number was selected until the predetermined number of respondents was achieved in each city.

Enumerators conducted interviews in person in East Jerusalem. Neighborhoods (Old City, French Hill and Sheikh Jarah, Shuafat and Isawiyya, Mount of Olives) were selected to ensure variation in both exposure to police integration (based on police officer demographic data) and political attitudes (based on author interviews). Streets were randomly selected from each neighborhood using a simple random sample. Houses were then selected from a set starting point on each street, and interviewers contacted every second house from this starting point. In multi-home buildings, each apartment was considered to be an individual unit for sampling purposes. Sampling continued on the selected street until the specified number of households was reached. If at that time a sufficient number of households had not been reached within the

TABLE A.7 *Survey sample statistics (Israel)*

Variable	Obs	μ	σ	Min.	Max.
Non-Jewish	804	.50	.50	0	1
Age	801	42.77	18.00	18	91
Male	804	.48	.50	0	1
Vote	803	.78	.41	0	1
Econ. satisfaction	790	3.20	1.11	1	5
Work public	803	.34	.47	0	1
In person	804	.13	.34	0	1

neighborhood in question, another street was chosen and interviews were conducted using the same method. Within each household, enumerators selected the resident with the most recent previous birthday. If the selected resident was unavailable, two additional attempts were made to contact them on future dates. If the selected resident still could not be reached, or if the resident refused to participate, the enumerator continued to the next household on the street.

Certain characteristics of this survey guard against social desirability bias. Adida et al. (2016) note that bias may be exacerbated when respondents and enumerators come from groups in conflict with one another. To avoid this possibility, phone interviews took place in the language selected by the subject with a fluent speaker of that language, and in-person interviews in Arab East Jerusalem used Arab enumerators. In-person interviews were conducted in respondents' homes, and phone interviews in a location of the respondent's choosing, in an effort to minimize discomfort and ensure a low-pressure environment. Finally, the design of the survey ensured that subjects' responses, as well as their participation in the survey, remained confidential, decreasing their incentives to answer untruthfully in the face of social pressures.

BIBLIOGRAPHY

Abraham Fund Initiatives. *Conference – Policing in a Divided Society: Arab Society-Police Relations in Israel.* 2013. www.abrahamfund.org/webfiles/fck/Conference_--_Policing_in_a_Divided_Society.pdf.

Abraham Fund Initiatives. *The Personal Security Index. Violence, Crime, and Policing in Arab Communities Report 2017.* 2018. https://www.iataskforce.org/sites/default/files/resource/resource-1578.pdf.

Adida, Claire and Amanda Robinson. Resisting assimilation: Passing, racial discrimination, and investments in cultural markers among African immigrants. *Working Paper*, 2019.

Adida, Claire L, Karen E Ferree, Daniel N Posner, and Amanda Lea Robinson. Who's asking? Interviewer coethnicity effects in African survey data. *Comparative Political Studies*, 49(12):1630–1660, 2016.

Akerlof, George and Janet L Yellen. *Gang Behavior, Law Enforcement, and Community Values.* Canadian Institute for Advanced Research, 1994.

al-Ali, Zaid. How Maliki ruined Iraq. *Foreign Policy*, June 2014. http://foreignpolicy.com/2014/06/19/how-maliki-ruined-iraq/.

Al-Jabouri, Najim Abed and Sterling Jensen. The Iraqi and AQI roles in the Sunni Awakening. *Prism*, 2(1):3–18, 2010.

Alesina, Alberto, Reza Baqir, and William Easterly. Public goods and ethnic divisions. *The Quarterly Journal of Economics*, 114(4):1243–1284, 1999.

Allport, Gordon W. *The Nature of Prejudice.* Addison-Wesley, 1954.

Andersen, Simon Calmar. From passive to active representation – experimental evidence on the role of normative values in shaping White and minority bureaucrats' policy attitudes. *Journal of Public Administration Research and Theory*, 27(3):400–414, 2017.

Ansorg, Nadine, Felix Haass, and Julia Strasheim. Police reforms in peace agreements, 1975–2011: Introducing the PRPA dataset. *Journal of Peace Research*, 53(4):597–607, 2016.

Ball, Portia M and Gordon N Cantor. White boys' raitings of pictures of Whites and Blacks as related to amount of familiarization. *Perceptual and Motor Skills*, 39(2):883–890, 1974.

Banerjee, Abhijit, Lakshmi Iyer, and Rohini Somanathan. History, social divisions, and public goods in rural India. *Journal of the European Economic Association*, 3(2–3):639–647, 2005.

Banerjee, Abhijit V, Raghabendra Chattopadhyay, Esther Duflo, Daniel Keniston, and Nina Singh. Can institutions be reformed from within? Evidence from a randomized experiment with the Rajasthan police. *CEPR Discussion Paper* (DP8869), 2012.

Bayley, David H. Post-conflict police reform: Is Northern Ireland a model? *Policing*, 2(2):233–240, 2008.

Becker, Gary S. Crime and punishment: An economic approach. In Nigel G. Fielding, Alan Clarke, and Robert Witt, editors, *The Economic Dimensions of Crime*, pages 13–68. Springer, 1968.

Ben-Porat, Guy and Fany Yuval. Minorities in democracy and policing policy: From alienation to cooperation. *Policing and Society*, 22(2):235–252, 2012.

Ben-Porat, Guy and Fany Yuval. *Policing Citizens*. Cambridge University Press, 2019.

Berman, Eli. Sect, subsidy, and sacrifice: An economist's view of ultra-orthodox Jews. *The Quarterly Journal of Economics*, 115(3):905–953, 2000.

Berman, Eli and Aila Matanock. The empiricists' insurgency. *Annual Review of Political Science*, 18:443–464, 2015.

Berman, Eli, Michael Callen, Joseph H Felter, and Jacob N Shapiro. Do working men rebel? Insurgency and unemployment in Afghanistan, Iraq, and the Philippines. *Journal of Conflict Resolution*, 55(4):496–528, 2011a.

Berman, Eli, Jacob N Shapiro, and Joseph H Felter. Can hearts and minds be bought? The economics of counterinsurgency in Iraq. *Journal of Political Economy*, 119(4):766–819, 2011b.

Besley, Timothy, Stephen Coate, and Glenn Loury. The economics of rotating savings and credit associations. *The American Economic Review*, 83(4): 792–810, 1993.

Biden, Joseph and Leslie Gelb. Unity through autonomy in Iraq. *New York Times*, 1:19, 2006.

Blair, Graeme and Kosuke Imai. Statistical analysis of list experiments. *Political Analysis*, 20(1):47–77, 2012.

Blair, Robert A, Sabrina M Karim, Michael J Gilligan, and Kyle Beardsley. Policing ethnicity: Lab-in-the-field evidence on discrimination, cooperation and ethnic balancing in the Liberian National Police. *Social Science Research Network*, 2016 https://dx.doi.org/10.2139/ssrn.2772634.

Blair, Robert A, Sabrina M Karim, and Benjamin S Morse. Establishing the rule of law in weak and war-torn states: Evidence from a field experiment with the Liberian National Police. *American Political Science Review*, 113(3):641–657, 2019.

Blaydes, Lisa. Compliance and resistance in Iraq under Saddam Hussein: Evidence from the files of the Ba'th party. In *AALIMS Comparative Politics Workshop*, 2013.

Boix, Carles and Milan W Svolik. The foundations of limited authoritarian government: Institutions, commitment, and power-sharing in dictatorships. *The Journal of Politics*, 75(2):300–316, 2013.

Boudreau, Cheryl, Scott A MacKenzie, and Daniel J Simmons. Police violence and public perceptions: An experimental study of how information and endorsements affect support for law enforcement. *The Journal of Politics*, 81(3):1101–1110, 2019.

Brainard, Lael and Derek Chollet. *Too Poor for Peace? Global Poverty, Conflict, and Security in the 21st Century*. Brookings Institution Press, 2007.

Byrne, Jonny and Lisa Monaghan. *Policing Loyalist and Republican Communities: Understanding Key Issues for Local Communities and the PSNI*. Institute for Conflict Research Belfast, 2008.

Cederman, Lars-Erik, Andreas Wimmer, and Brian Min. Why do ethnic groups rebel? New data and analysis. *World Politics*, 62(01):87–119, 2010.

Cederman, Lars-Erik, Nils B Weidmann, and Kristian Skrede Gleditsch. Horizontal inequalities and ethnonationalist civil war: A global comparison. *American Political Science Review*, 105(3):478–495, 2011.

Cederman, Lars-Erik, Simon Hug, Andreas Schädel, and Julian Wucherpfennig. Territorial autonomy in the shadow of conflict: Too little, too late? *American Political Science Review*, 109(02):354–370, 2015.

Chandra, Kanchan. Cumulative findings in the study of ethnic politics. *APSA-CP Newsletter*, 12(1):7–25, 2001.

Chapman, Chris. *Improving Security for Minorities in Iraq*. Minority Rights Group International, 2012.

Cole, Juan. Shia militias in Iraqi politics. *Iraq: Preventing a New Generation of Conflict*. Boulder, CO: Lynne Rienner, 2007.

Collier, Paul and Anke Hoeffler. Greed and grievance in civil war. *Oxford Economic Papers*, 56(4):563–595, 2004.

Collier, Paul, Anke Hoeffler, and Dominic Rohner. Beyond greed and grievance: Feasibility and civil war. *Oxford Economic Papers*, 61(1):1–27, 2009.

Condra, Luke N and Jacob N Shapiro. Who takes the blame? The strategic effects of collateral damage. *American Journal of Political Science*, 56(1): 167–187, 2012.

Crank, John P. *Understanding Police Culture*. Routledge, 2014.

Dawisha, Adeed. *Iraq: A Political History*. Princeton University Press, 2009.

de Figueiredo Jr, Rui JP and Barry R Weingast. Rationality of fear: Political opportunism and ethnic conflict. *Military Intervention in Civil Wars*, 1999.

Deflem, Mathieu and Suzanne Sutphin. Policing post-war Iraq: Insurgency, civilian police, and the reconstruction of society. *Sociological Focus*, 39(4):265–283, 2006.

Department of the Army. Counterinsurgency. *Field Manual*, 3–24, 2006.

DePue, Mark R. *Patrolling Baghdad: A Military Police Company and the War in Iraq*. University Press of Kansas, 2007.

Dodge, Toby. *Inventing Iraq: The Failure of Nation Building and a History Denied*. Columbia University Press, 2005.

Dodge, Toby. *Iraq: From War to a New Authoritarianism*. Routledge, 2012.

Dube, Oeindrila and Juan F Vargas. Commodity price shocks and civil conflict: Evidence from Colombia. *The Review of Economic Studies*, 80(4):1384–1421, 2013.

Ehrlich, Isaac. Participation in illegitimate activities: A theoretical and empirical investigation. *Journal of Political Economy*, 81(3):521–565, 1973.

Ehrlich, Isaac. Crime, punishment, and the market for offenses. *Journal of Economic Perspectives*, 10(1):43–67, 1996.

Eklund, Karna, Brendan O'Leary, and Paul R. Williams. Negotiating a federation in Iraq. *The Future of Kurdistan in Iraq*, pages 235–250, 2005.

Ellison, Graham. A blueprint for democratic policing anywhere in the world? Police reform, political transition, and conflict resolution in Northern Ireland. *Police Quarterly*, 10(3):243–269, 2007.

Enloe, Cynthia H. *Ethnic Soldiers: State Security in Divided Societies*. University of Georgia Press, 1980.

Fearon, James D. Ethnic war as a commitment problem. In *Annual Meetings of the American Political Science Association*, pages 2–5, 1995a.

Fearon, James D. Rationalist explanations for war. *International Organization*, 49(03):379–414, 1995b.

Fearon, James D and David D Laitin. Explaining interethnic cooperation. *American Political Science Review*, 90(04):715–735, 1996.

Fearon, James D and David D Laitin. Ethnicity, insurgency, and civil war. *American Political Science Review*, 97(01):75–90, 2003.

Fortna, Virginia Page. *Peace Time: Cease-fire Agreements and the Durability of Peace*. Princeton University Press, 2004.

Galbraith, Peter W. What went wrong. *The Future of Kurdistan in Iraq*, pages 235–250, 2005.

Gibson, Clark C and Barak D Hoffman. Coalitions not conflicts: Ethnicity, political institutions, and expenditure in Africa. *Comparative Politics*, 45(3):273–290, 2013.

González, Yanilda. Varieties of participatory security: Assessing community participation in policing in Latin America. *Public Administration and Development*, 36(2):132–143, 2016.

González, Yanilda. The social origins of institutional weakness and change: Preferences, power, and police reform in Latin America. *World Politics*, 71(1):44–87, 2019.

Grossman, Guy, Oren Gazal-Ayal, Samuel D Pimentel, and Jeremy M Weinstein. Descriptive representation and judicial outcomes in multiethnic societies. *American Journal of Political Science*, 60(1):44–69, 2015.

Gurr, Ted R. *Why Men Rebel*. Princeton University Press, 1970.

Habyarimana, James, Macartan Humphreys, Daniel N Posner, and Jeremy M Weinstein. Why does ethnic diversity undermine public goods provision? *American Political Science Review*, 101(4):709–725, 2007.

Haddad, Fanar. *Sectarianism in Iraq: Antagonistic Visions of Unity*. Columbia University Press, 2011.

Haim, Dotan, Matthew Nanes, and Michael W Davidson. Family matters: The double-edged sword of police community connections. Presented at the annual meeting of the American Political Science Association. Washington, DC. 30 August 2019.

Hardin, Russell. *One for all: The Logic of Group Conflict*. Princeton University Press, 1997.

Hartzell, Caroline and Matthew Hoddie. Institutionalizing peace: Power sharing and post-civil war conflict management. *American Journal of Political Science*, 47(2):318–332, 2003.

Hashim, Ahmed. *Insurgency and Counter-insurgency in Iraq*. Ithaca, NY: Cornell University Press, 2005.

Hasisi, Badi and David Weisburd. Policing terrorism and police–community relations: Views of the Arab minority in Israel. *Police Practice and Research*, 15(2):158–172, 2014.

Hasisi, Badi and Ronald Weitzer. Police relations with Arabs and Jews in Israel. *British Journal of Criminology*, 47(5):728–745, 2007.

Hassan, Mai. The strategic shuffle: Ethnic geography, the internal security apparatus, and elections in Kenya. *American Journal of Political Science*, 61(2):382–395, 2017.

Hoddie, Matthew and Caroline Hartzell. Civil war settlements and the implementation of military power-sharing arrangements. *Journal of Peace Research*, 40(3):303–320, 2003.

Horowitz, Donald L. *Ethnic Groups in Conflict*. University of California Press, 1985.

Humphreys, Macartan and Jeremy M Weinstein. Who fights? The determinants of participation in civil war. *American Journal of Political Science*, 52(2):436–455, 2008.

Jabar, Rega. Examining the Anbar crisis. *Stability Institute*, 2014.

Jablonski, Ryan S and Steven Oliver. The political economy of plunder: Economic opportunity and modern piracy. *Journal of Conflict Resolution*, 57(4):682–708, 2013.

Jensen, Steffen and Karl Hapal. Police violence and corruption in the Philippines: Violent exchange and the war on drugs. *Journal of Current Southeast Asian Affairs*, 37(2):39–62, 2018.

Kalyvas, Stathis N. *The Logic of Violence in Civil War*. Cambridge University Press, 2006.

Kalyvas, Stathis N and Matthew Adam Kocher. How "free" is free riding in civil wars? Violence, insurgency, and the collective action problem. *World Politics*, 59(02):177–216, 2007.

Karim, Sabrina. Restoring confidence in post-conflict security sectors: Survey evidence from Liberia on female ratio balancing reforms. *British Journal of Political Science*, 49(3):799–821, 2019.

Karim, Sabrina and Kyle Beardsley. *Equal Opportunity Peacekeeping: Women, Peace, and Security in Post-conflict States*. Oxford University Press, 2017.

Kennedy, Brandy A., Adam M. Butz, Nazita Lajevardi, and Matthew J. Nanes. *Race and Representative Bureaucracy in American Policing*. Palgrave Macmillan, 2017.

Kingsley, J Donald. *Representative Bureaucracy: An Interpretation of the British Civil Service*. Yellow Springs, OH: Antioch Press, 1944.

Krebs, Ronald R and Roy Licklider. United they fall: Why the international community should not promote military integration after civil war. *International Security*, 40(3):93–138, 2016.

Kubovich, Yaniv. In recruting campaign, Israel police discriminates against Arabs, ultra-orthodox Jews. *Haaretz*, May 13, 2007 https://haaretz.com/.premium-israeli-cops-show-bias-in-recruiting-1.5248075.

Laitin, David D. *Nations, States, and Violence*. Oxford University Press, 2007.

Lake, David A. *The Statebuilder's Dilemma: On the Limits of Foreign Intervention*. Cornell University Press, 2016.

Lake, David A and Donald Rothchild. Containing fear: The origins and management of ethnic conflict. *International Security*, 21(2):41–75, 1996.

Lasley, James R. Ethnicity, gender, and police-community attitudes. *Social Science Quarterly*, 75(1):85–97, 1994.

Lawrence, Quil. *Invisible Nation: How the Kurds' Quest for Statehood is Shaping Iraq and the Middle East*. Bloomsbury Publishing USA, 2009.

Levi, Amir and Daniel Suchi. The causes and consequences of Israeli government Resolution 922: A roadmap to accelerate economic inclusion of Arab communities in Israel. M-RCBG *Associate Working Paper*, (99):1–44, 2018.

Lijphart, Arend. Consociational democracy. *World Politics*, 21(2):207–225, 1969.

Lijphart, Arend. *Democracies*. Yale University Press, 1984.

Lipsky, M. *Street-level Bureaucracy: Dilemmas of the Individual in Public Services*. New York: Russell Sage Foundation, 1980.

Lohman, Charles M and Robert I MacPherson. *Rhodesia: Tactical Victory, Strategic Defeat*. Virginia: United States Marine Corps, 1983. www.rhodesia.nl/Rhodesia%20Tactical%20Victory.pdf.

Lott, John. Does a helping hand put others at risk?: Affirmative action, police departments, and crime. *Economic Inquiry*, 38(2):239–277, 2000.

Lyall, Jason. Are coethnics more effective counterinsurgents? Evidence from the Second Chechen War. *American Political Science Review*, 104(01):1–20, 2010.

Lyall, Jason, Yuki Shiraito, and Kosuke Imai. Coethnic bias and wartime informing. *The Journal of Politics*, 77(3):833–848, 2015.

Magaloni, Beatriz. Credible power-sharing and the longevity of authoritarian rule. *Comparative Political Studies*, 41(4–5):715–741, 2008.

Marr, Phebe. Iraq's identity crisis. *Bouillon, Malone and Rowsell (eds), Preventing Another Generation of Conflict*, 2007.

Matanock, Aila M. Bullets for ballots: Electoral participation provisions and enduring peace after civil conflict. *International Security*, 41(4):93–132, 2017.

Mattes, Michaela and Burcu Savun. Fostering peace after civil war: Commitment problems and agreement design. *International Studies Quarterly*, 53(3):737–759, 2009.

Mazerolle, Lorraine, Emma Antrobus, Sarah Bennett, and Tom R Tyler. Shaping citizen perceptions of police legitimacy: A randomized field trial of procedural justice. *Criminology*, 51(1):33–63, 2013.

McCoy, C. Enforcement workshop-affirmative action in police organizations-checklists for supporting a compelling state interest. *Criminal Law Bulletin*, 20(3):245–254, 1984.

McCrary, Justin. The effect of court-ordered hiring quotas on the composition and quality of police. Technical report, National Bureau of Economic Research, 2006.

McGarry, John. Police reform in Northern Ireland. *Irish Political Studies*, 15(1):173–182, 2000.

McGarry, John. Canadian lessons for Iraq. In O'Leary, Brendan, John McGarry, and Khaled Salih, editors, *The Future of Kurdistan in Iraq*. University of Pennsylvania Press, Philadelphia, 2005.

Meier, Kenneth J. Latinos and representative bureaucracy: Testing the Thompson and Henderson hypotheses. *Journal of Public Administration Research and Theory*, 3(4):393–414, 1993.

Meier, Kenneth J and Jill Nicholson-Crotty. Gender, representative bureaucracy, and law enforcement: The case of sexual assault. *Public Administration Review*, 66(6):850–860, 2006.

Meier, Kenneth J and Joseph Stewart Jr. The impact of representative bureaucracies: Educational systems and public policies. *The American Review of Public Administration*, 22(3):157–171, 1992.

Meier, Kenneth John. Representative bureaucracy: An empirical analysis. *American Political Science Review*, 69(02):526–542, 1975.

Messner, Steven F and Robert J Sampson. The sex ratio, family disruption, and rates of violent crime: The paradox of demographic structure. *Social Forces*, 69(3):693–713, 1991.

Miguel, Edward and Mary Kay Gugerty. Ethnic diversity, social sanctions, and public goods in Kenya. *Journal of Public Economics*, 89(11):2325–2368, 2005.

Miguel, Edward, Shanker Satyanath, and Ernest Sergenti. Economic shocks and civil conflict: An instrumental variables approach. *Journal of Political Economy*, 112(4):725–753, 2004.

Mosher, Frederick C. *Democracy and the Public Service*. Oxford University Press, 1982.

Muller, Edward N. Income inequality, regime repressiveness, and political violence. *American Sociological Review*, 50(1):47–61, 1985.

Mummolo, Jonathan. Militarization fails to enhance police safety or reduce crime but may harm police reputation. *Proceedings of the National Academy of Sciences*, 115(37):9181–9186, 2018.

Murphy, Kristina. Public satisfaction with police: The importance of procedural justice and police performance in police-citizen encounters. *Australian & New Zealand Journal of Criminology*, 42(2):159–178, 2009.

Nanes, Matthew J. Police integration and support for anti-government violence in divided societies: Evidence from Iraq. *Journal of Peace Research*, 57(2):329–343, 2019.

Nanes, Matthew J. Policing in divided societies: Officer inclusion, citizen cooperation, and crime prevention. *Conflict Management and Peace Science*, 37(5):580–604, 2020.

New Israel Fund. Arab sector: NIF grantees fight discrimination in Arab education. September 2005. http://archive.li/UWPYy.

Nordlinger, Eric A. *Conflict Regulation in Divided Societies*. Number 29. Center for International Affairs, Harvard University Cambridge, MA, 1972.

Norris, Pippa. *Driving Democracy: Do Power-sharing Institutions Work?* Cambridge University Press, 2008.

O'Leary, Brendan, B Roswell, D Malone, and M Bouillon. In David M. Malone, Markus E. Bouillon, and Ben Roswell, editors. Federalizing natural resources. *Iraq: Preventing a New Generation of Conflict*. London: Lynne Rienne, 2007.

Olken, Benjamin A. Monitoring corruption: Evidence from a field experiment in Indonesia. *Journal of Political Economy*, 115(2):200–249, 2007.

Olson, Mancur. *Logic of Collective Action: Public Goods and the Theory of Groups*. Harvard University Press, 1965.

Olson, Mancur. Dictatorship, democracy, and development. *American Political Science Review*, 87(03):567–576, 1993.

Østby, Gudrun. Polarization, horizontal inequalities and violent civil conflict. *Journal of Peace Research*, 45(2):143–162, 2008.

Ostwald, Kai. Using policy to engineer identity: How Singapore's national service shapes ethnic and civic identities to reduce the divisive potential of ethnic diversity. *Available at SSRN*, 2013.

Paige, Jeffrey M. *Agrarian Revolution*. Simon and Schuster, 1975.

Paoline III, Eugene A, Stephanie M Myers, and Robert E Worden. Police culture, individualism, and community policing: Evidence from two police departments. *Justice Quarterly*, 17(3):575–605, 2000.

Patel, David Siddhartha. ISIS in Iraq: What we got wrong and why 2015 is not 2007 redux. *Middle East Brief*, 87:1–8, 2015.

Perito, Robert. *The Iraq Federal Police: US Police Building under Fire*. US Institute of Peace, 2011.

Pfaff, Tony. Development and reform of the Iraqi police forces. Technical report, US Army War College Strategic Studies Institute, 2008. https://apps.dtic.mil/dtic/tr/fulltext/u2/a476462.pdf

Phillips, Phillip D. Characteristics and typology of the journey to crime. In Daniel E Georges-Abeyie and Keith D Harries, editors, *Crime: A Spatial Perspective*, pages 167–180, New York: Columbia University Press, 1980.

Polk, William R. *Understanding Iraq*. New York: Harper Collins, 2005.

Posen, Barry R. The security dilemma and ethnic conflict. *Survival*, 35(1): 27–47, 1993.

Raphael, Steven and Rudolf Winter-Ebmer. Identifying the effect of unemployment on crime. *Journal of Law and Economics*, 44(1):259–283, 2001.

Rayburn, Joel. *Iraq after America: Strongmen, Sectarians, Resistance*. Hoover Institution Press, 2014.

Rengert, George. The journey to crime. In Bruinsma, Gerben, Hank Elffers, and Jan de Keijser, editors, *Punishment, Places, and Perpetrators: Developments in Criminology and Criminal Justice Research*, chapter 11, pages 169–181. Routledge, 2004.

Robinson, Linda. *Tell Me How This Ends: General David Petraeus and the Search for a Way out of Iraq*. New York: PublicAffairs, 2009.

Rocha, Rene R and Daniel P Hawes. Racial diversity, representative bureaucracy, and equity in multiracial school districts. *Social Science Quarterly*, 90(2):326–344, 2009.

Roeder, Philip G. *Where Nation-States Come From: Institutional Change in the Age of Nationalism*. Princeton University Press, 2007.

Roeder, Philip G and Donald S Rothchild. *Sustainable Peace: Power and Democracy after Civil Wars*. Cornell University Press, 2005.

Rudnitzky, Arik and Itamar Radai. *Citizenship, Identity and Political Participation: Measuring the Attitudes of the Arab Citizens in Israel*. The Konrad Adenauer Program for Jewish-Arab Cooperation, 2017.

Russett, Bruce M. Inequality and instability: The relation of land tenure to politics. *World Politics*, 16(03):442–454, 1964.

Salehyan, Idean, Kristian Skrede Gleditsch, and David E Cunningham. Explaining external support for insurgent groups. *International Organization*, 65(4):709–744, 2011.

Samii, Cyrus. Perils or promise of ethnic integration? Evidence from a hard case in Burundi. *American Political Science Review*, 107(3):558–573, 2013.

Saunders, Jessica, Steven W Popper, Andrew R Morral, Robert C Davis, Claude Berrebi, Kristin J Leuschner, Shira Efron, Boaz Segalovitz, and K Jack Riley. *Effective Policing for 21st-Century Israel*. Rand Corporation, 2013.

Sawyer, Katherine, Kathleen Gallagher Cunningham, and William Reed. The role of external support in civil war termination. *Journal of Conflict Resolution*, 61(6):1174–1202, 2017.

Schedler, Andreas. The nested game of democratization by elections. *International Political Science Review*, 23(1):103–122, 2002.

Selden, Sally Coleman. Representative bureaucracy: Examining the linkage between passive and active representation in the farmers home administration. *The American Review of Public Administration*, 27(1):22–42, 1997.

Sharp, Jeremy Maxwell. Iraq's new security forces: The challenge of sectarian and ethnic influences. Congressional Information Service, Library of Congress, 2005.

Shayo, Moses and Asaf Zussman. Judicial ingroup bias in the shadow of terrorism. *The Quarterly Journal of Economics*, 126(3):1447–1484, 2011.

Shesterinina, Anastasia. Collective threat framing and mobilization in civil war. *American Political Science Review*, 110(3):411–427, 2016.

Skogan, Wesley. Fear of crime and neighborhood change. *Crime and Justice*, 8:203–229, 1986.

Skogan, Wesley G and Susan M Hartnett. *Community Policing, Chicago Style*. Oxford University Press New York, 1997.

Skolnick, Jerome H and David H Bayley. *The New Blue Line: Police Innovation in Six American Cities*. Simon and Schuster, 1988.

Smith, Brad W. The impact of police officer diversity on police-caused homicides. *Policy Studies Journal*, 31(2):147–162, 2003.

Smyth, Jim. Symbolic power and police legitimacy: The Royal Ulster Constabulary. *Crime, Law and Social Change*, 38(3):295–310, 2002.

Spain, Ted and Terry Turchie. *Breaking Iraq: The Ten Mistakes that Broke Iraq*. Palisades: History Publishing Company, 2013.

Stedman, Stephen John. Spoiler problems in peace processes. *International Security*, 22(2):5–53, 1997.

Strøm, Kaare W, Scott Gates, Benjamin AT Graham, and Håvard Strand. Inclusion, dispersion, and constraint: Powersharing in the world's states, 1975–2010. *British Journal of Political Science*, 47(1):165–185, 2017.

Sutton, Malcom. An index of deaths from the conflict in Ireland, N.D. https://cain.ulster.ac.uk/sutton/tables/Status_Summary.html.

Taylor, Brian D. Police reform in Russia: The policy process in a hybrid regime. *Post-Soviet Affairs*, 30(2–3):226–255, 2014.

Taylor-Robinson, Michelle M and Roseanna Michelle Heath. Do women legislators have different policy priorities than their male colleagues? A critical case test. *Women & Politics*, 24(4):77–101, 2003.

Tezcür, Güneş Murat. Ordinary people, extraordinary risks: Participation in an ethnic rebellion. *American Political Science Review*, 110(2):247–264, 2016.

Toft, Monica Duffy. *Securing the Peace: The Durable Settlement of Civil Wars*. Princeton University Press, 2009.

Toft, Monica Duffy and Yuri M Zhukov. Islamists and nationalists: Rebel motivation and counterinsurgency in Russia's North Caucasus. *American Political Science Review*, 109(2):222–238, 2015.

Tyler, Tom R. Procedural justice, legitimacy, and the effective rule of law. *Crime and justice*, 30:283–357, 2003.

Tyler, Tom R. Enhancing police legitimacy. *The Annals of the American Academy of Political and Social Science*, 593(1):84–99, 2004.

Ungar, Mark. *Policing Democracy: Overcoming Obstacles to Citizen Security in Latin America*. Johns Hopkins University Press, 2011.

United States Commission on International Religious Freedom. *Iraq Annual Report*. 2013. https://uscirf.gov/sites/default/files/resources/Iraq%202013.pdf

Walter, Barbara F. The critical barrier to civil war settlement. *International Organization*, 51(03):335–364, 1997.

Walter, Barbara F. *Committing to Peace: The Successful Settlement of Civil Wars*. Princeton University Press, 2002.

Warren, Patricia Y. Perceptions of police disrespect during vehicle stops: A race-based analysis. *Crime & Delinquency*, 57(3):356–376, 2011.

Weber, Max. *Politics as a Vocation*. Fortress Press, Philadelphia PA, 1919.

Weitzer, Ronald. *Policing under Fire: Ethnic Conflict and Police-community Relations in Northern Ireland*. State University of New York Press, 1995.

Weitzer, Ronald. White, black, or blue cops? Race and citizen assessments of police officers. *Journal of Criminal Justice*, 28(4):313–324, 2000.

Weitzer, Ronald and Badi Hasisi. Does ethnic composition make a difference? Citizens' assessments of Arab police officers in Israel. *Policing & Society*, 18(4):362–376, 2008.

Weitzer, Ronald and Steven A Tuch. Race and perceptions of police misconduct. *Social Problems*, 51(3):305–325, 2004.

Weitzer, Ronald and Steven A Tuch. *Race and Policing in America: Conflict and Reform*. Cambridge University Press, 2006.

Westley, William A. *Violence and the Police*. MIT Press Cambridge, MA, 1970.

Wilkinson, Steven I. *Army and Nation: The Military and Indian Democracy since Independence*. Harvard University Press, 2015.

Willis, Graham Denyer. *The Killing Consensus: Police, Organized Crime, and the Regulation of Life and Death in Urban Brazil*. University of California Press, 2015.

Wimmer, Andreas. Democracy and ethno-religious conflict in Iraq. *Survival*, 45(4):111–134, 2003.
Wood, Elisabeth Jean. *Insurgent Collective Action and Civil War in El Salvador*. Cambridge University Press, 2003.
Yogev, Dikla. Public attitudes towards the Israeli police. *Israel Ministry of Public Security: Bureau of the Chief Scientist*, https://gov.il/BlobFolder/reports/pub_eval_police_2010/en/pub_eval_il_police2010_sum.pdf 2010.
Zajonc, Robert B. Attitudinal effects of mere exposure. *Journal of Personality and Social Psychology*, 9(2):1, 1968.

INDEX

CAMBRIDGE STUDIES IN LAW AND SOCIETY

Books in the Series

Diseases of the Will: Alcohol and the Dilemmas of Freedom
Mariana Valverde

The Politics of Truth and Reconciliation in South Africa: Legitimizing the Post-Apartheid State
Richard A. Wilson

Modernism and the Grounds of Law
Peter Fitzpatrick

Unemployment and Government: Genealogies of the Social
William Walters

Autonomy and Ethnicity: Negotiating Competing Claims in Multi-Ethnic States
Yash Ghai

Constituting Democracy: Law, Globalism and South Africa's Political Reconstruction
Heinz Klug

The Ritual of Rights in Japan: Law, Society, and Health Policy
Eric A. Feldman

Governing Morals: A Social History of Moral Regulation
Alan Hunt

The Colonies of Law: Colonialism, Zionism and Law in Early Mandate Palestine
Ronen Shamir

Law and Nature
David Delaney

Social Citizenship and Workfare in the United States and Western Europe: The Paradox of Inclusion
Joel F. Handler

Law, Anthropology, and the Constitution of the Social: Making Persons and Things
Edited by Alain Pottage and Martha Mundy

Judicial Review and Bureaucratic Impact: International and Interdisciplinary Perspectives
Edited by Marc Hertogh and Simon Halliday

Immigrants at the Margins: Law, Race, and Exclusion in Southern Europe
Kitty Calavita

Lawyers and Regulation: The Politics of the Administrative Process
Patrick Schmidt

Law and Globalization from Below: Towards a Cosmopolitan Legality
Edited by Boaventura de Sousa Santos and César A. Rodríguez-Garavito

Public Accountability: Designs, Dilemmas and Experiences
Edited by Michael W. Dowdle

Law, Violence and Sovereignty among West Bank Palestinians
Tobias Kelly

Legal Reform and Administrative Detention Powers in China
Sarah Biddulph

The Practice of Human Rights: Tracking Law between the Global and the Local
Edited by Mark Goodale and Sally Engle Merry

Judges beyond Politics in Democracy and Dictatorship: Lessons from Chile
Lisa Hilbink

Paths to International Justice: Social and Legal Perspectives
Edited by Marie-Bénédicte Dembour and Tobias Kelly

Law and Society in Vietnam: The Transition from Socialism in Comparative Perspective
Mark Sidel

Constitutionalizing Economic Globalization: Investment Rules and Democracy's Promise
David Schneiderman

The New World Trade Organization Knowledge Agreements: Second Edition
Christopher Arup

Justice and Reconciliation in Post-Apartheid South Africa
Edited by François du Bois and Antje du Bois-Pedain

Militarization and Violence against Women in Conflict Zones in the Middle East: A Palestinian Case-Study
Nadera Shalhoub-Kevorkian

Child Pornography and Sexual Grooming: Legal and Societal Responses
Suzanne Ost

Darfur and the Crime of Genocide
John Hagan and Wenona Rymond-Richmond

Fictions of Justice: The International Criminal Court and the Challenge of Legal Pluralism in Sub-Saharan Africa
Kamari Maxine Clarke

Conducting Law and Society Research: Reflections on Methods and Practices
Simon Halliday and Patrick Schmidt

Planted Flags: Trees, Land, and Law in Israel/Palestine
Irus Braverman

Culture under Cross-Examination: International Justice and the Special Court for Sierra Leone
Tim Kelsall

Cultures of Legality: Judicialization and Political Activism in Latin America
Javier Couso, Alexandra Huneeus, and Rachel Sieder

Courting Democracy in Bosnia and Herzegovina: The Hague Tribunal's Impact in a Postwar State
Lara J. Nettelfield

The Gacaca Courts, Post-Genocide Justice and Reconciliation in Rwanda: Justice without Lawyers
Phil Clark

Law, Society, and History: Themes in the Legal Sociology and Legal History of Lawrence M. Friedman
Edited by Robert W. Gordon and Morton J. Horwitz

After Abu Ghraib: Exploring Human Rights in America and the Middle East
Shadi Mokhtari

Adjudication in Religious Family Laws: Cultural Accommodation, Legal Pluralism, and Gender Equality in India
Gopika Solanki

Water on Tap: Rights and Regulation in the Transnational Governance of Urban Water Services
Bronwen Morgan

Elements of Moral Cognition: Rawls' Linguistic Analogy and the Cognitive Science of Moral and Legal Judgment
John Mikhail

Mitigation and Aggravation at Sentencing
Edited by Julian V. Roberts

Institutional Inequality and the Mobilization of the Family and Medical Leave Act: Rights on Leave
Catherine R. Albiston

Authoritarian Rule of Law: Legislation, Discourse and Legitimacy in Singapore
Jothie Rajah

Law and Development and the Global Discourses of Legal Transfers
Edited by John Gillespie and Pip Nicholson

Law against the State: Ethnographic Forays into Law's Transformations
Edited by Julia Eckert, Brian Donahoe, Christian Strümpell and Zerrin Özlem Biner

Transnational Legal Ordering and State Change
Edited by Gregory C. Shaffer

Legal Mobilization under Authoritarianism: The Case of Post-Colonial Hong Kong
Waikeung Tam

Complementarity in the Line of Fire: The Catalysing Effect of the International Criminal Court in Uganda and Sudan
Sarah M. H. Nouwen

Political and Legal Transformations of an Indonesian Polity: The Nagari from Colonisation to Decentralisation
Franz von Benda-Beckmann and Keebet von Benda-Beckmann

Pakistan's Experience with Formal Law: An Alien Justice
Osama Siddique

Human Rights under State-Enforced Religious Family Laws in Israel, Egypt, and India
Yüksel Sezgin

Why Prison?
Edited by David Scott

Law's Fragile State: Colonial, Authoritarian, and Humanitarian Legacies in Sudan
Mark Fathi Massoud

Rights for Others: The Slow Home-Coming of Human Rights in the Netherlands
Barbara Oomen

European States and Their Muslim Citizens: The Impact of Institutions on Perceptions and Boundaries
Edited by John R. Bowen, Christophe Bertossi, Jan Willem Duyvendak, and Mona Lena Krook

Environmental Litigation in China: A Study in Political Ambivalence
Rachel E. Stern

Indigeneity and Legal Pluralism in India: Claims, Histories, Meanings
Pooja Parmar

Paper Tiger: Law, Bureaucracy and the Developmental State in Himalayan India
Nayanika Mathur

Religion, Law and Society
Russell Sandberg

The Experiences of Face Veil Wearers in Europe and the Law
Edited by Eva Brems

The Contentious History of the International Bill of Human Rights
Christopher N. J. Roberts

Transnational Legal Orders
Edited by Terence C. Halliday and Gregory Shaffer

Lost in China? Law, Culture and Society in Post-1997 Hong Kong
Carol A. G. Jones

Security Theology, Surveillance and the Politics of Fear
Nadera Shalhoub-Kevorkian

Opposing the Rule of Law: How Myanmar's Courts Make Law and Order
Nick Cheesman

Ironies of Colonial Governance: Law, Custom and Justice in Colonial India
James Jaffe

The Clinic and the Court: Law, Medicine and Anthropology
Edited by Ian Harper, Tobias Kelly, and Akshay Khanna

The World of Indicators: The Making of Government Knowledge through Quantification
Edited by Richard Rottenburg, Sally E. Merry, Sung-Joon Park, and Johanna Mugler

Contesting Immigration Policy in Court: Legal Activism and Its Radiating Effects in the United States and France
Leila Kawar

The Quiet Power of Indicators: Measuring Governance, Corruption, and Rule of Law
Edited by Sally Engle Merry, Kevin E. Davis, and Benedict Kingsbury

Investing in Authoritarian Rule: Punishment and Patronage in Rwanda's Gacaca Courts for Genocide Crimes
Anuradha Chakravarty

Contractual Knowledge: One Hundred Years of Legal Experimentation in Global Markets
Edited by Grégoire Mallard and Jérôme Sgard

Iraq and the Crimes of Aggressive War: The Legal Cynicism of Criminal Militarism
John Hagan, Joshua Kaiser, and Anna Hanson

Culture in the Domains of Law
Edited by René Provost

China and Islam: The Prophet, the Party, and Law
Matthew S. Erie

Diversity in Practice: Race, Gender, and Class in Legal and Professional Careers
Edited by Spencer Headworth, Robert L. Nelson, Ronit Dinovitzer, and David B. Wilkins

A Sociology of Constitutions: Constitutions and State Legitimacy in Historical-Sociological Perspective
Chris Thornhill

A Sociology of Transnational Constitutions: Social Foundations of the Post-National Legal Structure
Chris Thornhill

Genocide Never Sleeps: Living Law at the International Criminal Tribunal for Rwanda
Nigel Eltringham

Shifting Legal Visions: Judicial Change and Human Rights Trials in Latin America
Ezequiel A. González-Ocantos

The Demographic Transformations of Citizenship
Heli Askola

Criminal Defense in China: The Politics of Lawyers at Work
Sida Liu and Terence C. Halliday

Contesting Economic and Social Rights in Ireland: Constitution, State and Society, 1848–2016
Thomas Murray

Buried in the Heart: Women, Complex Victimhood and the War in Northern Uganda
Erin Baines

Palaces of Hope: The Anthropology of Global Organizations
Edited by Ronald Niezen and Maria Sapignoli

The Politics of Bureaucratic Corruption in Post-Transitional Eastern Europe
Marina Zaloznaya

Revisiting the Law and Governance of Trafficking, Forced Labor and Modern Slavery
Edited by Prabha Kotiswaran

Incitement on Trial: Prosecuting International Speech Crimes
Richard Ashby Wilson

Criminalizing Children: Welfare and the State in Australia
David McCallum

Global Lawmakers: International Organizations in the Crafting of World Markets
Susan Block-Lieb and Terence C. Halliday

Duties to Care: Dementia, Relationality and Law
Rosie Harding

Insiders, Outsiders, Injuries, and Law: Revisiting "The Oven Bird's Song"
Edited by Mary Nell Trautner

Hunting Justice: Displacement, Law, and Activism in the Kalahari
Maria Sapignoli

Injury and Injustice: The Cultural Politics of Harm and Redress
Edited by Anne Bloom, David M. Engel, and Michael McCann

Ruling Before the Law: The Politics of Legal Regimes in China and Indonesia
William Hurst

The Powers of Law: A Comparative Analysis of Sociopolitical Legal Studies
Mauricio García-Villegas

A Sociology of Justice in Russia
Edited by Marina Kurkchiyan and Agnieszka Kubal

Constituting Religion: Islam, Liberal Rights, and the Malaysian State
Tamir Moustafa

The Invention of the Passport: Surveillance, Citizenship and the State, Second Edition
John C. Torpey

Law's Trials: The Performance of Legal Institutions in the US "War on Terror"
Richard L. Abel

Law's Wars: The Fate of the Rule of Law in the US "War on Terror"
Richard L. Abel

Transforming Gender Citizenship: The Irresistible Rise of Gender Quotas in Europe
Edited by Eléonore Lépinard and Ruth Rubio-Marín

Muslim Women's Quest for Justice: Gender, Law and Activism in India
Mengia Hong Tschalaer

Children as 'Risk': Sexual Exploitation and Abuse by Children and Young People
Anne-Marie McAlinden

The Legal Process and the Promise of Justice: Studies Inspired by the Work of Malcolm Feeley
Jonathan Simon, Rosann Greenspan, Hadar Aviram

Gift Exchanges: The Transnational History of a Political Idea
Grégoire Mallard

Measuring Justice: Quantitative Accountability and the National Prosecuting Authority in South Africa
Johanna Mugler

Negotiating the Power of NGOs: Women's Legal Rights in South Africa
Reem Wael

Indigenous Water Rights in Law and Regulation: Lessons from Comparative Experience
Elizabeth Jane Macpherson

The Edge of Law: Legal Geographies of a War Crimes Court
Alex Jeffrey

Everyday Justice: Law, Ethnography, and Injustice
Sandra Brunnegger

The Uncounted: Politics of Data in Global Health
Sara L. M. Davis

Transnational Legal Ordering of Criminal Justice
Gregory Shaffer and Ely Aaronson

Five Republics and One Tradition
Pablo Ruiz-Tagle

The Law Multiple: Judgment and Knowledge in Practice
Irene van Oorschot

Health as a Human Right: The Politics and Judicialisation of Health in Brazil
Octávio Luiz Motta Ferraz

Shari'a, Inshallah: Finding God in Somali Legal Politics
Mark Fathi Massoud

Policing for Peace: Institutions, Expectations, and Security in Divided Societies
Matthew Nanes

For EU product safety concerns, contact us at Calle de José Abascal, 56–1°,
28003 Madrid, Spain or eugpsr@cambridge.org.

www.ingramcontent.com/pod-product-compliance
Lightning Source LLC
LaVergne TN
LVHW011812200926
848484LV00005B/1157
* 9 7 8 1 1 0 8 8 3 9 0 5 1 *